A Student's Guide to the Liberal Arts

A STUDENT'S GUIDE TO THE LIBERAL ARTS

Edited by WILBURN T. STANCIL

Rockhurst University Press
Kansas City, Missouri
2003

ISBN 1-886761-27-2 (cloth), 1-886761-28-0 (paper)

Printed in the United States of America
        07   5   4   3   2
First Edition

CONTENTS

PREFACE

APPROXIMATELY THREE-QUARTERS of all American colleges and universities have some type of first-year seminar for freshmen. These courses go by various names ("Freshman Seminar," "First Year Experience," etc.), have different goals and purposes (orientation to campus life, creation of community, introduction to the curriculum, etc.), and vary widely in their intensity (usually from one to three credit hours). Yet, all strive to help freshmen adjust to the rigors and responsibilities of college-level life.

Many of these programs explicitly seek to provide students with a broad orientation to the liberal arts. To such programs this book is directed. Though other introductory materials on the humanities exist, *A Student's Guide to the Liberal Arts* examines not only the nature of the liberal arts (chapter 1) and the goals of a liberal education (chapter 15), but also explores, in an introductory fashion, thirteen specific disciplines—communication, language, literature, music, art history, history, psychology, sociology, political science, philosophy, religion, mathematics, and science.

Contributors to *A Student's Guide to the Liberal Arts* are veteran faculty from liberal arts colleges and universities around the country. Each writes in an accessible and straightforward style, providing an introduction to the humanities for students coming into contact with college-level study for the first time. The focus of the volume is practical, not just theoretical. Each chapter gives guidance to students who are just beginning their study, while showing respect for the place of the student in his or her educational development.

Chapters have been written with a number of questions in mind. The study of foreign languages will serve as an example of the kinds of issues addressed in the chapters.

- What is the nature of language study?
- Why might a student be interested in studying a foreign lan-

guage? That is, apart from intellectual curiosity, why would a
business major or a student planning on entering a helping profession want to study a language? The chapter demonstrates how
studying a language can make students among the best-prepared
professionals in their career.

- How can students study languages successfully? The chapter offers numerous study hints, Internet resources, and other practical
  suggestions for effective, college-level study of languages.
- How does the study of a foreign language connect to the other
  disciplines in the liberal arts? The chapter points out the role of
  language study in helping students become more flexible, adaptable, and imaginative—qualities essential for success in most disciplines.
- How can students study foreign languages outside the classroom?
  The chapter offers a cornucopia of suggestions that take the student beyond the library and the classroom.
- What is the value of language study for a lifetime of learning and
  living? The chapter argues that the study of a language can literally transform students and enrich their lives, guarding them
  against xenophobia while helping them to become world citizens.

I wish to thank all of the contributors to this volume for their
exceptional work in the midst of a busy schedule of teaching.
Each writer is engaged in the full-time teaching of undergraduates
at a liberal arts college or university. Many of the writers are also
involved in working with first-year seminars on their campuses.
All write with expertise and passion about their discipline. I
would also like to thank Rockhurst University for a generous
Presidential Grant for the completion of this project. Finally, special acknowledgement is due to Sarah Lammers, manuscript assistant for the Rockhurst University Press, whose careful and
detailed work has made this a much better volume.

Wilburn T. Stancil

A Student's Guide to the Liberal Arts

1

What Are the Liberal Arts?

James V. Schall, S.J.

"Because," I said, "the free man ought not to learn any
study slavishly. Forced labors performed by the body
don't make the body any worse, but no forced study
abides in a soul."

Plato *The Republic* 536e

That there is to be education in music in such a way
that they will participate in the works [of music], therefore, is evident . . . What is appropriate and inappropriate for different ages is not difficult to define and
resolve, in response to those who assert that the concern
is a vulgar one. In the first place, since one should share
in the works for the sake of judging, on this account
they should practice the works when they are young,
and when they become older leave off the works, and
be able to judge the noble things and to enjoy [them]
in correct fashion through the learning that occurred in
their youth.

Aristotle *Politics* 1340b31–38

But in an orator . . . we demand the acuteness of a
logician, the profundity of a philosopher, the diction
virtually of a poet, the memory of a lawyer, the voice
of a performer in tragic drama, the gestures, you might
almost say, of an actor at the very top of his profession.

Cicero *On the Orator*

THE CLASSICAL TRADITIONS

IN THE *Crito* of Plato, during the month in jail awaiting the return
of the sacrificial ship that would occasion Socrates's execution,

Crito indicated that, from his personal wealth, he could easily provide a bribe to enable Socrates to escape. No one, even those who found him guilty as charged, really wanted Socrates to die. Besides, Crito, a rich friend of Socrates, would seem cheap in the eyes of the city if he did not come forth with bribe money to free Socrates. A convenient place to which Socrates might go in exile, Crito informs him, is Thessaly, famous for its barbarian ways. Socrates had already rejected the alternative of going to Thebes, a civilized city.

Nor would Socrates, contrary to his vocation, cease to philosophize so that he could remain in Athens, the cultured city that Pericles had called the freest. Socrates rejected going to Thessaly because, in such a society, he would have no one with whom to talk. The barbarian king would, of course, know of the big-city fame of Socrates, the philosopher. He would have asked him to his court to perform some amazing feat to impress his retainers. Kings often found hapless philosophers amusing, while philosophers were known to have conversed with kings.

Yet, for Socrates to be Socrates, the philosopher, he would need to engage in conversation, in dialectic. Such dialectic required someone genuinely interested in the higher things. Socrates preferred audiences that contained souls with some deep desire to know. He only undertook to give monologues before some corrupt, smooth politician like Callicles in the *Gorgias*. Callicles refused further to engage Socrates in conversation lest he, Callicles, have to question his own political life and its supposedly unlimited freedom to do whatever the politician wanted. As he tells us, he had gone to college in his youth; however, the young tyrant, by his own admission, rejected the principles of liberal education. He ceased all that academic nonsense when he went into the active life of politics. Nor was the barbarian king liberally educated. The former lacked virtue, the latter, culture.

The barbarians in Thessaly, then, although worthy enough in their own way, were not prepared systematically to examine their daily lives, the civic purpose that Socrates appointed to himself in *The Apology*. The barbarians would not have understood the point of such an "examined life." They were not "free" to know that they did not know. Socrates, who knew that he did not know, had to remain a private citizen even in Athens, lest he be elimi-

nated sooner. Still, his whole life was engaged in conversations
that could only take place in a city, albeit a disordered city. In this
city, philosophers and fools were not easily separated because no
principle of distinction was allowed. But in Athens, nevertheless,
philosophic *eros* might have some chance of attracting the souls of
potential philosophers who had not yet decided how they would
live their lives. Although philosophy was not necessarily or fully
at home in any existing city, including Athens, philosophers still
had to live in some place where they would not be killed, however much their killing might confirm their philosophic vocations
before the world. The cities in speech that they left us were designed to free us from actual cities even while living in them. To
have no articulated "city" in one's soul is the essence of an unfree
human being. To have one, placed there by argument, is to be
liberally educated (Chesterton, 53–58).

Likewise, in the New Testament, we read that Pilate, Christ's
Roman judge, hears that Christ is from Galilee, a place outside of
Pilate's immediate jurisdiction. In Galilee, the Romans had set up
Herod, a puppet king. Pilate, who knew this whole business of
executing Christ was messy, was delighted with the jurisdictional
excuse to put Christ outside of his legal authority. So he packs
him off to Herod's court for further judgment. Herod was
shrewd. He had, of course, heard of this Jesus and was anxious to
look him over. Like the barbarian king in Thessaly, Herod, too,
wanted Christ to be on stage. We can imagine the scene when
Christ is brought before Herod's court. Everyone is there, expect-
ing some feat, perhaps some miracle, about which many had
heard Christ to perform.

But before Herod, Christ remains in complete silence. He will
not "perform." He found nothing genuine in Herod, no place to
reach his soul. Herod evidently was sensitive enough to get the
point, so he returned Christ to Pilate. The gospel notes that up
until that time, Herod and Pilate, neither of whom was the absolute worst of men, were not on intimate terms, but now they
became "friends." They both experienced this Christ, silent before them, refusing to respond to unauthentic politicians. Theirs
was a friendship of complicity, of responsible men mutually rejecting their responsibilities, finding pleasant consolation in their,
to them, rather amusing, if lethal, jurisdictional game. If we are

liberally educated, we cannot help but see this "friendship" against the classical background of the friendship discussed by Plato, Aristotle, and Cicero.

Here, we have to recall a phrase that Leo Strauss has made famous, from Tertullian, both "Jerusalem and Athens" (Strauss, 147–73). That is, we have the two origins of our culture, the Greek heritage and the revelational response to its brooding questions to itself. And these origins belong together, however different each is. What is known as patristic and medieval thought is designed to explain how this relationship is possible, how the best in Athens can be seen as related to revelation and its unique terms. This seeing of this relationship is what Chesterton once called "the keenest of intellectual pleasures" (see Schall, "The Keenest of Intellectual Pleasures," 18–19). What is known as "modern" thought is largely the attempt to solve the classical human questions without recourse to either tradition (see Gilson). Any adequate concept of "liberal arts" and "liberal education" would, at the risk of intellectual incompleteness or dishonesty, require attention to the Greek and Roman classical traditions, to the Hebrew and Christian revelation, to the patristic and medieval experience, and, finally, to modern claims, especially those arising from science and politics, even when they claim to be "autonomous." Students who read Plato, Aristotle, St. Paul, and St. Augustine often are struck to find themselves more up-to-date, more knowledgeable about what is going on about them by reading these sources, than when they read *The New York Times,* or the latest textbook. The former possess a freedom and an intelligence that the latter somehow lack.

THE CONTRAST OF SLAVERY AND LEISURE

We are familiar with colleges that describe themselves as "liberal arts" colleges. We are also familiar with the distinction between things liberal and things servile. Work is sometimes designated, even in the church, as "servile," something to avoid on Sundays. Certain disciplines, particularly what is known from Aristotle as "metaphysics," are called freeing subjects. Such a "liberal" discipline is undertaken "for its own sake," that is, the purpose of the knowledge gained is not to "do" anything with it. Just to "know" something is in itself a pleasure, although it's often something we must learn to enjoy. The "useful" crafts and disciplines, even medicine and in its way art and law, are designed to "produce" or "make" something. The work, though worthy in itself, is "for" something else. The hammer can be in itself an artifact with ornate carvings, but is first intended to pound nails.

The notion of "slavery," in which someone was designated to perform "servile" work or labor, did not initially refer to something wrong with the slave, but something wrong with the work he was forced to perform. No one was willing to do it voluntarily. In the Book of Exodus, we read: "[the Israelites] were made to work in gangs with officers set over them, to break their spirit with heavy labor . . . So they [the Egyptians] treated their Israelite slaves with ruthless severity . . ." (Exod. 1:11–14). In short they made use of them as slaves in every kind of hard labor. Such slavery caused by conquest or other political means did not imply anything about the slave himself. Roman professors were sometimes Greek slaves.

The so-called "natural" slave, strictly speaking, was, unlike the captive slave, rather someone who was not *causa sui*. Such a person had some real and objective defect in body or mind that could not be remedied. He could not rule himself; he had to be ruled for his own good by another, be it family or state. Aristotle had already said, however, that if we could invent certain moving statues, perhaps it would be possible some day to make machines that would do much of this servile work that had to be done, like weaving or pounding. Such invention is indeed what eventually did happen in what came to be called the industrial revolution.

Much of the freedom from toil in the modern world is based on mechanical or technological "slaves" who do the work that is degrading for human beings to perform. Anyone who spends his time engaged in deadening or purposeless work, whether by coercion or by choice, would be considered by the Greeks to be a slave, however much we dislike that word. Moreover, as Yves Simon once remarked, if we contracted to pay a man a very high wage to dig a ditch six-by-six-by-six then fill it up again only to begin again and again, the man would soon go mad for being purposeless.

The main Christian commentary about this situation was, first, not to deny that there was back-breaking work, but, secondly, to affirm that the one who did it could nevertheless save his soul, that is, reach the highest things. Likewise, if a work needed to be done, even if it were drudgery, it usually had a worthy purpose, no matter how difficult or boring. It had the connotation of service to the poor, or to those who needed it, without which life could not go on. Even with adequate machinery, as modern totalitarian regimes have proved, without these two latter notions of personal salvation and objective service, legal slavery might never have been eliminated. Without them, slavery will no doubt return in some form or other. The worker has his dignity, the work has its purpose; but still there are things "for their own sake" that are neither drudgery nor directly the Beatific Vision. The order of things to be known and done in the world remains a worthy project even if we may, on occasion, save our souls without them. This too is part of revelation.

What is surprising about the sundry machines and devices from water wheels to computers that have been invented to do so many of the tasks that were otherwise considered inhuman and toilsome is that we end up, as even Hobbes suspected, with what is called "free time" and the problem of what to do with it. We have designed machines and techniques so that we do not have to do many necessary things that keep us alive and prosperous, things from sanitation systems to satellites. Is this time we now have left over merely "pastime"? Or are there things to be done that are not merely "useful"? This is the issue that Plato and Aristotle in ancient times and Josef Pieper in modern times have made famous under the notion of *skole,* or leisure (see Pieper). Ancient cities were criticized because they used slaves to do the servile work so at least a few could be free enough to pursue other, more noble things. Modern cities are often criticized because they are full of people with free time that is frittered away on frivolous things.

In a famous passage in *The Republic,* in the city he is building in speech, Socrates first sketches a city with a sufficiency of worldly goods and indeed with an abundance of luxurious goods, all of which came forth because of a demand caused by unlimited desire. Glaucon bitingly called this abundant economy "a city of pigs;" that is, it was a city with nothing higher in it than keeping alive and content. Glaucon's famous phrase was not a compliment, however worthy an accomplishment it might be to have both needed and luxurious things in existing cities. He was aware that what was most important about human life had not yet even been discussed in the city in speech. In the classical sense of the term, the "liberal arts" have to do with these things that exist in the midst of or beyond abundance. This does not deny that the intellectual and productive efforts to make this abundance come to pass—the free market, the rules of justice and law, the value of work—were also, in their own ways, freeing and noble ones.

The Liberal Arts Tradition Handed Down

"Liberal arts" have a history. The Greek and Roman experiences are, and remain in some sense, normative. To be free we must continue to study them carefully. The attentive reading of the Greek and Roman philosophical, literary, historical, and political traditions begins and continues a reflection into the heart of things that cannot be duplicated as easily or as elegantly by any other tradition. This is in large part because this tradition thought, however proud it was to be Greek or Roman, that it was addressing humanity as such. Metaphysics was not "Greek" metaphysics, but "metaphysics." The principles of "oratory" were not Roman, but universal.

Moreover, not only is this tradition worthy in itself; but it becomes doubly worthy because of the subsequent traditions that, themselves, read this initial source and commented on it, rewrote it, even objected to it. It was not an accident that Cicero, as he tells us in his *De Officiis,* sent his son, however unworthy, to Athens to study. Nor was it an accident that Augustine, as he tells us in *The Confessions,* decided, as a brash young man, to become a philosopher because of a now-lost Ciceronian dialogue. Likewise, it is not surprising that Augustine's major work is entitled *The City of God,* both because two Psalms speak of such a city (Ps. 46 and Ps. 87) and because Plato wrote *The Republic.* We cannot read Augustine without, at the same time, reading the Greeks, the Romans, the Hebrews, and the Christians. Augustine was a man of "liberal learning," who even wrote a dialogue featuring his own son entitled, *De Magistro*, "On the Teacher." Augustine still teaches us, if we but let him.

One of the men most responsible for what is known in the United States as "great books programs," themselves designed as efforts to "save" liberal education, was Mortimer Adler (but see Wilhelmsen, 323–31). "Liberal arts are traditionally intended to develop the faculties of the human mind, those powers of intelligence and imagination without which no intellectual work can be accomplished," Adler has written. He notes that:

> Liberal education is not tied to certain academic subjects, such as philosophy, history, literature, music, art, and other so-called "humanities." In the liberal-arts tradition, scientific disciplines, such as mathematics and physics, are considered equally liberal, that is, equally able to develop the powers of the mind. The liberal-arts tradition goes back to the medieval curriculum. It consisted in two parts. The first part, trivium, comprised grammar, rhetoric, and logic. It taught the arts of reading and writing, of listening and speaking, and of sound thinking. The other part, the quadrivium, consisted of arithmetic, geometry, astronomy, and music (not audible music, but music conceived as a mathematical science). It taught the arts of observation, calculation, and measurement, how to apprehend the quantitative aspect of things. Nowadays, of course, we would add many more sciences, natural and social. This is just what has been done in the various modern attempts to renew liberal education (Adler).

These medieval programs were called *trivium* and *quadrivium*, that is, they indicated the place where three *(tres viae)* ways or roads or four *(quatro viae)* roads of knowledge preparation crossed in the same person. The *quadrivium*, in particular, had to do with numbers—arithmetic meant "number in itself," geometry meant "number in space," music meant "number in time," and astronomy meant "number in space and time" (see "The Seven Liberal Arts"). Without preparation in such disciplines, we lack the intellectual tools to understand the world. They were each worthy of study in themselves, but once acquired, the student was "free" to stand before all things as a whole, both to know and to act. Hence the notion associated with "liberal arts" was "universal" or "general."

THE PLEASURE OF LEARNING AND THE UNEDUCATED PERSON

In order to be a complete human being, there were things worth doing and knowing. Man was an animal who freely needed to complete himself to be what he was intended to be. But this "self-completion" was not considered to be, although it could be, an act of pride or autonomy, that is, an act that made man the cause of the distinction in things. The fact that man had to "complete" himself to be what he was intended to be was itself a challenge in his own soul. It was a deference to his own initiative and freedom.

Education, moreover, was itself not a "thing." The word *educare* means to bring forth, or to complete something already begun by the very fact that one is a human being. We do not "make ourselves" to be human beings, as Aristotle constantly affirmed, though we do make ourselves to be good or bad human beings, complete or incomplete human beings. Yet, the freedom to become bad or evil is itself a kind of slavery, since it deflects us from our proper end. This is why the path to freedom in this classical tradition is always pictured as one of acquiring virtues and avoiding corresponding vices.

But the human mind itself had its own proper functioning. It was something *capax omnium,* something capable of knowing all the things it did not itself make or create. Aristotle had remarked that there is a proper pleasure attached to every human activity, including the activity of thinking, of knowing, as well as of willing, doing, and making. It would not be wrong, thus, to describe "liberal education" as the effort to experience the proper pleasure due to knowing, according to what they are, *all the things that are*—seeing, tasting, listening, touching, smelling, remembering, imagining, knowing, thinking, believing. "To be learning something is the greatest of pleasures," Aristotle remarked in a surprisingly open phrase, "not only to the philosopher but to the rest of mankind, however small their capacity" (*Ethics* 148b13–15). But since we can choose disorder, since we can reject the kind of being we ought to be, it is quite possible to be illiberally educated; indeed it is possible to acquire vices instead of virtues while knowing what both are. What would someone who does not acquire the proper formation of his soul look like?

We are fortunate to have three classical descriptions, without citing, in addition, Horace's famous description of the bore. Let me cite two portrayals—one from Plato, one from the English novelist Evelyn Waugh. In each of these descriptions, we find pictured a man who can certainly read and write, who is active in public, and who, no doubt, thinks he is properly educated. But in each description, it is clear that the person described lacks the very order of soul and mind that would enable us to call him "free" and judicious in his relation to the highest things.

In the eighth book of *The Republic,* Plato describes the soul of the democratic man, the man who is "free," that is, the man with no order of principle in his soul. What is his day like? And why? How does he appear before others? This is Plato's description:

> And he doesn't admit any word of truth into the guardhouse (of his soul), for if someone tells him that some pleasures belong to the fine and good desires and others to evil ones and that he must pursue and value the former and restrain and enslave the latter, he denies all this and declares that all pleasures are equal and must be valued equally.
>
> (Adeimantus) That is just what someone in that condition would say.
>
> And so he lives on, yielding day by day to the desire at hand. Sometimes he drinks heavily while listening to the flute; at other times, he drinks only water and is on a diet; sometimes he goes in for physical training; at other times, he's idle and neglects everything; and sometimes he even occupies himself with what he takes to be philosophy. He often engages in politics, leaping up from his seat and saying and doing whatever comes into his mind. If he happens to admire soldiers, he's carried in that direction, if money-making, in that one. There's neither order nor necessity in his life, but he calls it pleasant, free, and blessedly happy, and he follows it for as long as he lives (561b–d).

It would be difficult to find a more blunt description of what a liberal education is not. Such is the man who thinks his life to be pleasant and free when it is, by any objective evaluation, just the opposite.

Each point of the young man's disordered soul needs emphasizing: on occasion he jogs to keep in shape. Next, however, he is found with a beer lounging around mostly watching TV. One day, after seeing or hearing one, he desires to be a banker, the following day, a soldier, the day after, even a philosopher. He drinks heavily, then goes on a diet and drinks only water. He denies himself no pleasure, considers all pleasures equal whether they follow good or bad actions. In short, the man has no principle of order in his soul, no way to distinguish worthy and unworthy ways of life. Such a person endangers both himself and his polity precisely because his soul is disordered by a lack of discipline and knowledge about what human life is about. Plato never tired of reminding the potential philosopher that the condition of his city ultimately depended on the condition of his soul. No political reform could ever be successful without personal reform. No one who did not understand this relationship could be "liberally" educated.

Aristotle has a similar description in the *Politics* (1323a26–34) of a man whom no one would want to be if he could help it. One of the prime purposes of good literature is to enable us to encounter vicariously what disordered souls might look like before we ever decide to put them into our own lives, when it is too late. Again, because of lack of virtue, the man in Aristotle's graphic description is unable to do what he ought. And while Aristotle does not think virtue is a question of knowledge alone, still there is a knowledge component to virtue. That component is called prudence. Without this virtue, without the examination of the possible ends to which it might possibly be employed to examine the means to achieve it, the soul is continually engaged in pursuing false definitions of its own happiness and taking the wrong means to achieve it.

The man with a faulty understanding of what it means to be liberally educated is not free to do what he ought to do because, like Plato's democratic youth, he does what he wants, whatever it is. He denies himself no pleasure and refuses to acknowledge any distinction between good and bad not of his own making. Thereby he is "free" even to do what is wrong and call it virtuous. This position already anticipates the "freedom" of Machiavelli's prince, the apparently exhilarating but corrupting freedom to do wrong when "necessary," the freedom to reject Socrates's principle that "it is never right to do wrong."

The second passage I should like to cite in this consideration of what no one would want to be, of how one's faulty education will not really free him or teach him the truth of things, including human things, comes from Waugh's novel *Brideshead Revisited*. In the early part of World War II, Waugh had occasion to comment on the type of modern young man who comes into the army. He is clearly a young man of modern education and taste, a worthy successor to the men described by Plato and Aristotle. This young man's name is Hooper.

> Hooper was no romantic. He had not as a child ridden with Rupert's horse or sat among the camp fires at Xanthus-side; at the age when my eyes were dry to all save poetry—that stoic, red-skin interlude which our schools introduce between the fast flowing tears of the child and the man—Hooper had wept often, but never for Henry's speech on St. Crispin's Day, nor for the epitaph at Thermopylae. The history they taught him had had few battles in it but, instead, a profusion of detail about humane legislation and recent industrial change. Gallipoli, Balaclava, Quebec, Lepanto, Bannockburn, Roncevales, and Marathon—these, and the Battle of the West where Arthur fell, and a hundred such names whose trumpet-notes, even now in my sere and lawless state, called to me irresistibly across the intervening years with all the clarity and strength of boyhood, sounded in vain to Hooper (Waugh, 9).

Hooper evidently had a social science education, heavy on statistics and "facts." He did not know of the great events of history that ought to have filled his boyhood imagination. He was not liberally educated. He was not free.

In book four of Aristotle's *Ethics,* the word "liberal" initially had to do with material possessions. Aristotle saw that to be virtuous we needed a certain amount of material goods. He also understood that we reveal our souls by how we deal with the material goods, large or small, that we do have. The Greek word *elutheria* referred to that virtue by which we rule our material goods so that we can achieve our higher purposes by their proper use. The word is sometimes translated as "generosity" or "liberality." It has two aspects, the person with ordinary wealth and the person with immense wealth. Aristotle was not particularly worried that some people had more wealth than others. Rather he was concerned with how our wealth, whether little or great, was used. Liberality or generosity is a virtue precisely because it is designed to free us from ourselves to see that what we possess is also related to others not just for their good but for their enjoyment.

"Freedom to welcome truth, without hindrance on the part of our mind, certainly is a rare privilege," Yves Simon has written in a perceptive essay entitled, "Freedom from the Self."

> That human freedom should be restricted in this high order of the mind's relation to truth is a moral and metaphysical disaster of the first magnitude. Knowing is the creature's best chance to overcome the law of nonbeing, the wretchedness inflicted upon it by the real diversity of "that which is" and "to be." A thing which is not God cannot *be* except at the cost of *not being what it is not.* It cannot be except by being deprived of indefinitely many forms and perfections. To this situation, knowledge, according to St. Thomas' words, is a remedy, inasmuch as every knowing subject is able to have, over and above its own form, the forms of other things. This remedy is, so to say, complete in the case of intellectual knowledge, for intelligent beings can have the forms of all things and be all things spiritually, intentionally, transsubjectively, objectively (Simon, with a reference to Aquinas *De Veritate* 2.2).

Freedom from the self is first required that we might have a freedom for others, a freedom to know *what is.*

We cannot be the kind of being we are unless we are not other things. Thus, it is all right to be what we are. Yet, what we are contains this mind with its *capax omnium,* with its capacity to know *all that is.* It is this exciting freedom to take into our souls what we are not, to take it in without changing or destroying what we take in, that constitutes the purpose of liberal arts, which are designed to teach us how to be open to the various levels of being (see Schumacher on this point).

THE WAYS OF UNDERSTANDING LIBERAL ARTS

Robert Kagan has traced the various understandings given to the term liberal arts or a liberal education. Generally, the term included the ideas: (1) that knowledge was its own purpose, an end in itself, that it was good to know; (2) that liberty meant having the virtues whereby we could rule ourselves; (3) that knowledge included something useful, some worthy way of making one's way in the world; and (4) that this liberal learning had a political component, the ideal of living in a free society, of participating in ruling and being ruled (Kagan, 5). The Roman notion of education was more practically oriented than the Greek classical view. The Romans stressed the capacity of speech, of eloquence. Aristotle had said in his *Rhetoric* that a man should be as able to defend himself with his speech as with his arms.

The medieval university, having newly discovered Aristotle and being familiar with revelation and the classic heritage through the Fathers of the Church, considered that a liberal education dealt with already-discovered things. The source of truth was God, both as known by reason and by revelation. Logic and dialectic studies seemed the best way to prepare oneself for grasping what is known. The medieval *summae* and curricula, while not neglecting practical things, attempted to organize all of what men knew into one orderly, interrelated whole (see Lins for a still-masterly treatment of this topic). The Renaissance notion of a liberal education was, in part, an effort to return to the classics minus the addenda of revelation while minimizing the Greek notion of the contemplative life. There was a revival of the notion of the primacy of the city and its demands. The focus again became "this worldly." More particularly modern education was interested in what was not yet known. The "scientific method" stressed not what was revealed or what was previously learned or even what was useful for the city, but "new things." With the spread of "scientific method" into all disciplines, including the liberal ones, with its implication of "progress," it was again proposed that the secret to general education was at hand.

The modern university is "liberal" in the sense that it does not have any principle of priority. No department or branch of knowledge seems to have any priority over the other. Each discipline has in common only what each discipline maintains about itself. In this context, it becomes almost impossible to have a "liberal education" in the classical sense. Not merely do the great books seem to contradict each other, but so do the "truths" that are found in the disciplines (see Strauss, "What Is Liberal Education?" 3–8). The primacy of relativism as the ground for democratic education seems to flow from the condition of modern knowledge, as it flowed from Aristotle's notion that "democracy" was based on that understanding of liberty that had no order other than that of its own choosing. Universities are perhaps useful as a place for preparation especially of elite students who will, by a kind of aristocratic heritage, gain control of certain professions and offices in the economy and in politics. But whether there is in fact a genuine place of "liberal education" can be doubted in the present context. Not merely are the classics and revelation considered to be inadmissible as norms or canons for the education of all, but the sciences themselves never know what they might be in the future. The conclusion of this observation is not that there is no place for liberal learning, but that its place may not always, or even usually, be found in ordinary academic institutions (see Schall, *Another Sort of Learning* and *Student's Guide*).

THE PLACE OF ERROR IN LIBERAL EDUCATION

We are, of course, reluctant to admit that the case for "liberal education," for "liberal arts," for the things that free us from slavery to the self, from contentment with merely the useful, is hopeless. Liberal education is not a "speciality." It is not what is called a "major." Rather it is rooted in the kind of intellectual *eros* that we find in Plato, in the "wonder" that begins all thought in Aristotle, in the drive to know what reoriented the life of the young Augustine when he read Cicero. This *eros* lies behind all we do, since all things are worth knowing. "There is no such thing as an uninteresting subject," Chesterton once remarked, "but only uninterested people." Jacques Maritain put the issue bluntly: "Great poets and thinkers are the foster-fathers of intelligence. Cut off from them, we are simply barbarians" (Maritain, 85). That we be not barbarians, that we be not cut off from great poets and thinkers is what we mean by being "free" because we know the *things that are.*

  The liberal arts have something to do both with solitude and with the city. Cicero began the third part of his famous *De Officiis* (On Duties) with these memorable words: "Publius Cornelius Scipio, the first of the family to be called Africanus, used to remark that he was never less idle than when he had nothing to do, and never less lonely than when he was by himself" (159). We can likewise almost feel the draw of the city in this passage from Boswell. He and Samuel Johnson had stayed overnight at St. Albans. The following day, March 29, 1776, Boswell writes, "I enjoyed the luxury of our approach to London, that metropolis which we both loved so much, for the high and varied intellectual pleasure which it furnishes" (2.3). Again here we have that classic theme that there are genuine intellectual pleasures, that they are to be found in cities, without forgetting the fact that cities also kill philosophers and others of its own. One might almost say, in this context, that the reading and rereading of Cicero and of Boswell's *Life of Johnson* can, by itself, be considered a liberal education. There is more, but these are good beginnings, indeed good endings of such an enterprise.

Great thinkers, no doubt, can be and have been in error. Aristotle, who knew Plato's worry that the poets could corrupt us, understood that the knowledge of error, even great error, is not something that we should reject knowing. It is part of being free. "We must, however, not only state the true view," Aristotle observed, "but also explain the false views, since an explanation of that promotes confidence. For when we have an apparently reasonable explanation of why a false view appears true, that makes us more confident of the true view." (*Ethics* 1154a23–26). The history of error, the history of heresy (I think of Chesterton's *Heretics*), is as much a part of liberal education as the insight into truth. A considerable part of being intelligent and being virtuous consists in knowing what it is to be unintelligent and unvirtuous, especially knowing from graphic terms in which we see these in our literature.

Unless we can understand the arguments against truth, we do not fully understand it. And the arguments against truth can be very persuasive. Part of any liberal education is to know these arguments, and to know the truths to which they point. Josef Cardinal Ratzinger, himself a man of genteel and liberal leaning, gave a good example of this awareness that part of being free is to know where ideas lead. "The central problem of our time," he observed on October 6, 2001, at the Synod of Bishops in Rome, "is the emptying-out of the historical figure of Jesus. It begins with denying the virgin birth, then the resurrection becomes a spiritual event, then Christ's awareness of being the Son of God is denied, leaving Him only the words of a rabbi. Then the Eucharist falls, and becomes just a farewell dinner." We are reassured to see the connection of ideas and things, itself the result of our being free, being open to *what is*.

John Henry Newman, whose book *The Idea of a University* stands at the heart of any modern discussion of this topic, made this point about the difference between liberal education and salvation (144). Newman held that no matter how valuable natural virtues are, they do not, significant in themselves though they be, guarantee supernatural excellence. The gentleman, while perhaps being exquisitely refined, can still lose his soul (145). This is just another way of saying that man has a destiny higher than perfection in this world. Indeed, it implies that perfection even in this world is not complete without attention to his ultimate purpose. Any education can stop short of this higher purpose, but it does so at the cost of what is true at any level wherein something, in being itself, always points us higher.

Aristotle had indeed given many hints that something more was "due" to human nature than seemed given to it, although he was not quite sure what it was. "Such a (contemplative) life would be superior to the human level. For someone will live it not in so far as he is a human being, but in so far as he has some divine element in him." (*Ethics* 1177b27–28). This passage suggests why it may be "illiberal" not to include all that we can know of man in our "freeing" education of him. The best "natural" explanations of our condition as human beings seem to be aware that we are lacking something, not merely because of a certain "wickedness" of which even Aristotle was aware, but because nothing we find in our ordinary ways seems to satisfy us (*Politics* 1267b1). This again is Augustine's realism (see Deane).

Education that does not include explanations and understandings of what we are will rely on an education that lacks the necessary intellectual tools and information fully to explain man to himself. To explain man to himself is the central purpose of any liberal understanding of man. It is also, as Pope John Paul II often says, the purpose of Christianity. Christian literature presupposes certain unanswered, often brilliant questions that had already occurred to the human mind before Christianity itself came into being. The liberally educated man knows these classic questions as they arise in any soul, including his own. A liberally educated Christian cannot understand his own revelation if he, too, does not know the force of these classic questions.

Conclusion

In conclusion, liberal arts include the intellectual *eros* that is unsettled by not knowing what is true. If we read descriptions of this philosophic *eros* along side the revelational proposition that "man is not properly speaking human but superhuman" (*homo non proprie humanus sed superhumanus est*, Aquinas), we can at least suspect that this unsettlement that we find in human history is itself something put there from the beginning. To be free, that is, to be "liberally educated," to practice the truly "liberal arts" is to be open to something that is not ourselves, or not made by ourselves. Mankind is more a drama of receptivity than it is of its own creativity in cities and in arts.

The final word, I think, should be that of Aristotle, the man who made us most aware that there is an order in things. "For self-sufficiency and action do not depend on excess," he wrote in the *Ethics*, "and we can do fine actions even if we do not rule earth and sea; for even from moderate circumstances we càn do the actions expressing virtue" (1179a2–6). We do not have to rule the land and the sea to do fine actions. Ordinary people can do actions that express virtue, they can know *what is*. The revelational side of this same principle is simply that everyone, king or pauper, can, with grace, save his own soul. If we combine these two principles, we have the essence of what it is to be free, free both to know what the world is like and what is our destiny. We can, to be sure, choose to be "illiberal," to be "slaves" to ourselves, mindlessly to say whatever it is that comes into our heads. What it is to be "illiberal," in short, points us to "liberal arts," to what it is to be free enough to know the truth of things and to find pleasure in this truth.

Works Cited

Adler, Mortimer. "What Is Liberal Education?" Available: http://www.realuofe.org/libed/adler/wle.html.
Boswell's Life of Johnson. London: Oxford, 1931.
Chesterton, G. K. "On the Classics." In *Come to Think of It*. New York: Dodd, Mead, 1931.

Cicero. *Selected Works.* Edited by Michael Grant. Harmondsworth: Penguin, 1960.

Deane, Herbert. *The Political and Social Ideas of St. Augustine.* New York: Columbia University Press, 1956.

Gilson, Etienne. *Reason and Revelation in the Middle Ages.* New York: Scribner's, 1938.

Kagan, Donald. "What Is A Liberal Education?" In *The McDermott Papers.* Irving, Tex.: University of Dallas, 2001.

Lins, Joseph. "The Seven Liberal Arts." In *The Catholic Encyclopedia,* 1:760–65. New York: Appleton, 1912.

Maritain, Jacques. "Education and the Humanities." In *The Education of Man: The Educational Philosophy of Jacques Maritain.* Edited by Donald and Idella Gallagher. Garden City, N.Y.: Doubleday, 1962.

Newman, John Henry. *The Idea of a University.* Garden City, N.Y.: Doubleday Image, 1959.

Pieper, Josef. *Leisure: The Basis of Culture.* Translated by G. Malsbary. South Bend, Ind.: St. Augustine's Press, 1998.

Schall, James V. *Another Sort of Learning.* San Francisco: Ignatius Press, 1988.

———. *A Student's Guide to Liberal Learning.* Wilmington, Del.: Intercollegiate Studies, 1997.

———. "The Keenest of Intellectual Pleasures." *Gilbert!* 4 (March 2001): 18–19.

Schumacher, E. F. *A Guide for the Perplexed.* New York: Harper Colophon, 1977.

"The Seven Liberal Arts." Available: http://www.cosmopolis .com/villa/liberal-arts.html.

Simon, Yves. "Freedom from the Self." In *A General Theory of Authority,* 151–52. Notre Dame: University of Notre Dame Press, 1980.

Strauss, Leo. "Jerusalem and Athens: Some Preliminary Reflections." In *Studies in Platonic Political Philosophy.* Edited by Thomas Pangle. Chicago: University of Chicago Press, 1983.

———. "What Is Liberal Education?" In *Liberalism: Ancient and Modern.* Chicago: University of Chicago Press, 1968.

Waugh, Evelyn. *Brideshead Revisited.* Boston: Little, Brown, 1945.

Wilhelmsen, Frederick. "Great Books: Enemies of Wisdom?" *Modern Age* 31 (Summer/Fall 1987).

2

The Study of Communication

Daniel S. Brown

COMMUNICATION is among the oldest of the academic disciplines, yet it is one of the most recent additions to many college curricula. Its value in a modern liberal arts education is obvious, and even the ancient Greeks included the study of rhetoric in their trivium. The Egyptian wisdom writings entitled *Instruction of Ptah-Hotep* and the *Instruction of Ke'gemni,* that date perhaps to 3,200 B.C., comprise what are considered the oldest known books from the ancient world. The writings include practical, systematic advice about improving communication and relationships. The *Ptah-Hopte* and *Ke'gemni* texts take a form very similar to the Book of Proverbs, the collection that Judeo–Christian faith communities honor for its practical guidelines, including advice about communication. Despite its ancient roots, the study of communication is currently recognized as one of the fastest growing fields of study in higher education.

The many titles for communication departments—your college's department might be called the Department of Speech, the Department of Rhetoric, the Department of Communication Arts, the Department of Mass Communication and Journalism, or the Department of Media and Culture—signal the field's rich, diverse history as well as the breadth of interests of those who study and teach communication. The existence of so many monikers actually highlights the pervasiveness of communication in all of life. It is a broad field of study, without a doubt. Indeed, a recent publication from the National Communication Association (NCA) identified more than twenty concentrations or majors offered by communication departments. These range from applied communication to communication theory, from family communication to legal communication, from journalism to advertising, from gender communication to public relations, and from small group communication to semiotics. While diversity exists from campus to campus, communication is a comprehensive and well-defined academic discipline that enjoys a rich legacy.

This chapter is organized into three parts. In the first part, we focus on a core definition of communication and suggest a rationale for its centrality in the liberal arts. Second, we explore some basic approaches used to study communication in the early twenty-first century. This section also explains how communication is interdependent upon the other liberal arts and sciences. The third and final part of this chapter will suggest additional arenas where communication students can put their interests to work outside of the classroom.

WHAT IS COMMUNICATION?

I heard a delightful anecdote recently. Several years ago, a young professor of what was then called "speech communication" traveled through the British Isles during an academic break. His journey took him to an English pub one evening. It was one of those centuries-old, dark-paneled gathering rooms where no strangers were known. Welcomed by other travelers over a pint of ale, they shared their stories in turn.

"So what is it that you do, friend?" asked one of his new British hosts. "Well, I am from the States. There I teach speech at the university level." An awkward silence fell over the group. "Speech at the university, you say?" someone said. Another pause. "Over here, our children pick that up around the age of four or so."

The twinkle in the taunter's eye let everyone know this was a man of humor, but the laughter that followed also highlighted an important question. If we all "pick up" communication as children—if we all communicate as part of our human nature—why is it that we think we should study and teach it? More critically, what exactly do we mean when we talk about the academic study of communication?

I begin many of my courses with one of three exercises designed to help my students think about this question at the beginning of each term: "What exactly do we mean by 'communication studies,' anyway"? Sometimes, I assign my students to learning groups and ask them to "draw a model or a pictorial graphic" of what communication should look like in an interpersonal context. In other classes, I set my students loose on campus after asking them to interview seven or eight members of the college community. "Ask them, 'What do you think communication majors study?'" I instruct. At the next class meeting, their short papers synthesizing the responses they received provide a good gauge for how faculty, staff, and students view communication studies on our campus. As a third strategy, I sometimes ask two professors from very disparate disciplines—say biology and French—to present a brief talk about how communication courses impacted them when they were undergraduate students. What my students and I soon discover is this: communication means different things to different people at different stages in their life experiences.

Most basically, of course, communication involves the study of messages. Figure 1 shows a snapshot of a basic and simple model of communication. In order for communication to exist, four essential elements must intersect. There is a *source* that is motivated to share a *message*. The message is transmitted through a *channel* to a *receiver*. This is the S-M-C-R model that is popular in many basic textbooks. Often a "feedback loop" is also added to this simple and basic linear model of communication. But note that, according to this model of communication at least, it's all about the message.

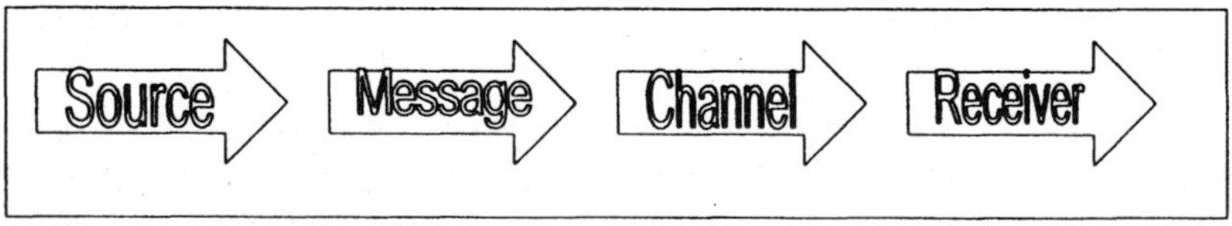

Fig. 1.
The S-M-C-R Model of Communication

Communication always involves more than these essentials, and scholars have produced literally hundreds of good definitions of communication. One such scholar, Harold Lasswell, the political scientist at the University of Chicago and later at Yale University, conducted original research on Germany's World War II propaganda in the early part of the last century. While conducting his research on propaganda, Lasswell fashioned a simple definition of communication that has become a classic. Lasswell claimed that communication studies focus on this question: *Who* says *what* through *which channel,* to *whom,* with *what effect?* This was one of the first widely accepted, contemporary definitions of communication. Obviously, his approach, and that of many scholars who followed him, favored the S-M-C-R model with the addition of a feedback loop.

Today, however, we recognize that the world of communication studies is much richer, much broader, and—frankly—much more complicated than Lasswell would lead us to believe. As we have noted, many basic media and speech communication textbooks still use Lasswell, or the S-M-C-R model, as a beginning point for their readers; but we are naïve if we do not look at the larger connotations of communication studies. As students discover during the first week of our classes, message creation and transmission are only part of what we are concerned with in communication.

In the mid-1990s, several members of NCA met to draft a definition of communication that would be understood by the general public. After months of work, the following definition emerged from their work: "The field of communication focuses on how people use messages to generate meanings with and across various contexts, cultures, channels, and media. The field promotes the effective and ethical practice of human communication" (*Pathways,* 1).

I like this definition because it calls our attention to the most common areas investigated by communication majors in their programs of study. Most programs in communication have a conscious emphasis on message analysis and creation. But each program also has a specialty or focus for which it is known; some emphasize broadcasting or film, others emphasize platform arts, face-to-face human interactions, or corporate communication.

Then, too, colleges and universities are increasingly turning to their communication faculties to assist all their students in developing their communication skills and generating a personal ethic of communication.

Messages occur in an abundance of locations, scenes, and settings, according to the NCA definition. For our study of communication to be worthwhile, we must understand that the world of communication is diverse and complicated.

Communication scholarship recognizes three dimensions in our field of studies. First, consider that communication may be either oral or written communication. Written communication is very often taught and studied in departments of English, while scholars who teach and study oral communication are typically housed in departments of communication. There is a great deal of cross-over to be sure, but the principles involved in effective writing and effective speaking differ significantly enough that we recognize this as a primary distinction in the world of communication.

The second dimension reflects our understanding that communication may be experienced either directly or indirectly. That is, communication can occur either face-to-face or in a mediated fashion. By mediated, we mean to refer to those messages that go through an electronic channel before reaching the receiver. Publishing, filming, broadcasting, or cybercasting a message means it is reaching the receiver indirectly, through a medium that replaces the face-to-face interaction that is basic to human relations.

You and I—the reader and the writer—have this book in common. While you and I do not share physical proximity, we are sharing a message. The strategies we use while engaged in this written, mediated communicative effort differ from the strategies that we would use if we were sitting in a coffee shop, one-on-one reviewing the same message. We also know that, depending upon the purpose of the message's source, the usefulness of mediated communication differs from that of direct communication. By this we understand that a book chapter is a better, more effective, or more cost-efficient means of communicating content or information. While it would be wonderful to meet each reader using the direct, oral mode, we instinctively understand the advantages of using the mediated, written mode in this case.

Communication, therefore, can be viewed as taking place in at least two different dimensions and in four different modes. These modes, visually demonstrated in figure 2, begin to highlight the variety of channels from which sources have to choose in order to communicate their message to the targeted receivers. Furthermore, students can begin to see how their communication interests fit together. A newswriting class, for example, focuses on written, mediated communication, while public speaking is a class that focuses, perhaps exclusively, on oral, direct communication.

As important as it is to understand these two dimensions of communication, a critical third dimension is also involved. Figure 3 shows what the world of communication looks like when we add six levels of communication to the four modes of communication.

Let us briefly reflect on each of the six levels of communication. The first level of communication is the interpersonal level. *Interpersonal communication* is often used synonymously with dyadic communication, that is, two people—a dyad—talking. Your Internet conversations with your mother, your telephone arguments with your best friend, your appeal to your dormitory assistant, a note passed in class, and your face-to-face "stupid question" asked

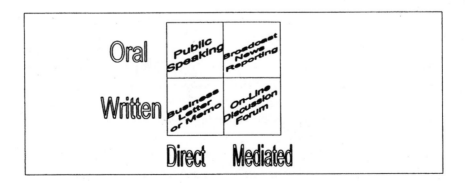

Fig. 2.
The Modes of Communication Including Examples of Contexts

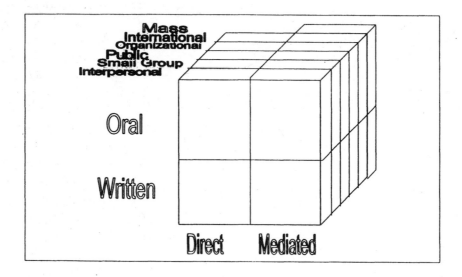

Fig. 3.
The World of Communication Including the Six Levels of
Communication

to the clerk at the local "Home Super-Store" are all interpersonal
communication.

Communication changes somehow, however, when you add a
third person to the mix. Have you ever been engaged in an exclusive conversation with another person when a third individual
wanders by and tries to jump into the dialog? It's an awkward
feeling for everyone, as the relationships and the communication
patterns need to be re-negotiated. The tone, formality, and even
the content will change. *Small group communication* takes place
when anywhere from three to eight individuals are engaged in
communication. Any time you find a group of three to eight
individuals who are sharing in the responsibility for a task, small
group communication is at work. Other hallmarks include group
members taking turns leading and following, members taking on
specific goals and chores for the good of the group, a clear divi-

sion of labor, and a sense of identity or cohesiveness among group members. Ad hoc committees, planning commissions, task forces, and hearing boards provide examples of small group communication.

If you have ever been part of a real-time Internet chat forum, you know that something happens as more people are added. Six or seven people in a chat forum are fine. It is difficult and takes concentration, but you can keep everyone's screen name straight; you can follow their trains of thought. The group is still depending on every member's contribution when there are eight members. Because of that interdependence, group members are respected and their contributions are solicited. The group will miss a member if she drops out of the chat for too long. As is the case when interpersonal communication becomes small group communication, small group communication goes through a change when a ninth or tenth member is added.

At some point, members begin to fall by the way. As a group grows in size, the reported satisfaction levels of individual members decreases. This occurs in part because they are no longer able to follow all the contributions to the group. Neither are they able to find an opening that allows them to make their own unique observations. They no longer are interested in the main discussion group. Perhaps they would rather follow a totally different discussion thread. Maybe they stop participating all together. The group can survive without them, they reason; and they are correct.

This phenomenon occurs in real-time groups as well as in chatrooms, of course. Without everyone focused and participating, the result will be less than desirable. This is why most large groups—say your college's Board of Trustees—will break themselves into small working groups or committees.

As a group grows to include nine or more members, communication begins to function differently. We call this level *public communication*. At this level, there is usually a clear leader in a larger group who is in charge of the setting—often called "the speaker" or "the author"—and an identifiable receiver—"the audience." These roles are fixed in public communication; small group members, as we have inferred, usually take turns at leading and following in the process.

The message in public communication is expected to be much

better prepared than it is in interpersonal or small group contexts. The level of formality increases in public communication settings as well. For these reasons, teleconferences being cablecast to an entire organization are much different than the Internet chat rooms described above.

A fourth level of communication is *organizational communication*. Currently one of the fastest-growing areas of interest among communication scholars and students, organizational communication focuses on the flow of messages through networks of interdependent relationships or groups in an ever-changing environment. Today's organizations are faced with rapidly changing internal politics and external pressures. How efficiently and effectively those organizations communicate both internally and externally will determine whether they exist in the future and whether they are successful in realizing their mission if they do exist in the future.

Another level of communication occurs when the participants are from different countries or cultures. *International communication* can be written or oral, of course. It can also be direct or mediated through an electronic channel of some sort. Misunderstandings that result from a lack of common language and shared history sometimes turn violent. Most often, but not always, cultural differences come into play with international communication. Participants in intercultural and international exchanges constantly must be cognizant not only of denotative meanings of the words and symbols they are using, but also the connotations that those words and symbols carry. Understanding develops between nations only as their representatives generate messages and create meaning with each other.

A final level of communication that must be addressed is *mass communication*. While mass communication certainly shares in many of the qualities and principles of the other levels of communication, it retains its own peculiarities.

Mass communication is treated distinctively from the other levels of communication for at least three reasons. First, the feedback loop operates at an extremely slow rate in mass communication. While a public speaker can instantaneously respond to the questioning look that he perceives in his audience's eyes, a journalist must depend on letters to the editor, and television broadcasters must depend on viewer mail that arrives long after a program is taped. Second, the messages of mass communicators are more generic and neutral than the messages of other types of communication. Why? The message is directed at a mass audience. That audience is large and diverse, and the message must be tailored to the lowest common denominator, to use a mathematics metaphor. Finally, mass communication varies from other levels of communication because of the channel that is utilized. By definition, mass communication is only mediated; figure 3 reinforces this fact. There is no such thing as direct mass communication. To reach the masses, you must utilize the mass media.

To summarize our discussion thus far, we assert that communication in any form—interpersonal, small group, public, organizational, international, or mass—is within the purview of communication studies. Communication messages occur across various contexts, cultures, channels, and media.

STUDYING COMMUNICATION IN THE TWENTY-FIRST CENTURY

It is simplistic to view communication only as a means of sharing information. This is where the earlier definitions of communication, particularly the S-M-C-R model, are weak. As we have noted, the message—content or information—is absolutely necessary for communication to take place, but communication between source and receiver serves a variety of additional functions as well. Communication students and scholars, therefore, explore the philosophical, psychological, and social processes and consequences of communication. This is why the NCA's definition of the field of communication insists that communication actually generates meaning.

The process of communication helps us make sense of the world. Some would argue that all we can know about reality is gained by means of the communication process. Others might go as far as to argue that truth is created by means of communication. Surely we all understand that communication is the fiber that holds together cultures, communities, groups, and relationships.

Robert Craig's essay on the organization and the development of communication as a disciplinary field identifies for the first time seven distinct "traditions" that co-exist in departments of communication. We, therefore, run the risk of oversimplifying the diversity and depth of interests in the discipline by focusing on only two main means by which communication is studied. We gain much by understanding that communication is studied both as part of the traditional humanities and the more modern social sciences.

More directly, because of its multi-faceted history and rich scholarship, the typical communication department provides students opportunities to study communication in both the humanistic tradition as well as in the social scientific tradition. Some communication departments identify most closely with the humanities. Other departments find their academic alliances in the social sciences. It can be argued that the humanistic tradition confronts communication events or acts and interprets them—or assigns meaning to them—by using pre-determined criteria.

On the other hand, the social scientific tradition within the communication field embraces the worldview of the modern scientific model. Social scientists, therefore, posit that "truth," "meaning," and "reality" exist independent of social phenomena and that they can be discovered or revealed by the application of the scientific method.

Communication traces its humanistic roots back to the ancients, including Aristotle's text *The Rhetoric* and Plato's dialogue *The Gorgias*. These evidence the Western world's obsession with and humanity's interest in the deliberate use of language and the power of words to accomplish political or social goals in public settings. Students in the humanities tradition may focus on great speakers or persuasive speeches. They also examine the rhetoric of campaigns, movements, and worldviews. Their interests include cultural studies, where political and social theories are applied to messages constructed by both leaders and common people. The humanistic tradition shares a kindred mind with the disciplines of literature, history, politics, philosophy, and others.

While humanists in the discipline are termed interpretivists, social scientists are considered observationists. The social scientific community emerged as a forceful and important way of uncovering truth, beginning in the early to mid-twentieth century. Science and modernity were the giants that shaped the world at that time. Research in mathematics and the hard sciences changed, and often improved, the quality of life throughout the world beginning in the 1920s. Many scholars argued that the scientific method, applied properly to human or social concerns, would lead to equally changed and improved human relationships.

With the coming and going of two World Wars, educated people began to question the influence of the media and its use by world leaders. Opinion polls, surveys, questionnaires, and field research became popular and valuable methods for studying the effects of the media. Later, these same methods were used to study the functions and effectiveness of small groups, organizations, and people groups. Thus, social scientific research as a means of knowing truth was promoted within the communication field. The social scientists in the communication discipline often identify closely and find linkages with colleagues in the sister disciplines of psychology, sociology, anthropology, and education.

One additional note should be apparent by now. Regardless of the general emphasis of a particular communication program, and regardless of the nomenclature used by the department on your campus, communication programs are dedicated to exploring communication effectiveness and promoting high ethical principles in all communication.

Let's be honest. Some people communicate better than others, and yet all people can improve their communication skills. Communication professionals realize that most of us are more effective in some communication settings than in others. One person is a born speaker while another suffers from public speaking anxiety. Many people enjoy working in small groups, and others dread teamwork. Then again, some are confident and effective as they craft a newspaper editorial, but struggle greatly with face-to-face interpersonal interactions. These are all matters of communication effectiveness.

Presumably, marginally effective messages can be made more effective. Communication students and scholars begin with this premise: our innate skills—forming ideas into words, concepts into symbols, and sounds into meaning—can be improved. By no means is this the only or even most important part of a communication department's role, but it is often the most visible role served by the department faculty. The study of communication includes skills development. College students are often required to enroll in public speaking and rhetoric courses. They may also enhance their communication effectiveness in newswriting, small group communication, audio-video production, public relations, and other skills-based courses. Most students who concentrate in communication studies will also serve their communities and earn academic credit toward their degree by completing internship and practicum experiences.

A final issue students grapple with is communication ethics. Communication is a moral act. That is, communication activity can be used for great good or for great harm. As such, communication in all its forms—interpersonal, small group, public, organizational, international, and mass—contains an ethical component. The public speaking of Osama bin Ladin, for example, resonated with certain of his followers through the late twentieth and early twenty-first centuries. His use of communication technology, his inspiration of a rag-tag team of misfit warriors, and his ability to rally support across international borders was—by some measure—"effective." But wait, asks the student of communication, he was an effective communicator, but was he a "good" communicator? The apparent mastermind of the September 11, 2001 attacks on the Western world is an obvious example of an "effective" communicator who is not a "good" communicator. Adolf Hitler would be another; Harold Lasswell's propaganda research quickly reminds us of this.

Let us for a moment, however, move from the international stage to the corporate boardroom. Can the mid-level manager be effective in her presentation to the board of directors without being "good"? Move now to the Christian pulpit. Can our pastor approach his holy task and find success—some level of effectiveness—without being a "good" communicator? As a husband, can I communicate with great "effect" but still fall short "ethically"?

Those who study communication ask these questions and others:

- Who is setting the standard and telling us that one person is a "better" communicator than another?
- Who says one person or group is "more articulate" than the next?

- Who sets the standards by which we "dress for success" and communicate nonverbally?
- By whose standard shall we define what "news" is?
- What makes for "successful" television programming?
- What does the effective and ethical use of the Internet look like?
- How and why do these principles change over time?

STUDYING COMMUNICATION OUTSIDE THE CLASSROOM

Communication students search for the answers to these questions because the field of communication is where individual personalities, culture, race, history, literature, politics, linguistics, and organizational theory—along with that innate human ability called speech—converge. The fact that all people communicate—that "children pick that up around the age of four or so"—is sometimes used as a rationale for *not* engaging in the serious, advanced study of communication. Just the opposite conclusion should be drawn, of course. Those who understand that communication is basic to what it means to be human desire to know more about how that process works and how it can be improved.

Students often wonder why I don't just "tell them the right definition of communication" up front rather than going through the exercises I described earlier. The study of communication is adaptable and flexible because, as we now understand, communication is:

- Dependent on the context (is it mass communication? international communication? organizational communication? public communication? small group communication? or interpersonal communication?);
- Dependent on the channel (is it delivered face-to-face? via web-based technology? in print? through broadcast? or on film?);
- Dependent on the objective (is it designed to inform? entertain? persuade? or inspire?); and
- Dependent on the relationships (is the speaker known to her audience? a favorite speaker? a despised demagogue?).

Students of communication, therefore, study, critique, produce, and practice communication in a variety of forms. This raises a question, does it not? Inquirers need to know "To what

end is all this studying of communication?" "What can I do with
the communication courses I take?" And, most importantly,
"What happens to me when I explore the field of communication?"

Of course, communication is an excellent major for those who
plan to enter the business professions of sales, marketing, and
management. Many find they are well prepared for the helping
professions of counseling and social work. Law schools, seminaries, schools of business administration, and other professional institutions encourage communication as a major among their
prospective students. *Pathways to Careers in Communication* provides excellent ideas and advice to help students combine their
intellectual interests with studies in the field to prepare for careers
in technology, health care, legal affairs, government, international
relations, education, as well as the more traditional communica-
tion-focused opportunities that include advertising, dramatic arts,
journalism, the various media, and public relations.

Read articles or books on the contemporary workplace. Employers are increasingly telling pollsters and college career-placement
officers that they need people who are effective and ethical communicators. A 1997 study reported in *Association Trends* found that
executives with Fortune 500 companies want to hire college
graduates with strong communication skills and the ability to
work in teams and with people from diverse backgrounds (4).

Furthermore, the National Association of Colleges and Employers (NACE) recently issued its annual report based on surveys
of human resource professionals and other managers who would
be hiring college graduates in the next year, and they titled their
announcement "Employers Want Their New College Hires to
'Get Along.'" No one was surprised when the NACE revealed
that "communications skills top the list of personal qualities/skills
employers seek in new hires." Additional most-sought-after characteristics in this study were "honesty/integrity," "teamwork
skills," "interpersonal skills," and "motivation/initiative."

Communication professors are confident that their students are
gaining these skills. Expertise in effective and ethical message creation—what the field of communication is all about—is essential
to meet the challenges of the marketplace.

Communication is an important field of study. It should not be entered into lightly. Communication students must be disciplined individuals who read broadly and think deeply. In addition to understanding current events that shape our world, communication students must have a good working knowledge of history.

Communication, by its very nature, lends itself to service-learning and internship opportunities beyond the walls of the classroom. Students completing my interpersonal communication course during their second year of college often report that the course has changed their lives. This often surprises me, but I know it shouldn't.

The intensive, serious study of communication during one's college years should be life challenging, if not life-changing. Opportunities abound to relate the field of communication to all of life. The typical college students will make several life-shaping decisions within a period of just four years. Like others before you, you will likely decide whom you will marry, what career options you will pursue, what faith-commitments you will make, whether you will explore graduate school options, and what tone you will maintain in your relationships with your parents. All this occurs within a period of less than forty-eight months—less time than it takes to pay off a new automobile—that is book-ended by freshman orientation and college graduation. Understanding and utilizing quality communication is vital at this point of your life.

The theory and research basis in the communication discipline is solid, and the field provides students with multiple opportunities to put that theory into practice. It is surely impractical and probably impossible not to apply communication theories and principles to life outside the classroom. Interpersonal relationships, small group meetings, public presentations, organizational contexts, even intercultural and media opportunities exist for serious students of communication. Thus, the study of communication can change lives.

The field of communication was among the first in the nation to begin the purposive cultivation and identification of practicum and internship opportunities for their students. In the past decade, my own students have completed learning experiences for academic credit by working in numerous professions. These include assignments with the local chamber of commerce, a statewide festival committee, a local pastoral counseling team, and a congressional candidate's election campaign. Students discover continued success working and learning at local radio and television stations, newspapers, and magazines. I have placed learners with local businesses and industries. In all cases, the students negotiated a learning/work contract with an internship sponsor by whom they were mentored on the job. Students then earn academic credit—up to a full semester's worth of credit in some cases—for documenting that they have learned new skills and developed new knowledge beyond what they gained inside the traditional classroom.

Students who study communication find there are ample opportunities for learning in and out of the classroom, for applying new understanding on and off campus, and for gaining practical work experience. They may do so for academic credit or simply for building their professional resume.

Concluding Thoughts

Communication is more than an event in our lives. It is a lifelong process. Indeed, communication is also at the core of who we are. Perhaps the insight of communication scholars Sarah Trenholm and Arthur Jensen best illuminates this idea:

> If we try to understand a river by analyzing a bucket of water drawn from it, we are not studying the river as a whole. The same is true of communication. Individual sentences, words, or gestures make sense only when we see them as part of an ongoing stream of events. To understand communication, we have to look at how what we do and say is connected to what others do and say. We have to view communication as an ongoing process (5).

Understanding what it is that we study is neither an easy nor an unimportant task, but we commit ourselves to the task because communication makes a difference. I really believe that. Marriages fall apart because of communication problems. Managers miss promotions because they are ineffective at communicating with their work team. Children are frustrated because their teachers are not communicating "at their level." Businesses find their way into bankruptcy courts because their strategic communication plans did not meet with success. Multi-million dollar contracts are discontinued because of failed communication. Lives are lost because communication plans fall short in times of crisis. Communication matters. It matters because the best communicators generate meaning effectively and ethically.

WORKS CITED

Aristotle. *The Rhetoric of Aristotle.* Translated by Lane Cooper. Englewood Cliffs, N.J.: Prentice-Hall, 1932.

Craig, Robert T. "Communication Theory as a Field." *Communication Theory* 9 (1999): 119–61.

"Employers Want Their New College Hires to 'Get Along.'" National Association of Colleges and Employers. Bethlehem, Pa., 2002. Available at: http://www.naceweb.org/press/display.asp?year=2002&prid=138

"Graduates Are Not Prepared to Work in Business." *Association Trends* (June 1997).

Instruction of Ptah-Hotep and the Instruction of Ke'gemni: The Oldest Books in the World. Translated by Battiscombe G. Gunn. Kila, Mont.: Kessinger Publishing, 1998.

Lasswell, Harold. "The Structure and Function of Communication in Society." In *The Communication of Ideas,* 37–51. Edited by Lyman Bryson. New York: Harper and Row, 1948.

Occupational Outlook Handbook, 2002–2003. Department of Labor: Washington, D.C.

Pathways to Careers in Communication. 5th ed. Washington, D.C.: National Communication Association, 1998. Also available at: http://www.natcom.org/pubs/Books/default.htm

Plato. *Gorgias.* Translated by W. C. Helmbold. Indianapolis: Bobbs-Merrill, 1952.

Trenholm, Sarah and Arthur Jensen. *Interpersonal Communication.* Belmont, Calif.: Wadsworth, 1988.

3

The Study of Language

M. Kathleen Madigan

How I Fell in Love with Languages

I HAVE JUST RETURNED from Europe where I taught students in Paris and participated in a seminar for teachers in Salamanca, Spain. During that time, I also traveled and met people from many parts of the world. Since I travel frequently, it is nothing new for me to be immersed in foreign languages and cultures. Because of the depth of the encounter with other cultures, whether here or abroad, that learning a language can facilitate, my enthusiasm has never been higher for learning languages.

When I was a freshman in college, I confess, I enrolled in a language class my first semester mainly to get the requirement out of the way. Thank God for that requirement, because it changed my life! Prior to being enrolled in that college class, I had certainly taken some language courses, but was anything but enamored with them, until perhaps my senior year of high school. My family had moved to another state and I found myself in a new school, in the presence of a dynamic teacher who scared me at first, because she really expected that we would speak in the target language during class. However, I quickly became used to her way of teaching, and I learned rapidly. But in spite of this very positive experience, I still in no way planned to make languages an integral part of my life, let alone my profession.

So there I was, signed up for this French conversation class, with no idea that I would later study at the Sorbonne in Paris, live in France for a year while teaching English, spend a year doing research in Germany, and then begin to guide students on studying abroad. An older sister had studied languages, so there was precedent, but as a college freshman, the serious study of language still seemed like a "foreign world" to me. Art and science classes were the ones that I planned to continue, and I had written on my application form to college that I wanted to become a medical illustrator, as that seemed to be a practical yet creative way in which I could use my talents in the service of others.

My respect for those who dedicate their lives to curing the sick through discoveries in medicine has only increased with time; likewise, my interest in art has only grown and expanded. But what I began to see that first year in college is that, no less than medicine, the human spirit needs to express meaning in order to reach its greatest potential, and that one of our most vital vehicles of such expression is the language of literary art. In order to enter into the fullest understanding of this expression of humanity, we must learn how to cross cultural borders and to transcend linguistic barriers.

That first semester in college, while creating and presenting dialogues in class with other students and learning songs in French, I also continued the study of literature in my own language, English, and came to a new appreciation of its unique properties and richness. It did not take long before it became clear how the study of one language complemented appreciation of other languages. Certain sounds, structures, or ways of thinking simply do not exist in other languages and cultures, so the effect of certain groupings of words cannot be conveyed in another tongue. The more I learned about foreign languages and literatures, the more I wanted to see how they compared with literature in English, and vice-versa. And I realized that literary critics are unable to do justice to literary works without reading knowledge of foreign languages. Finally, I became more interested in cultural immersion and began to consider studying abroad.

This was quite a development, as travel overseas had never figured prominently as a goal in my plans, either. Even if someone had convinced me of the benefits of living in another country, with six sisters and brothers, some also in college at the time, it did not seem like a financial possibility. However, that door opened with time. Meanwhile, I discovered the value, including the comparative affordability, of some university programs abroad. Also, the more I continued with my studies, the more I wanted to "dive in" and experience what I'd heard about, putting to use my preparation and practice. So I studied in Paris. I have never regretted that investment decision.

Because I have benefited so much from the study of language, it is natural that I would want as many students as possible to have similar opportunities. One of the most rewarding experiences that I have had as a language professor is watching my students use their language skills abroad. During our Paris program last summer, my students not only communicated in French with those they met, but also taught English to middle-school French pupils. While the Parisian students were quite advanced in their language study and English was spoken during most of the class, our students needed their French at times to understand a question or to understand why certain concepts were more difficult than others. However, our university students are the first to say that they are the ones who learned the most from the experience, as the French children voiced their perceptions about our country and culture and invited the university students to see their own lives from a French perspective. Every year, as I watch the development of the students who say "yes" to languages and reach out with all the life within them to learning about others, I see them rewarded in turn with fuller knowledge of themselves and their own language and culture as well.

In my case, however, even as my adventure with languages may have come full circle as I watch my students teach, my own learning has certainly not come to a dead end. On the contrary! There is always something new to learn about a language, or it is time to start learning another one. I had completed my doctorate in Comparative Literature, which involved the study of several classical and modern languages, and had already been teaching full-time for years when I started studying Spanish. I mention this now, because in this way I can encourage those just beginning a language and can demonstrate that although optimally language learning begins early in life, it can continue at any age. It does take time and determination, but in the following paragraphs I will try to explain further why I think it is well worth the effort. Finally, I will also offer some suggestions that I hope will help you to succeed in your study and enjoyment of languages for life.

YOUR EXPERIENCE WITH LANGUAGES

I don't know what your experiences have been with taking languages, but I hope that you will keep an open mind about beginning or continuing with them. Because languages are something we "perform," like playing a musical instrument, sometimes we develop strong feelings with regard to our perceived abilities or past experiences. If you have enjoyed your courses up until now and have strong motivation for continuing, that's great! The more courses you take, the more your life will be enriched and you will prepare for rewarding cultural exchanges. You should enroll for language classes as soon as possible, in order to develop and maintain your skills.

On the other hand, perhaps you are still not sure why you should continue with the study of languages. What do foreign languages have to do with your life, especially if they seem unrelated to your major? Or perhaps a language class that you took before was not your favorite. Let me address those who have developed some attitudes already with regard to language study, and I will come back to those just beginning.

I understand initial ambivalence towards the idea of registering for more courses, because remember, for the first three years of my study of modern languages in high school, I was not particularly interested and languages did not begin to come alive for me until my fourth year. And it was not until I was in college that I developed a passion for them. So give it a chance! Realize that no matter what your past experience, if you have already taken a language, you have something valuable to build upon, whether it be a certain amount of vocabulary, grammar, knowledge of culture, oral proficiency, etc. The extent of our knowledge of a language, including our native tongue, is never complete, so try to avoid an "all or nothing" attitude and instead work on improving your skills step by step and enjoy what you learn along the way.

Below, I will give you specific suggestions on how to improve these skills, but first I would like to explain a bit more about the study of language and how it fits in with the other liberal arts. I believe that you will be more motivated to study languages if you consider just a few philosophical and practical justifications for the effort. So let us first consider the scope and purpose of language study.

THE GOALS OF LANGUAGE STUDY

When learning a language, we are studying one of the most precious means we have been given to express our desires and identities, our sufferings and dreams, and our view of the world. Different theories may exist about whether we structure language or it molds our thinking, but few would dispute our need to be able to understand others and ourselves and how this process may be enhanced through language. One of the main ways we relate to others, whether in verbal or non-verbal situations, is through language, and language is formed in community. As Joan Kelly Hall writes, "Communication is at the heart of all social life" (16).

Communities change with the times and their language with them. That is one of the more exciting characteristics about language development. One of the reasons you will never be bored studying even just one foreign language is because of its dynamic nature. Even if you are studying a classical or "ancient" language, you can trace changes in pronunciation, spelling, usage, etc., for the length of the time it was spoken.

Because language "lives" along with the people who speak it, and is so closely connected to the ways of life, thinking, and culture of that people, language and culture cannot be separated. Therefore, in a truly mutual relationship, each person would make an effort to understand the language of another culture. This does not mean that all are equally gifted or educated, but we cannot claim to want to understand those of another culture without showing respect for, and at least some level of interest in, their language, which is part of their identity. It works both ways: in order to get to know others of another culture well, one must learn their language, and one cannot become linguistically proficient without understanding the culture or what to say in certain situations.

Helene Zimmer-Loew includes both linguistic and cultural dimensions in the multiple and interconnected reasons she lists for learning a foreign language:

Students' primary goals are to communicate in languages other than English, to gain a knowledge and understanding of the cultures where the languages are used, to provide a connection to other bodies of knowledge, to be able to compare and contrast the language being studied with other languages, and to participate in multilingual communities here and abroad . . . Thus, the purpose of learning a language is *to know how, when, and why* to say *what to whom,* to engage in meaningful human interaction, moving from an emphasis on how (grammar) to say what (vocabulary)—still critical elements—to the sociolinguistic and cultural aspects of language (2063).

In other words, the study of language requires the use of "nuts and bolts" (vocabulary, grammar, structures, phonetics, etc.), but also integrated knowledge of the culture in which the language is spoken. Several areas of competence must be developed in order to perform adequately in a particular setting.

Communicative competence requires not only knowledge about "syntactic, morphological, lexical, phonological, and orthographic systems," but also knowledge such as "the context, stylistic appropriateness, and the nonverbal and other background cultural knowledge that communicators rely on to understand and contribute to any particular communicative activity" (Hall, 21). In addition to grammatical competence, sociolinguistic competence, or "the extent to which the second language can be used or understood appropriately in various contexts to convey specific communicative functions" must be developed; attitude and style play a key role in any particular setting. Discourse competence, or the ability to communicate cohesively, and strategic competence, or ways of overcoming linguistic limits, also play a key role in communicating in a foreign language (Hadley, 6).

Standards articulating what students should know and be able to do in foreign languages as developed in recent decades include the "5 Cs," which, in addition to *Communication* and *Cultures,* include *Comparisons*—"to develop insights into the very nature of language and culture as systems or patterns," *Communities*—"to search actively to test . . . new competencies in venues beyond the school," and *Connections*—"to explore interdisciplinary content" (Phillips, "Standards," 3). The importance of cultural understanding for good communication has been stressed, as well as comparisons in terms of the knowledge of our own language and culture, which the study of language enhances. As we make the effort to meet those of diverse backgrounds on their own territory, whether in our country or as part of study abroad, we will encounter communities that challenge and nurture our development. The goal of acquiring a connection to other bodies of knowledge or disciplines, also mentioned above, is one that deserves special consideration in this context, which we will now consider under the heading of the liberal arts.

LANGUAGES AND THE LIBERAL ARTS

It is commonly accepted that the study of the liberal arts can free us from ignorance and develop our minds and spirits. I am a proponent of the study of the liberal arts, because such study provides a framework like none other within which we can expand our horizons and knowledge base, as well as take a broader view about the meaning and purpose of our lives. We can learn from the wisdom of the ancients as well as contemporaries, and reflect on the past as we learn to live in the present and contribute to the future. Above all, we can learn how to learn, so that learning becomes a lifelong process.

As to the study of languages within this framework, I am convinced that such exposure helps to free us from much ignorance while simultaneously supporting other fields. Perhaps most importantly, the study of language helps to free us from unwarranted fear of others and enhances the potential for mutual understanding, assuming good will and an open spirit. When we study the language of another culture, we get "out of the box" of the limitations of our own culture as we learn to do things in different ways, from pronouncing new sounds to constructing meaning in new structures. Since a particular language associates itself with the identity of a people and their history, customs, wishes, practices, and habits, while immersing ourselves in it, we become more open to other ways of accomplishing tasks, interacting with others, and indeed, ways of living.

Reflecting on this a bit, it is not difficult to see why those who speak a foreign language become flexible, adaptable, and imaginative, and therefore some of the potentially best-prepared professionals in any field. They may have gained a deeper sense of what is relative and what is universal; aware, for instance, of what may be global themes in literature while also having discerned what could only be produced in one particular language. For instance, a particular structure or grouping of words expressing a key concept may not even exist in another language. This means of expression, as well as the idea itself, may resonate with a particular people because of the context in which it is used. The foreigner must literally enter into a different linguistic world to fully understand the meaning of a text in a different language. Yet if the foreign language student is willing to enter into this text in depth, then not only linguistic, but also human barriers drop.

Because the study of language and the study of all that makes us human are interconnected, knowledge of any one field can support understanding of another. In fact, some fields are so closely related that one simply cannot obtain mastery of a given topic without the study of another. For instance, any time the history of a nation is studied, certain terms will emerge in the language of that people, because they are the most linguistically expeditious ways of expressing a concept. The term in the original language will connote a wealth of associations, emotions, and other factors which can only be understood through further study of the culture embedded in the language. If one learns that language in depth, then one will gain not only a better grasp of the concepts, but also the whole linguistic context, influenced by other fields, from which the terms emerged. Because our ways of thinking and belief systems are expressed through language, most fields of study are replete with such terms.

As another illustration of the connection between languages and the other fields of the liberal arts, let me offer the example of my university's Summer Program in Paris, in which students have the opportunity to take a course in communication in an international setting. Of course, the setting is ideal, because nowhere more than in a foreign country does it become clear that communication does not always work in the same way as in our own country. Awareness of cultural norms for communication becomes heightened as other ways of relaying and receiving messages are observed, and the observers become more conscious of their own means of communication. Participants learn that efforts to use the foreign language and to approximate norms established by the culture are usually very much appreciated and can open doors, and even improve international relations on a small scale, as each "citizen diplomat" (Vetter, 203) demonstrates interest in and knowledge of the people and customs of that culture. Thus, communication is improved, which is one of the main goals of study abroad.

Practical Paths and Rewards

Practical benefits of language study, such as increased root recognition (for vocabulary understanding), problem-solving ability, flexibility, creativity, and adaptability have already been suggested, and these are marketable skills. Cultural sensitivity, tolerance, and open-mindedness may also be developed, as those exposed to new cultures move through stages defined by Dale L. Lange as "defense against difference" to "adaptation" and "integration of difference" (75). But that's not all: "Did you know that studying a second language can improve your skills and grades in math and English and can improve entrance exam scores . . . GREs, MCATs, and LSATs?" (MLA brochure available at http://www.mla.org/.) So the study of a language has many applications and benefits in other domains.

But in addition to these personal benefits, there are compelling professional reasons to study a language extensively. Because of the increasing multi-cultural interaction in many professions, the question once posed, "What can you do with a language major?" has quickly been replaced with "How can one do without languages?" With the acute shortage of language teachers in the U.S. at present, language majors currently have little reason for employment concern. But foreign language speakers are also in demand in many health care professions (physical and occupational therapy, speech communication and disorders, nursing, etc.), in the legal field (court translation, law enforcement, etc.), in development programs, international journalism, diplomacy, teaching, general translation, ministry, etc.

As you acquire a good liberal arts base, bilingual students have a real advantage in pre-professional majors. In the business world, for instance, the Association to Advance Collegiate Schools of Business (AACSB International), the main accrediting agency for colleges of business in the United States, affirms the value of knowing a language:

> International communications are the responsibility of all parties. Everyone needs to develop proficiency in at least one foreign language, and the language of business is logically the language of the customer . . . All business majors must learn to speak at least one foreign language well and to have exposure to foreign cultures sufficient to gain an appreciation for cultural differences (Voght, 273).

Business executives do well to encourage future and current employees to continue with their study of languages, realizing that even small steps taken can help to form a bridge of humanity rather than create the image of simply wanting to succeed in a deal. For those committed to justice, it is easier to obtain fair dealings when the value system within the culture is understood.

Considering further the moral dimension of cross-cultural exchanges, it is important to note that as a practical consideration, many companies do genuine service to their cross-cultural clients by hiring foreign language speakers and compensating them for their skills. For example, a retirement funds company may send out a representative to explain fair investment strategies to recent immigrants who have little background in this area and who are just beginning their studies in English. My students have reported that even in summer jobs, some phone and airline companies routinely pay more for those who speak a second language, and this makes sense, because the foreign language speaker is better equipped to serve the customer both linguistically and culturally. Therefore, your language study may pay off in practical as well as personal ways: your life will be enriched, and you may have more and better employment opportunities to choose from. These benefits may also be taken into consideration when deciding which language to take and at which level.

WHICH LANGUAGE(S) AND WHICH LEVEL?

In my view, it matters less which language you take than your firm commitment to study at least one, because any language will open your mind and deepen your understanding of those of other cultures as well as your own. Having said that, here are just a few practical reasons to support taking some of the languages offered. Following each language is a web site where you may obtain more information; many more follow at the end of this chapter.

French is the second most commonly used language at the United Nations and is spoken on every continent as a first or second language (http://aatf.utsa.edu). German-speaking countries play an important economic role in the European Union and boast an extraordinary record of Nobel laureates in physics, chemistry, and medicine; knowing German will allow you to read many scientific reports (www.dartmouth.edu/artsci/german). The study of Latin affords a sound basis for the study of other languages and will help with recognizing vocabulary, since the majority of English words are derived from Latin (www.promotelatin.org).

While Spanish is the official language of Spain and most Latin American countries, it is also spoken ever more widely in the U.S., and for communication with neighbors as well as active trade throughout the Americas, it should be considered (www. amerispan.com/amer.live/shyspnsh.html). However, other languages (for instance, Arabic, Chinese, Greek, Hebrew, Korean, Italian, Japanese, Portuguese, Russian, Swahili, Navajo, etc.!) are also good choices, even if taught less frequently, for that very reason. If fewer prospective employees speak or read that language, you may be in more demand for your unusual skill. Also, as the international relations and business scene shifts, the perception of the relative importance of certain languages may also change.

You may wish to discuss this choice with your advisor, as you explore options for your major(s). But it may also be a good idea to begin with the language that attracts you the most, because then your motivation will be high at the outset and later you can add another language. If you are continuing with a language you have studied before, start at a level that is challenging but not overwhelming. The mistake that some freshmen make is to take a basic course when they are already fully prepared to start at a higher level. The result is that they are bored and may unwittingly intimidate those who have never studied the language.

Take courage and get into the level where you will learn the most. You will probably perform better in an atmosphere in which you are engaged rather than bored. If your school offers a placement test, do the best that you can on it and ask for the wisdom of your advisor and the department about the right level for you. Otherwise, you may be placed on the basis of your high school courses, in which case you can go to the college class and make sure that the level is sufficiently challenging. Do not hesitate to discuss your placement level with your instructor.

How to Study Languages

Acquiring a language involves learning a skill, not unlike learning to play a musical instrument. When it comes to performance in other domains, practice and perseverance, but also a relaxed sense of play, translate into success. In order to feel comfortable with a language, adequate time has to be allowed for review and practice; most students need about two hours of study for every hour of class. Whereas in some fields and projects it may be possible to read intensively for a particular period of time in order to attain one's goal, with languages the opposite practice will be most productive: frequent study for shorter periods of time and daily usage will support learning much more than long but irregular periods of concentration. If you keep in mind the "performance" model, this makes sense. Like learning chords and playing scales, at first your learning may seem controlled and contrived, but later you will be able to build on the stages of imitation and repetition and become more "improvisational" or spontaneous, as you become aware of the range of possible exchanges in a given situation.

In order to avoid frustration, you should not set fluency as a goal for the end of your first year, let alone the first few years, unless you have the privilege of studying abroad. Fluency comes with a number of years of practice, along with other factors, which will vary for individuals. While the earlier you start a language the better, if you are beginning later, take heart: if children imitate with almost flawless accents and repeat without inhibition, adult learners may gain quicker insight into cultural difference, due to experience.

The profession of teaching languages has made great strides

over recent decades and a variety of approaches are currently available, from the functional (task-oriented) or "TPR" (total physical response, or movement in response to commands), to the natural (emphasis on acquisition and the affective) and humanistic (community learning, silent way, etc.) ways (Hadley, 106–29). What does this mean for you and your studies? If emphasis is given to oral proficiency, it is likely that the target language will be used during much or most of the class. Don't panic; a simulated immersion climate is ideal and with time you will understand more and more. Do not worry if you do not understand every single word; instead, watch facial expressions and gestures and try to get the idea or "gist" of what is being said. Think positively, relax, and try to absorb and respond as much as possible.

The building blocks of a language are its words, which you will use most appropriately and probably retain best if learned in a context. Some new vocabulary may be introduced first in a dialogue, in phrases, or in a specific situation. Then you already have an idea about how and when to use these words. If you can visualize when and under what circumstances a word was used, you will more likely remember the word or the expression's meaning.

But perhaps as part of an expansion of the unit or in order to identify new vocabulary, you may also be confronted with a list. How to remember all those words? If tapes or software packages with a listening component for use at home or in a laboratory are part of your program, you should consider using these for even more time than required, because they will give you the opportunity to hear the correct pronunciation of the words and to repeat them, which will also help you to retain them. The advantage of having your own set of tapes, if available to you, is that you can also play them in the car, your room, or put them into a portable tape player. You may also wish to invest in a software program with an audio component as a supplement, if your lab or library does not already own one (see resources below).

Besides listening to tapes and using techniques such as reviewing the words you have to learn in context, it may help you to write out the words; you can copy them onto index cards (you can cut these down to smaller sizes), with the translation on the other side. These cards can be used for review between classes, while waiting for an appointment, while exercising, etc. For me, the more active the study the better the results: I learned a lot of ancient Greek vocabulary and verb forms with my vocabulary cards while walking around Manhattan one summer while taking an intensive course. Other ways to retain vocabulary include highlighting in different colors according to gender, drawing a picture, or writing down another word association (for example, based on the sound of the word, etc.), which helps you to call up the foreign word. However, try to learn vocabulary in context as much as possible in order to learn in what sorts of situations particular words are used.

With the first set of words, in addition to listening and speaking, you may also begin reading and writing. Most likely, you will start with dialogues and brief cultural readings, and you may also be asked to begin writing exercises. If you are not already doing so as part of your course, you can supplement these assignments by finding a pen pal (see web resources below) willing to exchange messages in the target language. One of my students had the good fortune to find a native speaker who, as a favor to the student requesting it, always replied with a corrected copy of my student's message in addition to a reply. Free tutoring! Accept corrections as a matter of course: no one expects great prose when you first start writing. However, you will probably find that a similar quotient exists between reading and writing as in listening and speaking: the more you read, the more you may write with appropriate vocabulary and expressions.

What to read? In addition to valuable textbook material, check your library's holdings for foreign newspapers and magazines. Start with brief sections, such as headlines, captions, or announcements. Although the articles in newsmagazines may seem difficult at first, the fact that you may already be aware of some of the events reported in them will help you to identify the topic. Other popular magazines may also prove useful for learning colloquial language. Finally, access the Internet for a wealth of material (see web resources below). Essayist, economist, and writer, Jacque Attali, has pointed out that although English was pervasive on the Internet in early stages, it is already decreasing proportionately to other languages, and the 'Net will ultimately lead to significant diversity in languages accessible to all (cited in Pinet, 460).

The more of the foreign language you can "take in," the more you will be capable of producing. So in addition to fun reading and writing, take advantage of the opportunity to participate in language tables, conversation clubs, or international film discussion groups on and off campus. If you have cable TV or a dish network, you can make use of the foreign news; with the pictures as an aid, often you can figure out what topic is being discussed, even if you do not understand everything that is being announced. You can also rent foreign language videos or check them out from your university or public library. Foreign language CDs may be available as well.

Find out if your area or university hosts any foreign language radio programs. Through these you may also hear about special cultural events, where you can meet native speakers or others interested in speaking the language. Don't wait to become an advanced language student to help with organizing such events. Volunteer to support these activities while your schedule is still fairly flexible. The more activities in which you participate, the more personal contact and support you will find, and these activities will boost your spirit and fuel your desire to learn more.

LANGUAGES FOR LIFE

I began this chapter by telling you about how I thought that my need for languages would be short-lived as I entered college, but then I realized that this plan was shortsighted. Retrospectively, I can't imagine having lived as full a life without the study of languages, which has afforded me a bridge to others from cultures around the world, as well as to others not met but encountered in their own words through literature. I can say that any period of frustration or discouragement encountered in the study of language has been worth it and more than offset by the joy of a friendship developed in a different culture or the awe inspired by a poem so moving in the beauty of the original language that no translation can do it justice. May you, too, catch the fire of the love of languages and other cultures, while better understanding and encountering another part of humanity so similar and yet so unique. Experience how renewing and rewarding it can be not only to speak but to live in another culture and language.

If what I have said about study abroad does not seem to be possible for you right now, I believe that if you persist in your study of language and actively seek a way to go, you will find a path. Volunteer and work opportunities in other countries abound. Another possibility is to find a position at a company or organization in need of employees willing to work abroad in the future. If nothing else, as soon as you are able, take a shorter study or service trip to the country that fascinates you. But don't rule out study abroad during your college years if at all possible; a financial aid officer at your institution may be able to work with you to make this possible through loans, grants, or allocated funds. Find out where your Study Abroad Advisor is located and make an appointment soon to find out about how to apply for a program.

I wish you much joy in the study of language! With a little persistence, you will soon make progress. Remember, you did not learn to speak your maternal language in a semester. If you make languages a part of your life, you will benefit from them enormously on multiple levels, more than you ever imagined. You will reach signposts that before your studies would have been indecipherable, but will come to signify deep meaning for you. Foreign countries or even another cultural section of town can become a place where your friends live, and their language and culture can become a part of you. I challenge you to think of your study of languages as a lifetime journey, which will transform you and increase your understanding and appreciation of your own language and culture, while enabling you to enter into wonderfully untranslatable exchanges with others. These you will simply have to experience for yourself.

¡Buen viaje! Bon voyage! Gute Reise! Gokigen yoroshuu! Etc.! Etc.! Etc.!

WORKS CITED

Hadley, Alice Omaggio. *Teaching Language in Context*. 3d ed. Boston: Heinle and Heinle, 2001.

Hall, Joan Kelly. "The Communication Standards." In *Foreign Language Standards: Linking Research, Theories, and Practices*. Edited by June K. Phillips and Robert M. Terry, 15–56. National Textbook Company, 1999.

Lange, Dale L. "Planning for and Using the New National Culture Standards." In *Foreign Language Standards: Linking Research, Theories, and Practices*. Edited by June K. Phillips and Robert M. Terry, 57–135. National Textbook Company, 1999.

Modern Language Association brochure available at: http://www.mla.org/

Phillips, June K. "Standards for World Languages—On a Firm Foundation." In *Foreign Language Standards: Linking Research, Theories, and Practices*. Edited by June K. Phillips and Robert M. Terry, 1–14. National Textbook Company, 1999.

Phillips, June K. and Robert M. Terry, eds. *Foreign Language Standards: Linking Research, Theories, and Practices*. National Textbook Company, 1999.

Pinet, Christopher P. "From the Editor's Desk." Introduction. *The French Review* 74, no. 3 (2001): 459–60.

Vetter, Charles T., Jr. *Citizen Diplomacy*. Provo, Utah: Brigham Young University, 1995.

Voght, Geoffrey M. "New Paradigms for U.S. Higher Education in the Twenty-First Century." *Foreign Language Annals*. 33, no. 3 (2000): 269–77.

Zimmer-Loew, Helene. "Looking Backward, Looking Forward: MLA Members Speak." *PMLA*. 115 no. 7 (2000): 2063.

Web Resources

This list is meant to show you some examples of the kinds of resources available, rather than to attempt to be comprehensive. You may locate other addresses by using a search engine and typing in key words, such as "Spanish AND language resources" or "French AND exercises." You may also type in Yahoo plus the first two letters of the language you are studying to find additional sites (for example, Yahoo.fr for French or Yahoo.ge for German). Some of the following addresses may change, but others will remain the same, so try another address if one does not work. Also, while web dictionaries are listed, you should buy at least one good portable dictionary.

General/Several Languages

Information about the European Union: http://www.europa
.eu.int/
E-mail partners: http://www.stolaf.edu/network/iecc
Dictionary for translating Dutch, French, German, Italian, and
Spanish www.allwords.com

By Country

(Remember, these are just some samples. If the country that interests you is not listed, search it on the web, for example, "Brazil AND Portuguese language resources")

Austria's history, geography, politics, etc.: http://www.aeiou.at/
aeiou
Canada (news from Canada in French): http://www.matin.qc.ca/
China (courses, links, resources, radio, and software information,
etc.): www.webcom.com
France: Tutorials www.frenchlesson.org and www.frenchtutorial
.com; French grammar help online www.geocities.com/sohlhaut;
French newspaper www.lemonde.fr/; French music information http://www.ircam.fr/index-e.html; tourist information
http://meteora.ucsd.edu/~norman/paris; weather report from
France http://www.meteo.fr/; not just for children . . . a dictionary, stories, etc. http://www.imaginet.fr/momes/; clothes
shopping http://www.laredoute.fr; Science and Industries
Center (Paris) http://www.cite-sciences.fr/; weekly Paris happenings http://pariscope.fr/; Paris metro in cyberspace http://
www.paris.org.:80/Metro/
Germany: Reference grammar www.travlang.com/languages/
german/ihgg; for German students, with an online magazine
http://www.goethe.de/z/jetzt/deindex.htm; links to libraries,
news, culture, tourism, etc. http://www.goethe.de/dservlis.htm;
Ask your professor to set up a class partnership! http://www.
goethe.de/z/ekp/deindex.htm; radio programs from Bayern

http://www.br-online.de; radio from the Southwest Südwest-funk http://www.swf.de/; Tagesschau news magazine http://www.tagesschau.de; Netmagazine www.eurozine.com; German Television Network http://www.ard.de; Deutsche Welle News http://www.dwelle.de; The President's News http://www.bundespraesident.de/; Inter Nationes: video magazine, film data bank, etc. http://www.inter-nationes.de/; Study, Research, and Scholarships http://www.daad.org

Israel (Judaism and Resources includes Hebrew): http://shamash .org/trb/judaism.html

India (News): http://www.indolink.com

Italy: Vatican exhibit http://www.christusrex.org; Vatican tour http://www.Vatican.va; Literature http://www.crs4.it/HTML/Literature.html; Sardinia: video spots, slides, map, etc. http://www.crs4.it/zip/sardinia/sardinia.html

Japan: Lessons, virtual class, history of language www.jiskha.com/foreign_languages/japanese/; thirteen Katakana lessons www.charm.net/tomokoy/japaneselesson.html; Japanese bookstores, news articles, etc. www.trussel.com; page for beginners, phrase of the day, etc. www.japanese.about.com

Latin America (see also Mexico and Spain for Spanish): Grammar, travel, culture, etc. www.studyspanish.com; politics, career center, Hispanic organizations, education, etc. http://www.hispanic online.com/res&res/index.html; chat, forums, shopping, etc. http://www.demasiado.com; current events links, networking, etc. http://lib.nmsu.edu/subject/bord/laguia; Latino sites, museums, geography, etc. http://www-personal.si.umich.edu/~rlwls/andes.html; grammar, regionalisms, dictionaries, chat, etc. www.about.com; dictionary http://dictionaries.travlang .com/SpanishEnglish/; culture, newsletters, schools http://edb518ea.edb.utexas.edu/html/LatinAmerica.html; MSN News, chat, publicity, etc. http://www.msn.com.mx; art and culture, health, sports, etc. http://espanol.yahoo.com/; news, etc. http://espanol.fullcoverage.yahoo.com/

Mexico (News): www.univision.com; http://www.jornada .unam.mx/index.html

Quebec: French in Quebec, business French, etc. http://www.olf.gouv.qc.ca; official government tourist site http://www.tourisme.gouv.qc.ca

Russia and former Soviet Union: Russian http://www.geocities
.com/CollegePark/Bookstore/3230/
Spain: Culture and games http://cvc.cervantes.es/portada.htm;
http://www.uco.es/cordoba/prologo.html; electronic magazine
http://www.cec-spain.org.uk; daily news from Spain http://
www.elpais.es/www.estrelladigital.es; Spain, Latin America, and
more: government, media, exchange rates, etc. www.ibermundo
.com

Classical Languages

Latin: Dictionaries, study helps, literature http://www.csbsju.
edu/library/internet/latin.html
Greek and Latin: Grammar aids, etc.http://www.cs.utk.edu/
~mclennan/OM/grk-lat.html

Software, Cassettes

http://www.worldlanguage.com; www.agoralang.com

Study Charts

Contact your bookstore or BarCharts, Inc. at (800) 226–7799

Study Guides

Available at http://www.bn.com (Barnes & Nobles); http://www.
amazon.com; etc.

Study Abroad

Check with a campus advisor and http://www.centerforstudy
abroad.com

Volunteer Work Abroad

International Volunteer Programs Association http://www.
volunteerinternational.org; Jesuit Volunteer Corps (work with

the poor) http://www.jesuitvolunteers.org; Peace Corps http://www.peacecorps.gov

Work Abroad

Info@councilexchanges.org; Internships Info@cdsintl.org

Work for Foreign Language Speakers

http://www.latpro.com; http://bilingual-jobs.com

4

The Study of Literature

Robert D. Hamner

LITERATURE MUST be among the most elemental of the liberal arts because its medium is language. Whereas the initial purpose of language is practical (transmission of information—whether factual or emotional), literature intensifies and extends usage into imaginative applications. The creative writer composes and gives meaningful expression to selected portions of life in verbal form. In order to fulfill the basic requirements of all the arts, to instruct and entertain, the creative writer has license to exploit every rich ambivalence, connotation, equivocation, figure of speech, and nuance of linguistic trickery. Consequently, it becomes necessary to develop our ability to interpret literature, to learn to appreciate its special relationship both to reality and to the whole range of liberal arts. As is the case with all the fine arts, literary truth is not the same as literal fact. Artists are free to incorporate facts into their works. Whatever particulars they may adopt, however—a painter's landscape, a musician's assimilation of bird calls, a novelist's historical setting—the standard by which artists are to be measured is not their superficial reflection of actuality, but rather, their memorable revelation of the underlying principles of life. Their figurative presentation may then be valued in so far as it leads us to discover a fictional, nonetheless, reliably truthful insight.

PHILOSOPHICAL BACKGROUND

At the risk of oversimplifying the complicated relationship between reality and literary truth, it may be helpful to refer to three philosophical models in the history of Western aesthetics. One of

the earliest and best-known analyses of the artist's function is offered by Aristotle (343–322 B.C.) His *Poetics* argues for the Mi-
metic Theory: that the artist is an imitator of nature. Thus the
sculptor molds in clay or carves in marble copies of the physical
specimens he observes, and the playwright draws upon the interactions and conversations he witnesses among mankind in order
to generate plot and character for the stage. After 2,400 years, this
classical paradigm remains influential today, and there is hardly a
recognizable alternative until the late eighteenth century when
European Romantics began to consider a more organic model.

Reacting against the overly intellectual approach of neoclassical
predecessors in the late 1700s, Romanticists such as Johann von
Goethe in Germany, Alexandre Dumas in France, and English
poets Wordsworth and Coleridge preferred to view the artist as
being part of and emotionally responsive to the natural world
as a living entity. In his 1801 "Preface to the *Lyrical Ballads*,"
Wordsworth describes the ideal of poetry as "emotion recollected
in tranquility." M. H. Abrams symbolizes the difference between
the two schools of thought in the title of his seminal book *The
Mirror and the Lamp* (1953). The mirror represents the classical
ideal of the artist as objective reflector of physical appearance. The
lamp suggests the artist as a receptacle of experience who then
illuminates the world by expressing his subjective reactions. Since
there was never a time when writers could claim pure objectivity,
the focus on expressiveness signals a shift in attention to self-
consciousness in the artistic process.

By the 1940s, the freedom of personal expression is carried to
its logical extreme with a third model. In asserting the difficulty
of ever truly knowing the essence of reality, Existential theory
questions the very possibility of meaning outside the subjective
person's frame of reference. One result is literature of the absurd.
In an irrational universe, man becomes the creature who interro-
gates the grounds of his own being. The physical world is depicted as surreal in the paintings of Salvador Dali, in plays of
Eugène Ionesco, Samuel Beckett, and Jean Paul Sartre. Applying
Existential criticism to such established texts as the book of Job,
and Abraham's dilemma when he is commanded by God to sacrifice his only son Isaac, the reader is asked to consider the tenuous-
ness of faith and ethical paradoxes. That militant degree of doubt

at first appears to rule out all sources of value and meaning. Rather than descend into chaos, however, the existentialist insists on the inescapable burden of responsibility that comes with absolute freedom. Losing confidence in external sources of value and meaning, the individual is condemned to a radical dependence on faith. Paradoxically, as with older conventional schools of thought, everything depends ultimately on that in which one believes. In order to achieve an authentic existence, even the atheist who denies a supreme being must answer to a personal code of conduct.

Whatever theory philosophers may adopt regarding the relationship between art and reality, the general consensus is that art instructs and entertains but also challenges our capacity to understand the world and our place in it. That leaves students of literature with the task of interpretation. Classical approaches to serious reading have included comparative examinations of similar works; genre studies (classifying works in terms of conventional types: epics, ballads, novels, for example); biographical or psychological analyses of texts for insights into the life of the author or of fictional characters. In an attempt to refine criticism and focus on creative writing isolated from such extraliterary forces as society or the author's intentions, a loose movement called New Criticism arose in the 1930s to call for exclusive attention to the interrelationships of elements within each unique text. Its insistence on close reading, or *explication de texte,* has the advantage of bringing out the minutest intricacies of a work, but it soon had to yield to an unavoidable fact. Literature is not created in a vacuum; the author writes within a specific cultural environment. Linguistic and anthropological Structuralists in the 1960s, particularly in France, began to apply the scientific methodologies of their fields to the study of poetry and fiction as social documents. In their wake, a host of Poststructuralist schools, from Deconstructionists to Feminists, have emerged to point out the oversights and inadequacies of all finite systems of analysis and evaluation.

PRACTICAL VALUE OF LITERATURE

Taking such uncertainties into consideration, it is more important than ever that an educated person understand the pragmatic advantages of literary study. No matter what the subject matter of a novel, play, poem, or short story may be, a work of literature is never merely *about* some aspect of life. It is an *experience* of life in and of itself. This sets it apart from and gives it an advantage over discursive prose. Discursive prose addresses specific experiences and facts directly, unequivocally, whether it is to recount an actual sequence of events (narration), describe a person, place, object, or idea (description), convey information (exposition), or persuade (argumentation). The writer of fiction, on the other hand, presents the reader or audience with a persona, or a cast of characters involved in actions and feelings in an appropriate setting. The latter's advantage is that rather than explain about life, the author appeals to all the reader's faculties. When the connection is made, the individual becomes engaged in a vicarious experience from which each derives his or her own insight into some truth about humanity.

Furthermore, the fictional creation has potential advantages over actual experience. When life grows hectic, the turmoil around us can become incomprehensible. We may easily misunderstand the words and intentions of those who are closest to us, not to mention our own unconscious motives, so that the flow of activities with which we are surrounded may become incoherent, preventing us from being able to discern priorities and see meaningful connections. Of course, the world of the novel can replicate accidents and scenes of chaos, but the novelist purposefully selects all the details of a fictional composition. However complicated the sequence of events, an organizational pattern is more accessible there than in the profusion of life. Depending on the point of view, of course, the author can access the subconscious thoughts of characters, open yet more far-reaching insights through dialogue and the exploitation of allusion, metaphor, and symbol. With structure and meaning thus assured, there is still more to be gained than the informational and entertainment value of vicarious experience.

Being able to read with discernment is no luxury. It should be recognized for its usefulness. The discipline of reading interpretive literature forces us to bring into play all of the ingenuity of reason and powers of intuition that are required to survive not only in school but in society, the market place, and the professions. Textbooks supply concepts, working vocabularies, and the raw data that equip people to enter just about every field in the modern world. Nevertheless, a standard history would be hard put to make us feel what it would have been like to live through Napoleon's invasion of Russia more vividly than Leo Tolstoy's *War and Peace* (1864–69). The advantage of its subjective view is that, instead of diagnosing relevant causes and charting statistics, the novel puts us in scenes among the people whose lives were being affected. When Sigmund Freud (1856–1939) broke ground in the field of psychoanalysis, prototypes for many of the psychoses he was diagnosing among his patients were already extant in the Greek tragedies of Sophocles (496–406 B.C.). The Oedipus and Electra complexes are anticipated dramatically in the title characters of *Oedipus Rex* and *Electra*. Lawyers, physicians, and military authorities find such astute portrayals of their specialties in Shakespeare's drama that they believe the playwright might well have had experience or training similar to their own.

The literary component of a liberal education affords students an unparalleled opportunity to weigh their own prospects in the light of a diversity of possibilities. As Emily Dickinson points out, "There is no frigate like a book / To take us lands away." Through the advantage of translation, without having to book passage, or having a time machine, readers can drop in on cultures, races, alien galaxies, and times that cannot be reached in any other way. Without having to risk the vagaries of the stock market, future businessmen can participate imaginatively at any level in the economic environment from the maintenance closet or the secretarial pool to the executive suite. With selected reading, providers of social services can preview invaluable, realistic experiences among the mentally, socially, and financially troubled clients they will eventually serve in the field. The minister contemplating an inner city mission has a twofold opportunity. Not only can the priest gain vicarious insights into the problems confronting his multifarious parishioners, but when he speaks before his congregation, a library full of authors offers endless anecdotes and allusions to supplement biblical passages. Aside from these certified professions, those choosing a future in industry or the trades sell themselves short if they overlook the life of the mind. The knowledge, reason, and taste that are enhanced through the challenges of literature are available to anyone willing to invest the time and effort.

UNDERSTANDING LITERATURE

When philosophers and scholars find cause for disagreement, we might well ask where the neophyte may be expected to begin the study of literature. Despite the technicalities and finer points over which experts may argue endlessly, the prospect is not hopeless. From the outset it is essential to keep in mind the fact that while no analytical method is infallible, any approach can be fruitful in so far as it yields useful insight. It is wise to expect the necessity of reading the best works from more than one perspective and to anticipate the possibility of multiple levels of meaning. The fact that much of the reading in university classes is assigned does not eliminate the student's right to have qualitatively determined preferences. While the established canon remains serviceable, it has been opened up more and more to dissenting voices. Recent critical theorists have demonstrated that cultures in the past tended to favor the view of dominant groups while marginalizing or idealizing others: victor over victim, male over female, white races over darker races, industrial societies over less-developed societies, Christian over non-Christian. It is understandable that a social group or nation tends to think that its own position is superior on a variety of grounds, including moral and ethical; but in order to arrive at an aesthetic judgment, it is necessary to evaluate a work of art in accordance with aesthetic principles.

To allow a literary work of art a fair estimate of value, it is essential that a reader be willing to assume an objective position regarding his or her personal beliefs. Otherwise a person succumbs to prejudice. Discriminating taste in art requires an honest attempt to comprehend a work, whether we agree or disagree with the subject matter or opinions being expressed. Undervaluing a poem or story without first reaching an informed understanding reflects a reader's inadequacies, not those of the text in question. A reasonable procedure is to delve into the work in a flexible, step-by-step manner, whether studying prose fiction, a play, or a poem. On the simplest level, it is a matter of taking into consideration the content, the structure, and the style of a given text, three components that can be isolated temporarily for the purpose of analysis. The author's subject matter and type of material usually rise to the surface on first reading, but getting at the deeper meaning of complex texts often requires closer scrutiny by an experienced, or at least perceptive, reader. Consequently, while it may be convenient to begin by recognizing the superficial nature of the work, it is usually necessary to postpone forming a statement of theme (the meaning) until the later stages of interpretation.

In order to reach the combined goal of understanding a work on its own terms and being able to estimate its relationship to other established works of art, a reasonable point of departure is to divide the task into manageable steps. More than one reading may ultimately be required, but the first step is to look at what is happening to whom in the context of the action. The second step is more technical and involves looking into implications that emerge through resolution of the action. In other words, cautiously steering around the "intentional fallacy" of trying to decipher the writer's mind, it is still possible to see whether the work creates a moment of light entertainment without suggesting serious application to life, or evokes a provocative experience that engages and enlightens the reader. The combination of the thought content and the literary devices creates a range of expectations within the reader. To this point, we are taking stock of the ingredients in order to establish the nature of the object under examination. Stage three involves critical appraisal. Here it is necessary to assess how successfully the work fulfills expectations it has created. If the thoughtful reader reaches the conclusion that the work achieves its effects legitimately and that it offers insights into life that are worthy of further consideration, then and only then is it profitable to move to the last stage: comparing the piece to other examples of literature that have been generally recognized to have lasting aesthetic qualities.

Fortunately, in spite of the incredible variety of literature from which we have to choose, the basic elements of creative writing, along with the accompanying critical concepts and vocabulary, are consistent and fairly easy to grasp. In order to generate and sustain interest, a writer must launch an action among characters in a setting of his own invention. The action, or sequence of events which comprise a plot, must somehow overcome inertia and cause us to anticipate a conclusion. The action of a poem may be nothing more than a leaf in flight that eventually leads to a reflection on the brevity of life. On the other hand, it can multiply into the interlocked subplots of an epic or a novel. In either case, the reader should experience a sense of dramatic suspension until matters come to rest or conflicts are resolved. That drama, whether it be subtle or violent, played out internally or externally, may involve an individual against him or herself, against another person, society, or some natural or supernatural force.

Whatever the nature of the conflict, those who are acting or being acted upon are the author's fictional characters. The leading figure, about whose fate we become concerned, is called the protagonist, and any obstruction with which he or she must contend stands as an antagonist. In order for the unfolding of character interactions to be convincing, readers have the right to expect an author to adhere to terms of existence that, although alien to us, are consistent with the fictional world being portrayed. At the same time, we cannot impose preconceived restrictions drawn from outside the parameters of the work. Effective writers, for example, are at liberty to indulge in fantasy, to insert surprises and accidents, expose values of which we disapprove, even leave issues inconclusive for an open-ended plot. However, because they have poetic license, a power of selection greater than in life itself, true craftsmen do not unfairly manipulate details that would ordinarily be comprehensible to a reader who is engaged in the unfolding scene.

Whether they are drawn from history, mythology, the lower animals, or outer space, for characters to be effective we have a right to ask that they meet rudimentary criteria. They should be sufficiently developed not only to accomplish their function in the plot, but also for us to be able to understand their behavior. Their personalities can be revealed in a number of ways. A narrator or other characters can comment directly; we hear them converse, perhaps drop into their inner thoughts; and their actions sometimes expose more than their words. Second, if they are sufficiently developed, we should be able to perceive the motive behind their behavior and determine its appropriateness. In the end, adequately developed and motivated characters behave consistently, both in terms of their perceived traits and in response to the circumstances that provoke their reactions.

Of course, the characters play out their story against a background, a third structural element of the author's imagined world: setting. Setting involves both chronological and emotional time, as well as place and atmospherics. A lyrical poem may capture only a moment while a novel might well span centuries, the writer choosing a beginning point with the option of filling in past, present, and future episodes in any pattern that suits his narrative purposes. In shorter works, timing must be unobtrusively but more rigidly controlled than in expansive stories. One classical ploy to pique the reader's interest is to begin in the midst of things, with the action having reached a critical point. Information regarding crucial preceding events (called antecedent action) and necessary features of the characters' personalities is then interspersed as we are propelled forward by complications in the story line. Whatever the chronological period and the geographic location, the writer is free to select details as elaborately or sparsely as required for the effect he or she wishes to achieve. Beyond the physical logistics, it is often necessary also to take into account the time and place in a character's emotional life. It is not unusual for a writer to employ the setting in time to reinforce mood or themes, selecting the fall of the year, evening of a day, or an appropriate ceremony in a character's waning life to signify old age or death. Place is sometimes equally significant as informative background for customs and behavioral patterns within which characters must function.

Indispensable as plot, character, and setting are to the interpretive process, these structural elements are inevitably conveyed to us in a manner and tone that affect the way we see the content. It would be difficult to overestimate the influence of the author's chosen point of view. The narrative voice, of course, should never be attributed unreservedly to the author in his or her real life. At its autobiographical optimum, the writer's persona must necessarily be a self-projection composed merely of fragments that are consciously assembled to serve the poem or story. Each of the four available points of view is a representational device that lends its own cohesiveness: first person, limited omniscient, omniscient, and dramatic. Thus the "I" of a fictional piece, whether a disembodied voice, a participant among the cast, or purporting to be the "author," remains a functional invention.

The first-person narrator has the advantage of being the most directly accessible, relating matters in the participant's own words. What this narrator says must be weighed carefully, however, because his or her powers of observation, intelligence, and articulation may be limited. Restrictions are also attached to the limited omniscient point of view in that the author allows us to overhear the private thoughts of one or two characters, and these may be minor characters on the sidelines of the central plot. Nevertheless, these inner revelations usually imply that they are unfiltered and can be trusted. Equally candid and credible are the editorial kinds of exposition that accompany the omniscient perspective. As though God were commenting on the unfolding scene, the narrator can be anywhere at any time to expound at leisure from various angles. The shortcoming is that the intervening commentary threatens the basic flow of the action. The last of the four points of view is the dramatic or objective form of presentation. If the first three perspectives offer a guiding hand, the dramatic point of view takes the risk of leaving the audience or reader to draw unassisted conclusions. All the data available to the viewer for processing is that which might be captured by camera and microphone. Action is unimpeded, but the audience is totally dependent on its ability to analyze and comprehend.

A basic accounting for the major structural elements of a literary work yields basic answers to the question of how we are being shown what is happening to whom in particular settings, but thorough reading of a literary text should include examination of its style and any underlying figurative devices. Characters and events presented fancifully in a manner that takes liberties with the laws of reality create expectations that are different from those arising from a naturalistic form of representation. Either method of creating a vicarious experience of life can be equally effective, and both require the ability to deal with figures of speech and imagery. Turns of phrase that occur in everyday conversation are a staple of imaginative literature. Many words have, in addition to their denotative (dictionary) definitions, connotative associations that bear on the way they are felt and must be understood.

There are some exceptions, such as the word play in novels of James Joyce and Vladimir Nabokov, but the more realistic versions of prose fiction generally do not test the limits of verbal expression. Poetic usage on the other hand differs from prose in the degree to which it exploits linguistic forms in order to generate the most intense, economically rich language possible. Novels and short stories utilize such devices as puns, metaphors, similes, imagery, irony, and symbols just as they may well resort to slang and vernacular. Communication in stage plays ranges from the silently expressive gestures of Japanese Noh theater and Shakespeare's poetic lyricism to Samuel Beckett's nonsequiturs and Eugène Ionesco's provocative absurdity. By its very nature, poetry stretches the possibilities of meaningful expression and also imposes the greatest demands on a reader's ingenuity.

Through imagery, poetry appeals to all the physical senses so that we imagine more vividly sights, sounds, odors, tastes, and the feel of things. Similes expand our way of connecting ideas by using the words "like" and "as," while metaphors identify seemingly disparate things with each other in ways we might not otherwise discover. To speak symbolically is to draw attention to the fact that some component in the text (a name, object, person, place) is being used to indicate significance on a broader scale outside its literal appearance on the page. Allusions to notable events, persons, or quotations function similarly to increase associations without having to go into elaborate explanations. Irony requires special caution because it can be very deceptive. Whether it be verbal, situational, or dramatic, each form of irony involves a discrepancy between appearance and reality and can be easily misread. To say one thing and actually mean another is to use verbal irony. When results go against what we want, expect, or think should happen, the situation turns ironic. Dramatic irony occurs when we as observers enjoy the advantage of knowing more than what is evident to the individual characters engaged in the action being portrayed.

Added to the difficulties of accounting for such common figures of speech and devices, the poem also incorporates the intricacies of metrical design. At least to some extent, the reader should take note of the measure of lines, stanzas, and the overall pattern that often distinguishes poetic genres. Free verse is duly calculated even if it does not have to conform to the rigidities of a sonnet. The traditional sonnet must have exactly fourteen lines of iambic pentameter and be rhymed in one of two specific sequences. Ideally, the thorough reading of which I spoke earlier (an *explication de texte*), would require an accounting of every pertinent turn of phrase, figurative usage, device, and rhythmic feature throughout the work. Practically, however, for the purpose of determining what expectations are being generated within a text, a basic understanding of the steps in the process should be sufficient to arrive at a sensible interpretation.

Once the structural and stylistic factors have been accounted for, it is then reasonable to begin consideration of how successfully a given work satisfies the expectations it has created. At this stage of analysis, the elements of plot, character, setting, and point of view have to be evaluated in order to determine the degree to which they work together credibly within the parameters of the work. In competently executed literature, every aspect of the work eventually leads toward some insight into life, the central theme or constellation of ideas that provides coherence. The sequence of events may be expected to unfold through causal forces. Characters should be developed to the extent that we can determine their behavior to be consistent and we can believe them to be plausibly motivated. The point of view that frames and exposes events, whether that of a first-hand narrator, an omniscient God, limited omniscient, or a camera, must fairly admit the audience to all that transpires and be available from the given perspective. Because they are instrumental in creating both the entertainment and instructional value, all of these structural elements must be taken into consideration in order to support thematic interpretation. The ability to discover and articulate theme improves, of course, with practice and maturity, but even relatively inexperienced readers can validate significant inferences applicable to life based on evidence within the composition.

When it has been determined that the four primary structural elements and the important stylistic devices cohere in an aesthetically meaningful whole, the fourth step in the process of interpretation is to consider the relative significance of what the work has accomplished. Qualitative assessment takes into account the fact that while many poems, plays, and stories may share common devices and deal with similar subjects not every one is equally significant. One poem engages us in enjoying the pleasures of spring. A play evokes laughter at the foolishness of lovers who are constantly at odds over slight misunderstandings. In a novel we see the best of intentions leading to disaster. Each work is a unique experience and must be taken for what it has to offer; nevertheless, the overall effect of each may be more or less consequential. Without taking away from the legitimate effects mentioned in these three examples, we may still envision a scale of value that depends on the breadth and profundity of a work that is already remarkable for its aesthetic accomplishments. Both qualifications must be met. Insight on a minor scale is useful, while a manipulated truth inevitably fails careful scrutiny. Obviously, in the court of literary debate, there is no monopoly on taste, and theories of beauty change. The field of interpretation and judgment is as open today as it was for Homer's listeners when he sang of the adventures of Odysseus nearly three thousand years ago.

INTERNET RESOURCES

Theories and approaches aside, the advent of the Internet has made an invaluable contribution to students of literature and literary criticism. With access to the World Wide Web, information on an author, a work, a bibliography, full-text research, and the catalogs of entire libraries are at our disposal. Electronic versions of primary texts make it much easier to locate key words and passages than manually turning pages. Digital forms of all kinds of works are continually being added to the thousands that are already accessible at the click of a key. Useful new sites appear at such a rapid pace that the list is continually outdated. Nevertheless, a few examples suggest the types of instruments that are currently being offered. *Project Gutenberg* at http://promo.net/pg/ helpex makes available, without charge, the texts of an extensive list of standard titles. While currently copyrighted material is legally prohibited, the Gutenberg collection does offer many selections up to the early 1920s, including an English translation of Dante and works by such recognized authors as Shakespeare and Edgar Allen Poe.

The commercial site for *Questia* at http://www.questia.com inventories over 35,000 titles that are available for a subscription fee. In addition to its digitized primary texts, for research assistance *Questia* hyperlinks its collection through bibliographies and footnotes. It also provides accessories such as a dictionary, thesaurus, encyclopedia, and means whereby the student may highlight passages and make marginal notes, with footnotes and a bibliography automatically generated. Many more sites provide secondary resources. The Internet Public Library's free *Online Literary Criticism Collection* at http://www.ipl.org/ref/litcrit is connected to thousands of Web sites, critical commentaries, and biographies on authors and their works that can be located by name, title, period, and nationality. The scope is international, ranging beyond the major European groups, including former colonial possessions, to Japanese, Chinese, classical Greek and Latin, African, Middle Eastern, Indian, and South East Asian. The Modern Language Association of America's bibliographic Web site at http://www. mla.org, to which many libraries maintain a subscription, is equally international in coverage. The database, which begins with 1963, is updated ten times annually. It now encompasses over 3,500 journals, series, books, essay collections, working papers, proceedings, dissertations, and bibliographies covering the fields of literature, criticism, drama, languages, linguistics, and folklore.

Among the several databases listed by Gale publishers at http://www.gale.com are *Contemporary Literary Criticism Select,* with its vast array of critical essays on contemporary writers, and *DIScovering Authors Modules,* a bio-bibliographical, multinational guide to over 1,200 writers from Muhammad to Amy Tan. *American Authors on the Web* at http://www.lang.nagoya-u.ac.jp/~matsuoka/ Amelit-G.html is confined to literature of the United States, but its alphabetical listing of links brings together interest sites such as comparative literature, drama, poets, syllabi of courses being taught at different universities, indexes, directories of scholars, digitized libraries, Native American writers, women authors, and postmodern culture. *NoodleBib* at http://www.Noodletools.com, which advertises itself as an "MLA Composer," alleviates the mechanical difficulties attached to the creation of bibliographies by automatically formatting entries drawn from linked databases.

These are but a sampling of the tools available on line that students will find helpful in locating material and keeping abreast of developments in literary studies; but nothing can replace individual readers' intellectual and emotional investment of themselves in the experience of a book, play, poem, or story.

LITERATURE IN THE LIBERAL ARTS

Since creative writing is capable of representing the vast range of human experience, it is intimately related to all of the other disciplines in the liberal arts. The instruments and methodologies of rational analysis, analogical thinking, grasping relationships, detecting patterns, reaching logical conclusions, and the ability to convey ideas intelligibly are valuable in every course of study. Because at its best, literature gets us involved vicariously through nearly every aspect of our being, it is arguably more accessible than the musical and plastic forms of the fine arts. Architecture, dance, music, painting, sculpture all affect us directly, but our grasp of them eventually has to be articulated in a vocabulary that requires a certain level of specialized training. Through its own medium, each of these arts instructs and entertains, emerges from the same sources, and engages in the identical processes that give rise to creative writing. Critical biographies can record the legacies of great performers, and interpretive theses can illuminate us regarding the qualities unique to these spheres of aesthetic expression. At the same time, an author's intriguing plot involving a musician, a sculptor, or an aspiring performer can draw us vividly into an equally enlightening fictional setting.

While there is no substitute for the textbooks and publications devoted to specific majors, conscientious students can still profit greatly from seeing their field of study in a context larger than case reports, laboratory experiments, statistics, and data, no matter how thoroughly they may be processed, illustrated, and explained. Although the aim of expository prose is to produce unequivocal clarity whatever its subject matter, its ventures into the more esoteric recesses of a specialization can bring into play the same imaginative, critical reading skills that have to be developed in literature courses. The social sciences of history, psychology, and sociology, with their strategic approaches, are based on the need to understand the unpredictable vagaries of human behavior. Despite their experimental protocols and regimented classification systems, physical scientists from biologists to geologists are studying and deriving factual explanations in the same environment as that surrounding Henrik Ibsen's Peer Gynt and Herman Melville's Captain Ahab. Businessmen and economic theorists concentrate on the same socio-political forces in the market place that also influence the fates of characters in Maxim Gorky's *The Lower Depths* and Victor Hugo's *Les Miserables*. Issues expounded upon by philosophers, ethicists, and theologians become the points of contention and the underlying factors motivating the dramatic personae from Sophocles to Bertolt Brecht. Above and beyond the entertainment value of fictional literature, then, obstacles confronted by protagonists and the resolutions of their conflicts yield examples of options taken by people in a greater variety of cultures and situations than are likely to be encountered otherwise in the academic environment. The vicarious experience of recreated times, places, and characters takes on additional value as it brings into play our analytical skills and increases the breadth and depth of our perspectives.

LITERATURE FOR LIFE

In the end, the essence of a liberal arts curriculum is not the content of a single discipline so much as establishing a foundation for continual learning. Outside academia, literature continues to function as adjunct to professional careers and daily life. Anyone who finds it necessary to communicate with other people, individually or before an audience, can tap the vast communal storehouse of literature for concrete examples to support ideas that might otherwise be vague or unfamiliar. Pertinent anecdotes and allusions are the stock in trade of statesmen, ministers, jurists, and public speakers everywhere. By the same token, it behooves educated citizens to avail themselves of the recorded wisdom of the world's creative writers. In fact, the literary community is very much alive outside the covers of books. Just as oral historians and genealogists scour old records and interview survivors of past decades in order to add to our knowledge, folklorists seek and record lyrics, memories, and stories from overlooked sources that are in danger of being lost to future generations.

It should come as no surprise that the most active areas of creative writing and criticism since the end of the Second World War have grown out of newly empowered women, emerging minorities, and authors from former colonial possessions. Their revising of established standards and rewriting of accepted themes has brought about an overdue reconsideration of the old masterpieces. A person need not be interested in becoming a creative writer in order to appreciate the enlightenment and pleasure attached to discovering a new voice, whether from a Native American tribe or from a Pacific island. No more does an avid reader have to be a scholar in order to participate in professional organizations, interest groups, or chat rooms available on the Internet. There are many sites devoted to individual authors, genres, periods, movements, and critical schools of thought. Although libraries and bound volumes appear to be destined to remain available for the foreseeable future, the number of electronic texts becoming available each year is growing exponentially. The only requirements are literacy and a desire to become involved.

Since no subject matter is outside its scope of depiction, literature is capable of reflecting all walks of life. From the earliest recorded examples, writers have represented not only the moment in which they lived, but the various ways in which they saw themselves and the past, present, and potential worlds around them. When we look back, the ebb and flow of humanity's understanding of reality and art may appear to follow a causally explicable pattern, that is, until we get too close to our present. Hindsight has always been more easily focused than the contemporary scene crowding in on us, as we have to make immediate decisions. This perception is probably not as unique as we might like to think; the advent of computer technology in this information age only exacerbates the difficulty humanity has always faced of being able to discern meaningful relationships among the whirl of responsibilities and opportunities that inundate us on a daily basis. Given the accelerating pace of change in the modern world, the study of literature can be particularly useful over the full span of life.

What begins as the burden of having to learn how to comprehend the intricacies of interpretive literature in school turns out to give us the advantages of entertainment with instructional value during the period when we must earn a living. The entertainment value derives from the vicarious experience of being many people in incalculable places and times without ever having to leave home. That is worth a great deal, but the instructional advantage works on more than one level. Not only do we get to practice all the analytical skills required to survive in the actual world from the safe distance of the den or bedroom, but the insights we discover increase our competency to handle real problems. When we must cope in a workplace where obsolescence is the rule, the literary component of a liberal arts education might help to prepare us not for a task, a job, even a career, but for a lifetime of learning. The initial problems of reading primary texts and "reading reality" go hand in hand with the additional challenge of keeping up with the changing ways of understanding what we think we know.

Thanks to Sigmund Freud, as well as the likes of playwrights such as Luigi Pirendello, we know that behind the masks we wear, the roles we play, and the narratives we weave about the events of our lives, reside the fragments from which we construct our identities. In the past, conceptual models of reality depended on presumably verifiable physical principles. Certainty has slowly given way to dependence on calculations of probabilities. A rudimentary appreciation of Albert Einstein's theory of relativity, Max Planck's quantum mechanics, its accompanying uncertainty principle, and the implications of chaos theory alerts us to the uncertainties of existence and to the urgency of mental dexterity. No wonder that in the relatively orderly world of literature, Poststructuralists such as Feminist and Deconstructive critics strive to equip us to remain flexible, to respect alternative interpretations, and to keep reexamining our conclusions.

5

The Study of Music

C. Randall Bradley

MUSIC IS inescapable! At the mall, at the grocery, in the elevator, the doctor's office, restaurants, home, and car—it's everywhere. While walking down the street, we're bombarded with someone's car stereo; even when we're on hold on the telephone waiting to be transferred, someone has chosen music to keep us calm while waiting or to create an image of the company we're contacting. We listen to music on personal headsets, on the Internet, and on compact discs. We hear live performances in concert halls, parks, and in places of worship. We participate in music by singing in choir, playing in a band, or making music for our individual enjoyment. Sometimes the music that we listen to is of our own choosing; too often it's chosen by someone else. We live in a time when we're overly exposed to music, perhaps to our detriment. Undergraduate students will most likely not encounter any subject to which they have more exposure and have been so highly influenced as when they begin the study of music, for by the time they reach college age, most students are already strongly attached to their favorite music and musicians. Yet with all our exposure, few of us can claim to be literate musicians, and few of us know very much about music outside our own preferences.

Some think our attachment to music has reached epidemic proportions, for music often controls our actions, chooses our friends, and determines our values. Allan Bloom, in a critique of American higher education, stated, "Nothing is more singular about this generation than its addiction to music. Today, a large proportion of young people between the ages of ten and twenty live for music. It is their passion. Nothing else excites them as it does. They cannot take seriously anything alien to music. When they are in school and with their families, they are longing to plug themselves in to their music" (68). While this analysis may be somewhat overstated, it nevertheless has truth for American society.

Music's role in society is further seen by the sheer influence that music sales have on our economy. Music is big business, and young people are often the target audience. Although we all choose aspects of our music listening, too often we purchase only what has been marketed to us without any knowledge of our alternatives.

While music's presence in our lives is at an all-time high, according to some studies participation in music is decreasing. Even as we depend on music to be present in every waking hour, we're often not interested or willing to participate in music making ourselves. In addition, as society cocoons, concert attendance has decreased and some of the musical stalwarts of our society—orchestras, church choirs, community bands, choruses, etc.—often struggle for existence. These and other issues deserve our best attention and should be considered in a study of music.

WHAT IS MUSIC?

There are many technical definitions of music; however, music is uniquely personal and can be defined in many different ways. It can be described in terms of melody, harmony, rhythm, meter, tempo, timbre, etc. Music notation is determined by bar lines, clefs, staffs, note values, etc. While all of this is important, music often proves to be a mystery for many people because music uses a language that is complex and, for the most part, unique to its discipline. The languages of music are often intimidating and difficult to decipher even to the trained musician who may be discussing music that falls outside his/her own specialty. Yet with minimal knowledge, music can be appreciated, understood (as a novice), participated in, and loved.

Music is difficult to define beyond technical definitions, for most of us discuss it in terms that are personal and experiential. Music is described as the universal language because it is a superb way of breaking down barriers and building rapport, and it doubtless has universal appeal. However, music is different for everyone, certainly from culture to culture. It is probably much more accurate to say that music is universal, but it is not universally understood, for every culture has music; however, each culture assigns its own meaning to its music. Every culture in the world has its own musical forms, instruments, vocal sounds, and functions. Even when the same instruments are used and vocal technique is similar, the musical output may be very different. Differences between music from culture to culture are similar to differences among dialects in spoken language; even though the same language is used, it has regional differences in inflection, pacing, and understanding. Music understanding is usually based on our experiences, and "what music is" is determined by how we've previously interacted with it. Since we assign meaning, then that meaning is determined by the experiences that we've associated with the music, its role in our culture, and our own preferences and prejudices.

KINDS OF MUSIC

There are as many sub-sets of music as there are variations in language usage, however, music can be categorized in order to gain a fuller understanding.

Western Classical Music

This is the music that dominates most college-level introductory music courses and supplies the core repertoire of most performances in major concert halls in North America, Western Europe, and in many other parts of the world. This broad category has its roots in Western Europe, in the church traditions of the Middle Ages, and was further developed in the Renaissance. Genres include traditional church music, opera, symphonic works, choral masterpieces, and many others. Composers such as Palestrina, Bach, Handel, Mozart, Haydn, Beethoven, Brahms, and hundreds of others are in the forefront of music in this tradition. This music is what we often refer to as "art music" or "classical music." Western art music is divided into musical periods that help us delineate stylistic, compositional, and performance characteristics. These periods include Renaissance, Baroque, Classical, Romantic, and Twentieth Century. Sound clips from all of these styles are easily accessible on the Web.

Folk Music

Every culture has its own folk music, for every group has its song and dance. Every culture has its rituals, ceremonies, and celebrations; and usually these events utilize music. Folk music is considered by many to be the true music of the people; often it cannot be traced to an original source because it goes through many variations as it reaches its current form. Folk music is usually passed on through oral tradition and is in constant revision. Moreover, folk music is usually performed differently from region to region even within a country. These different forms are known as variants. Folk music forms include ballads, work songs, lullabies, love songs (of many types), spirituals, dances, games, play parties, etc.

Popular Music

Popular music can be identified as music written and produced for its popular appeal. Popular music as we know it is a relatively new phenomenon, for prior to the nineteenth century, art music and popular music were not so easily distinguished from each other. Until that time, the style of music for the concert hall, home, or church tended to be similar even if its purpose or instrumentation differed. With the development of a sizeable middle class and increased industrialization in the nineteenth century, art and popular music became more distinct. In addition, music printing became cheaper, and composers wrote for the masses instead of specific patrons. In the nineteenth century and well into the twentieth century, popular music was disseminated through printed music (sometimes call "broadsides"), which were sung and played in homes, civic groups, etc.

With the wide-scale use of printing and eventually of recordings, the use of popular music has dramatically expanded. In the twentieth century, as radios became common in homes, recordings quickly spread the popularity of songs. Although radio continues to be a staple in the propagation of popular music, the role of television and the Internet is enlarging. As our society has become more visual, we want to see our music acted out as well as to hear it. Increasingly, the Internet is becoming the primary source of listening to and interacting with music of many styles. Types of popular music include rock, country, rhythm and blues, soul, rap, and many others. It is music that is quickly disseminated and understood by the dominant culture. The number of popular songs that are released each year is staggering. Although some become hits on radio stations that appeal to many people, others are short lived. Since much popular music is aimed at youth culture, it is constantly changing and recreating itself.

Jazz

A unique American musical form, jazz deserves a category of its own, for while it has many of the qualities of popular music, it is in many aspects similar to art music and folk music. Jazz developed out of the music of the African-American people of the South, and its roots can be found in cities along the Mississippi River. Partly due to recordings, jazz was quickly assimilated into more popular genres; its influence is broad and runs deep. There are many different styles of jazz, although all involve improvisation. Some of these styles reflect its development, and, overall, jazz has become more sophisticated as it has progressed. Jazz styles include big band, cool, bebop, fusion, etc. Jazz is widely studied and is often the primary focus of music students in colleges and universities. Significant also is jazz's influence in art music, for many composers of art music have included jazz idioms in their compositions. As you can see from this brief summary, jazz has progressed from folk music, to a popular idiom, to art music.

Religious Music

Religious music, like jazz, deserves a separate category of its own, although nearly every genre of popular music has its religious counterpart. Religious music also includes art music and utilizes many folk music styles. Throughout history, the church has sometimes led in the development of the culture's music, although more often it has imitated the popular culture of its day. Genres such as spirituals and styles such as gospel are uniquely rooted in the church. With the radical changes that occurred in American religion in the 1960s and the advent of Contemporary Christian Music in the late 1970s and early 1980s, religious music (in the broadest sense) has moved beyond music for worship and now includes music with religious texts in every style of popular music, including heavy metal and rap! In America and other industrialized Western cultures, religious music tends to be mostly Christian, but that is not the case in other cultures or countries.

World Music

As mentioned earlier, each culture has its own unique musical forms and genres. While there are similarities between musical cultures, these similarities usually relate to the function of music in people's lives. However, the role that music plays in the daily lives of the people may vary widely. Even though techniques and resources may be similar, the resulting music may be very different. World music is often distinguished by categories similar to the following: South Africa/West Africa, South Asia/Indonesia/East Asia, North America/Latin America, and Persia/Middle East. While the study of world music is vast, and often the music is unfamiliar to us, the music is an important component for those intent on understanding the world and its peoples. The Web provides many opportunities for interacting with music of different cultures.

MUSIC'S ROLE IN LIFE

Entertainment

In American culture, the most common use of music is to provide entertainment. When we attend a symphony concert, a rock concert, an opera, or hear jazz in a club, our primary motivation is usually to be entertained. While entertainment sometimes implies passivity, we do become involved as we interact intellectually, move to the beat, or respond in some other way. One of music's greatest contributions to our lives is to entertain us by moving us beyond our day-to-day existence and to help us better connect with ourselves and with others.

Rituals

Music plays a significant role in many of the most important events of our lives. It is difficult to imagine a wedding without music or a graduation ceremony without a processional. We use music to celebrate milestones in our lives such as anniversaries and birthdays, and to grieve losses such as death and national tragedy. Through music, we both celebrate and mourn. Music can give voice to life experiences that are too profound for language.

Community

Music plays a primary role in the building of community. It draws us together and unifies us. We are drawn together to support our favorite team through a fight song. We're moved to national pride through patriotic music. We are called to worship through songs that express the beliefs of our community of faith. Music is used in political campaigns to rally people, and it has played a major role in every war effort. Freedom movements such as the ending of apartheid in Africa used songs to further their causes, and music figured prominently in the American Civil Rights Movement in the 1960s. However, not all causes for which music has been used to unify community have been noble. A vivid example is Hitler's use of music to rally support for the Nazis in Germany. Music's ability to move us to action is powerful. According to Peter Kivy, ". . . music has always had, throughout the history of the human tribe, this enormous power of creating cohesion. There is no culture that does not use music to that end" (91).

MUSIC REPRESENTS ITS CULTURE

Culture is the sum total of the thoughts and actions of a people; therefore, to study music is to study people. For instance, to understand the development of the African-American spiritual, it is necessary not only to understand the texts, musical nuances, and historical context, but also to understand the plight of African-Americans in a slave culture. It is important to understand their lives, their backgrounds, their struggles, and their joys. Conversely, the lives of African-American slaves are much better understood through a knowledge of their music. When we study their lives from historical documents, we comprehend the facts of their existence. Music provides the soundtrack that completes the scene.

When discussing architecture, Frank Lloyd Wright, the great architect, said, "We shape our environment and our environment shapes us." Similarly, it may be said of music that we shape our music and our music shapes us. We are strongly influenced by the music that we hear, sing, and play. On the other hand, our experiences strongly shape the music that we choose and create. Because of music's strong influence in our individual lives and our culture, it is difficult to separate ourselves from the music that we value. Furthermore, music influences both conscious and subconscious thought and action. Perhaps we should be more conscious in choosing the music that we listen to. The next time you get into your car and turn on the radio or walk into your room and begin playing music, stop and analyze the music that you've selected. What influenced your musical decision? Did you choose music that reflects your mood, or music that has the potential to change your mood? These questions are worth your consideration.

Because of music's power and its ability to influence us and others, it is imperative that we study music in order to be good stewards of its potential and power.

BROADENING OUR MUSICAL PALETTE

Western approaches to music usually involve a Euro-centric approach, where the dominant music of Western culture is seen as normative, and any deviation is viewed with suspicion and may be perceived to have lesser value. In reality, Western music is not "better" than music of other cultures and shouldn't be viewed as normative for another culture. In other words, Western music should not be the point of departure. A much better approach would be to learn to value all music—music from one's own culture and from the cultures of others. With this approach, we are on our way to genuine music appreciation.

In order to broaden the musical palette, we must learn to think culturally; for example, in much the way an ethnomusicologist would approach studying music from a culture other than his/her own. In order to understand the music, an ethnomusicologist attempts to understand the people, the role of music in their lives, their language, their rituals and ceremonies, the elements of their music, etc. After this information is obtained and processed, a culture's music can be better understood. This approach is equally applicable when attempting to accept the preferred music of a neighbor in your dorm or of a sub-culture on another continent. Comprehending music that is new for us always involves seeking to learn about the people who create, perform, and listen to that music. *Understanding music is always a process of understanding people.* If your musical appreciation is limited to popular music, in order to begin to understand art music, a similar approach is recommended. On the other hand, if you are a serious student of art music and want to understand popular forms, the same is true for you.

In order to value music from other cultures, it is important to gain a global perspective. We often discuss music with such terms as "good," "bad," "pretty," "ugly." Language such as this shows a lack of respect of both the music and the people who perform and create it. It does not build bridges through which understanding can occur. We must learn to move with ease from our dominant culture. We must not see our culture as the norm with everything else being inferior, and we must learn to think in terms of "different" instead of using qualitative language. However, we must realize that we will find some music easier to identify with, much the same way that languages that share similar construction with our own are easier to learn.

RESPONDING TO MUSIC

Whether we realize it or not, we respond to all music, even if we tune it out. Indeed, to fail to respond is also a response. Our culture sometimes suffers from aural pollution; for example, our ears are over-stimulated, which causes an unhealthy aural environment. We have too many sounds competing for our attention; solitude is scarce. Sometimes we have difficulty hearing music because we so seldom have silence. Silence is, after all, the reference point for sound. In the next few days, secure a block of time (an hour or more) when you can be alone. While sitting quietly, write down the sounds that you hear. You may be amazed by what you discover even when there is silence.

The way we respond to music is determined by the ideas we associate with the music. All of our past experiences affect our responses. Music's ability to renew feelings is with us throughout our lives. When we hear a particular song, it may remind us, many years later, of falling in love for the first time, attending the funeral of a close friend, or of winning the state championship. Often, our musical opinions are a good gauge of our experiences from childhood, youth, and the present.

Music in Dialogue

One of the ways we respond to music is through discussing music with others. We often talk with our friends about music, read about music on the Internet and in books, and write about music through critiques and other forms. To talk about music is a form of musical interaction. Contemplating how music affects our lives is a worthy endeavor and should consume more of our time. When we study music, we gain a broader vocabulary through which we can discuss music.

Music As Participation

The best way to learn about and experience music is to participate in music making. To play music in private or to join with others in making music can be enriching. Music calls for participation. In cultures where music recording and playback are not commonplace, more people are involved in hands-on music making. Music helps us to express our emotions, and our need to express ourselves through music is most fulfilled by participation. Peter

Kivy says, ". . . to listen to music without having performed it at some level, as a singer or player, is like seeing *Romeo and Juliet* without ever having been in love" (90).

I strongly encourage you as a college student to consider musical participation. Perhaps you may want to sing in a choir, play in a group, learn to play an instrument, or improve your singing or some other musical skill. When you participate in music, you are using many of your senses (hearing, seeing, touching, etc.) to involve yourself in music; thus, the experience will be more profound. In addition, you will be utilizing both your right (emotional) and left (logical) brain hemispheres.

Music As Listener

Most of us commonly participate in music as listeners. Daily, we are accustomed to listening to music; for some of us music is hardly ever absent. However, as we study music, we should attempt to move beyond passive listening; for example, listening that requires no thought or music that is primarily background. As you study music, I challenge you to listen to music in the foreground, where it is closer to you and you can think about what you're hearing. Granted, some music is intended to be used as background and thus fulfills its purpose; however, other music should involve active listening. Developing listening skills is a part of what music study is designed to accomplish.

Generally, we enjoy music that we understand. Therefore, as we comprehend music more fully, we have greater potential for enjoyment. Music is created and performed with varying degrees of complexity; some music cannot be understood without a conscious effort to react with it intellectually. I challenge you to practice active listening each day, and as you gain more understanding, your range of listening repertoire will broaden. When you listen to music, you will want to listen for changes in tempo, dynamics, and instrumentation. Be aware of changes of mood and attempt to decide how they occur. Consider broadening the styles and types of music that you listen to. Soon your appreciation of music will be expanded.

MUSIC AS A PART OF LIFE

A primary goal of music study is to discover additional ways that music can be integrated into your life. Music is used throughout our lives as a learning tool. For example, most of us learned our ABCs through music. Theologians agree that we learn much of our theology through the music that we sing in worship; music influences our values as well. Music therapists help us to deal with emotions and to overcome illnesses by using music. Advertisers use music to encourage us to buy products, and restaurants utilize music to lure us inside. Discovering new music, gaining a deeper understanding of music, and experiencing the joy of music as a life-long pursuit is worth the time that you invest.

Music As Life-Long Enrichment

Through the difficulties and celebrations of our lives, music can become a valued source of enrichment. A quick analysis of music on a popular radio station gives us a sense of the role that music plays in different times in our lives. We immediately recognize life themes such as lost love, transition in employment and location, being misunderstood, etc. Whether the station is rock, country, or soul, the themes are similar. The power of music to sustain us in grief, uplift us in sorrow, and give voice to good fortune is compelling. As we discover new musical forms, the menu from which we choose our life's music is much broader, therefore, our lives are enriched.

Being Involved in Music

All of us are involved in music, even if we don't choose involvement intentionally. No one goes through life without singing "Happy Birthday" to a family member or "Auld Lang Syne" on New Year's Eve. When we participate in worship, we sing. When we go to sporting events, we sing. When we hold babies, we sing. When we listen to the radio, we interact with music. When we attend concerts, we interact with music. Intentional involvement in music making helps us to discover each other and ourselves in new ways. Few activities in life are more intimate than the bond that is established through making music with others.

Becoming Bi-Musical

The term bi-musical (Nettl, 5) is used to describe a person who understands more than one language of music in the same way that a bilingual person understands more than one spoken language. Becoming bi-musical, or multi-musical, requires effort. Without its being intentional, we can go through our lives only enjoying the kind of music with which we grew up. While the music of our childhood and youth may be meaningful, it will not provide us with the broadness that would enrich our entire lives. Enjoying new styles of music is much like learning to enjoy new types of food. I once heard a story of a university voice teacher whose student was complaining that he had to sing art music for his voice lessons. The teacher simply replied, "I grew up eating peas and cornbread, too; however, I've learned to like other foods." Broadening our musical menu involves sampling various kinds of music, learning to appreciate their flavors, seeking to understand those who make the music, and discovering why other people have their preferences. When processes such as these are followed, we usually find ourselves enjoying the variety that our new discoveries bring.

Accepting New Forms

We usually like what we know and understand. My high school choir director would forbid us to complain about the musical selections that he had chosen until after we had memorized them. Interestingly, we never complained about the selections, for once we had memorized them, we understood and loved the music. The challenge, then, is for us to learn about music and seek to understand it. Therein lies the key to enjoying music throughout life. Many of our preferences and ideas about life become fairly set during college and early adulthood. These years are ideal for expanding our musical horizons, thus benefiting us through a life of deeper understanding and more enriching experiences.

MUSIC AND THE LIBERAL ARTS

Music is closely related to other areas of liberal arts study, although it has many characteristics that are not shared. As discussed earlier, music is one of the primary ways that we know a people. We learn about music through observing their work, their rituals, their likes and dislikes; and we learn about people when we hear the way in which they integrate music into their lives. Consequently, music provides this same supportive role to other areas of the liberal arts. When we study history, there is always music that corresponds. With visual arts and drama, music closely resembles their development. In studying literature, music lends much to this understanding, even when the music does not involve texts. Music is closely related to language because music is concerned with subtle nuances and inflection. Furthermore, much great literature utilizes language from many cultures. When compared with other liberal arts, music can present many paradoxes. According to Elliot Schwartz:

> [Music] can be, perhaps next to architecture, the most scientific and mathematical of the arts, since it often deals with measurements, proportions, and acoustic properties. But in performance it offers the most immediate, sensual, and perishable of experiences: a few fragments of sound in the air, heard and then gone. Music has often been associated with rigorous logic and precision, but it has also played a vital role in our celebration of the irrational and unknowable: consider its importance in magical and theatrical ceremonies. Music suffers from the stigma of an elitist calling, whose mysteries are penetrable only by those possessing special skills; on the other hand, it is the most accessible and popular of the arts, capable of evoking a response in every one of us no matter what our level of experience. (3)

However, much liberal arts study in our culture is related to gaining knowledge, and in this area music may be in a field of its own. For while knowledge is a part of understanding music, it is only one component. Peter Kivy supports this idea when he states:

> We have chosen the wrong paradigm. We pattern the teaching of what used to be called "music appreciation" on the way the English

department, for example, would teach the nineteenth-century novel. But that is to make three crucial mistakes. First, it is to treat music as a "content" art, whereas I have been arguing that it is, rather, a "ritualistic" art, if you will. Second, it is to treat music as a "private" art, whereas, I have been arguing, it is a "community" art. And third, it is to treat music, from the appreciation side, as a "passive" art, whereas I have been arguing that even where one plays the role of passive auditor, it is a "participation" art. (91)

Someone can understand music technically, have a good grasp of music's history and performance practice, and yet not really understand music, for music is ultimately experiential. Through music, we understand ourselves more deeply and become more human as a result; therefore, interacting with music intimately and emotionally is important if music is to be fully understood. To understand music only from an intellectual perspective is in many ways to have missed the point. However, to internalize music and be moved in your spirit, yet fail to understand its construction, history, and background seems to me to be a much lesser offense.

As children, we were drawn to music by what it did to our spirits—it gave us reason to clap our hands, dance, play happy games, and voice our celebrations. Lullabies calmed us when we were afraid and helped to pass the feverish night. Work songs taught us simple growing-up tasks, and funny songs helped us to laugh with our friends. We were drawn to music because we couldn't help ourselves. I challenge you to reconnect with the child within you and allow music to work its miracle on you again. This innate need for music will not grow from classes, extra reading, additional listening, or concert attendance. It will grow because it is nurtured and cultivated at each stage of life. At this innate involvement level, music both connects with other liberal arts and departs from them. While music is in an area to itself, the humanizing that it does for us may help us to discover deeper truths in other liberal arts curricula.

CONCLUSION

Music's influence in our lives is undeniable. We are influenced by music both when we choose to be and often when we don't.

Music permeates almost all aspects of our society and plays a role in most of the important times in our lives. The study of music is closely aligned with the study of anthropology, in that music cannot be accurately understood without an understanding of the people who perform it and a concept of the reason behind its creation. Music helps us to understand a culture. Conversely, an understanding of a culture enhances our understanding of its music.

Each culture has its own music that is only accurately understood from the perspective of its people. It is easy to misperceive music when it is not understood within its cultural context. To understand a broad range of music, we should avoid placing value judgments on music and seek to see music as different rather than "good" or "inferior." However, it is important to remember that we will always view another culture through culturally-tinted glasses. According to Malcolm Floyd, "Nothing can change that. We can only be aware of the likely tints and shades that make up the glasses" (45).

The study of music should be a life-long process. Music can help us to transition through various stages in our lives and to express more adequately our accompanying joys and grief. With the proper foundation, our appreciation of music can increase as we mature, and music can provide a lifetime of enrichment.

Music can help us become more human and draw us together in community, both as we participate in music making and as we join with our neighbors in listening to music in concerts, civic events, religious ceremonies, and other places. Our experiences will be richer and more meaningful as we allow music's power to permeate our emotions and our intellects. The study of music has the ability to be life changing when begun now and continued throughout life.

Works Cited

Bloom, Allan. *The Closing of the American Mind.* New York: Simon and Schuster, 1987.

Floyd, Malcolm, ed. *World Musics in Education.* Brookfield, Vermont: Scholar Press, 1996.

Kivy, Peter. "Music and the Liberal Education." *Journal of Aesthetic Education* 25 (1991).

Nettl, Bruno. *Excursions in World Music.* 2d ed. Chicago: Prentice Hall, 1997.

Schwartz, Elliot. *Music: Ways of Listening.* New York: Holt, Rinehart and Winston, 1982.

6

The Study of Art History

Roger C. Aikin

LEONARDO DA VINCI'S FAMOUS PAINTING of *The Last Supper* (figure 4) depicts thirteen agitated men at a dinner table. Even if you are not of the Christian faith, you probably know that a man called Jesus dined with his followers the night before he was arrested and that a man named Judas betrayed him. You may be able to identify Jesus, some of the apostles, and the figure of Judas, who is clutching his money and shrinking back. During this meal, Jesus instituted the central sacrament of the Christian Church, called the Eucharist or the Lord's Supper, when he instructed the apostles and all future Christians to break bread and drink wine "in remembrance of me." Jesus also said that one of the apostles would betray him, and that appears to be the moment that Leonardo has chosen to represent: Christ at the quiet center of the storm of surprise and agitation that breaks out. Question: Why has Leonardo chosen to represent the moment Christ speaks of betrayal rather than the moment he blesses the bread and wine? Wouldn't it make more sense to depict the sacramental aspect of the event, especially since the painting is in the dining room of a monastery? These are the kinds of questions that art historians love to ask. Do you have any answers?

Now consider this: what if all copies of the Bible and all knowledge of Christianity had somehow been lost, and we encountered this painting without any of that knowledge? We would probably assume that the painting simply represents some people at a dinner table who are upset about the food, the place settings, or the size of the bill. We could not possibly understand the meaning of the expressions and gestures without knowing the story—even if we suspected that the formal and symmetrical look of the painting made it likely that it represented some important ritual or illustrated some lost text. Could we possibly "appreciate" the picture based solely on its color, light, composition, space, and the rendering of emotion in the faces and gestures without knowing the story? Such an appreciation would be incomplete and hollow, wouldn't it?

Take another example, the famous little painting in London's National Gallery called *Portrait of Giovanni Arnolfini and his Wife*, popularly known as *The Arnolfini Wedding* (figure 5), that has enchanted and mystified generations of museum visitors. An inscription above the mirror on the back wall tells us that it was painted in 1434 by the Flemish master Jan Van Eyck, and it depicts a man and a woman holding hands in an interior setting. The man gestures in greeting, and the couple seems to be formally presenting themselves as if asking us to recognize their relationship. So far, so good. But what shall we make of the many objects in the room that clearly have been put there on purpose—the single candle, the little carved figure on the bedpost, the shoes, the fruit on the window, and the small dog in the foreground? Why are all these objects here, and what is the purpose of this picture?

If we try to interpret Van Eyck's *Arnolfini Wedding* by simply describing what we see, the results will not be very satisfying, because decoding the significance of the many puzzling objects in the picture clearly requires some knowledge our own eyes and cultural experience do not give us. So we have to turn to literary texts and other paintings from that era, and these tell us that the objects in the Van Eyck picture are all *symbolic:* the candle stands for the presence of God; the carving represents Saint Margaret, a patron saint of childbirth; the fruit indicates fertility; the shoes are removed because the couple is on "holy ground" in the presence of God; and the dog is the ancient symbol of fidelity (a common name for a dog used to be "Fido").

The world of the fifteenth century was a world of symbols. That culture believed that the only really important things were in heaven, and that life on this earth was a pale and corrupt reflection of the eternal world. So almost every plant, animal, flower, or object in nature signified something else more important, usually a person or an idea. Everyone living in Van Eyck's time had these mental habits and would have recognized the significance of these objects, but we have to *reconstruct* this world

Fig. 4.
Leonardo da Vinci, *The Last Supper*, fresco and wax, 1497. (*Santa Maria delle Grazie, Milan.*) © *Archivi Alinari/ Art Resource.*

Fig. 5.
Jan Van Eyck, *Portrait of Giovanni Arnolfini and his Wife,* oil on oak, 32³/₈
in. × 22⁵/₈ in., 1434. Signed, inscribed and dated *Johannes de eyck fuit
hic, 1434. (London, National Gallery, NG182.)* © Alinari/Art Resource.

because we don't live in it any more. Art historians have invented a special word, "iconography," that means the study of subject matter, texts, and symbols in art. Today about the only thing left from this coded language is flower symbolism. Most of us know that red roses mean "love," yellow roses mean "friendship," and lilies are for funerals. So, if your date shows up with lilies instead of roses, the relationship is in trouble!

Using this knowledge of Renaissance symbol language, can we expand on our description of Van Eyck's picture and work toward a comprehensive interpretation of it? In fact, we know from other sources that the man in the painting was Giovanni Arnolfini, a representative of the Medici bank in Bruges, and his wife was a woman named Jeanne de Chename. A famous art historian named Irwin Panofsky argued that Jan Van Eyck's painting was intended as a kind of "visual marriage contract" in which the couple swears mutual "fidelity" before God and two witnesses (who are actually reflected in the tiny convex mirror on the back wall), and also before us, across the centuries. If this interpretation is correct, the painting certainly means more than we thought at first.

Now compare a more recent work, the small collage or "paste-up" made in 1955 by Richard Hamilton (figure 6), called *Just What Is It That Makes Today's Homes So Different, So Appealing?* Here is another young couple in a domestic setting, except this time all the objects in the room are consumer goods and brand names. The man holds a Tootsie Roll Pop as if it were a barbell (he's pretty well "pumped-up"), and the busty woman is posing seductively (she's all real: implants had not yet been invented). Hamilton's collage seems to invite comparison to the Jan Van Eyck, but, unlike the solemn Renaissance couple, these two love-birds don't even seem to notice each other. They are totally absorbed in themselves, their bodies, and their consumerism.

The tape recorder on the floor between the couple, which is positioned exactly like Van Eyck's dog, also seems to invite comparison. Why is it there? You may recall a phrase used in 1950s advertising to describe audio equipment that reproduced sound very accurately, which was, that's right, "high *fidelity*." Clearly Hamilton wants us to connect his work to the famous painting by Van Eyck, but how does he want us to think about the relationship? If his picture (one of the first examples of the style we call "Pop Art") is not just an inside joke, could it be a sly commentary on the emptiness of popular culture and modern relationships—since "fidelity" is probably not high on this couple's list of virtues? This interpretation is just a plausible guess, but it seems to make sense, and we like it because Hamilton's collage now seems to mean more: it becomes a critique of consumerism and materialism, suggesting that modern life and relationships suffer by comparison to the world of values and commitment depicted by Jan Van Eyck.

There are several important points to be made here. First, it is an article of faith in art history that *no artwork stands alone*—that all works of art and all human actions have a historical context. The artist may be making an intentional and purposeful comparison with an older work of art, or the similarity may be unintentional or unconscious. (Is Hamilton's work *intentionally* based on the Van Eyck, as we have supposed? How do we prove that? Shall we ask the artist? What if he's dead, doesn't remember, wasn't consciously aware of what he was doing, or just doesn't want to tell us?) This principle that all artworks depend on each other also holds true in music and literature: writers and poets, especially good ones like Bob Dylan or the Beatles, love to make clever references to other artists because that makes their own songs mean more.

Second, it may seem obvious that these two artworks are related, but nobody saw this relationship until 1990, and we would not have seen it unless we knew the Van Eyck picture and somehow made the connection. That is why the humanities are so difficult and so much fun. Ask the right question and the answer will jump at you, but asking the right question is an art in itself, and there are no rules to tell us how. Like all insights, new interpretations of artworks result from the combination of informed memory, creativity, and vigilance. I follow the rule first proposed by the great Yankee catcher, Yogi Berra, who said, "You can observe a lot just by looking."

By the way, nowhere is it written that you have to have a Ph.D. to propose new interpretations of artworks. Every year sharp students in beginning art history classes make observations that suggest new meanings for well-known artworks. Try doing that in

Fig. 6.
Richard Hamilton, *Just What Is It That Makes Today's Homes So Different, So Appealing?*, collage, 10¼ in. × 9¼ in., 1955. *(Kunsthalle, Tübingen, Germany)*

Physics 101! In fact, "research" in the humanities is often nothing more than finding out if anyone else has already put in print what you see. That is why I must tell you that the observation about the dog in Hamilton's collage is not mine, much as I wish it were. Graham Smith published it in 1990 in *Source: Notes in the History of Art*. Scholars build on each other's work, and we expect other scholars not to steal our ideas. Not to credit and *correctly cite* someone else's idea is about the most dishonest thing a scholar or a student can do. It amounts to theft, and you can lose your job or get an "F" if you do it!

We can make some funny mistakes if we unthinkingly apply our own contemporary, cultural standards and expectations to artworks of the past. As we look at the young woman in Van Eyck's picture, we may conclude from her posture and the symbols in the painting that she is pregnant—and that this marriage is a bit late. In fact, she is probably *not* pregnant. Our current standard of beauty prefers both men and women to have flat stomachs (washboard "abs"), but the cultural ideal in 1434 preferred bellies that protruded, even in women who were not pregnant, and women's fashions of that day reflected those ideals. You can see these dresses in museums: they are made of yards of layered cloth, weigh up to twenty pounds, and force the wearer to bend backwards and hold up heavy folds of extra material in front to keep balance, thus making the belly even more emphasized. The symbols in the painting emphasize fertility because that was woman's chief purpose in that era.

The history of art shows us that ideals of human beauty are cultural, not biological, and the ultra-thin or muscular body types celebrated in our media and advertising are, historically speaking, extreme and unusual. Also, popular ideals of beauty now change almost yearly, urged on by whole industries in media, fashion, cosmetics, surgery, hairstyling, and bodybuilding that pander to our obsession with youth and appearance. The Renaissance believed that human beauty was a rare gift from God, but we have come to think of it as everyone's right and have placed physical beauty above almost every other aspect of personality and character. That may be another message of Hamilton's Pop Art collage.

We cannot really understand art—as opposed to "enjoying" it—without history, because our human experience is limited by our own time and place: the farther back into the past we go, the more we have to *reconstruct* the historical context of a work of art if we are going to have any chance of knowing why it was made or how it changed the way people thought about art. Art history aims to understand the human condition, past and present, by studying works of art, and art historians may range widely into other aspects of human civilization such as politics, religion, philosophy, literature, music, and vernacular history. This is done in order to illuminate the social context of artworks, but the basic task must be to try to get the facts right and try to figure out the makers' intentions. However, we can never be sure that we know the ultimate meaning of any artwork, because many older artworks like *The Arnolfini Wedding* appear to present us with puzzles we can't read without documents or artifacts to guide us. That is why there can never be final "right answers" in art history—or in any of the humanities, for that matter—only *interpretations* that are more or less likely, more or less interesting, or more or less well expressed.

Art *critics,* on the other hand, make *judgments* about art their primary goal. They try to evaluate the quality, importance, or significance of artworks, especially new works. Like the movie reviewer or music critic, the art critic is true only to his own opinions, which he tries to justify to us. The art historian is not supposed to be interested in the quality of artworks, but in how art reveals the mind of the artist and her society (although, in fact, the best artworks are always more revealing and more interesting). So, if I say that I like Georgia O'Keeffe and do not like Cindy Sherman, and you say the opposite, we can argue about the "relative merits" of these two artists—and it is fun to do so, if our arguments are not based on willful ignorance—but we can never "prove" that one of us is right, because *de gustibus non disputandum est:* "you can't argue about taste." To take an example from classic rock and roll, I can and will claim that the Beatles are better than the Rolling Stones (who I think should have retired a long time ago), and I might give as reasons for my opinion that the Beatles were more original, complex, and funny, and were also important social critics. I also think they were better musicians. But if you were to say, as you very well might, that the Stones simply *rock* better and that their music touches you personally in a way that the Beatles' music does not, no one can argue with you. This is a problem for criticism, not history, where our first responsibility is to suspend our personal judgments.

Most paintings in the Western tradition are not as difficult to unravel as the Van Eyck or the Hamilton. *Stacks of Wheat (End of Day, Autumn),* popularly known as *Haystacks,* by Claude Monet (pronounced "moe-nay") in the Chicago Art Institute (figure 7) appears to present no puzzles or hidden meanings. Unless we are badly mistaken or do not know what haystacks are, our own eyes tell us what is being represented, and we can also appreciate that the artist wants to portray the effects of light and atmosphere at a particular time of year and time of day. The painting *pleases* us. We can imagine being there. We may even know that this art-work is an example of the art movement called "Impressionism" that flourished in France after 1870. What our eyes do *not* tell us, however, is that Impressionism is not the only way to paint a landscape and that when this painting was new, most people found it difficult to look at, if not downright objectionable: they did *not* like the bright colors, which were different from the paint-ings they were used to; they did not like the bold brushwork, which contradicted the accepted view that a painting should look "finished"; and they also thought the subject was too ordinary— that is, not elevated, refined, imaginary, or historical. In short, they reacted the same way most people react when they encoun-ter something new and startling—they hated it. Try to imagine how Beethoven, Stravinsky, Elvis, Jimi Hendrix, or House Music sounded at first. Exactly. Many listeners, especially the older gen-eration, hit the roof. (The day will come when *you* will hit the roof!)

Art is an acquired taste. European college students are exposed to painting and sculpture at an early age and come to think of their great artworks as national monuments—something like our Liberty Bell or the Grand Canyon. Europeans even have famous artists, musicians, and writers on their money. In contrast, when we Americans think of "Art" with a capital "A," we tend to think of old, boring objects that are anything but fun, useful, or important. However, if somebody mentions popular music, mov-ies, or television we perk up and discuss these media as if we were experts. We all have opinions about modern entertainment, and

Fig. 7.
Claude Monet (French, 1840–1926), *Stacks of Wheat (End of Day, Autumn)*, 1890–91. Oil on canvas, 65.8 × 101 cm. Mr. and Mrs. Lewis Larned Coburn Memorial Collection, 1933.444, image © The Art Institute of Chicago.

we don't believe we need any special training or credentials to make our judgments because these media are important parts of *our* lives and *our* world. We'd be very upset to lose them. Painting and sculpture were the movies and television of the past, and people in those societies took them as seriously as we take our own entertainment.

Furthermore, we Americans are a practical people. We value things that *work* and have less interest in things that are beautiful but useless. If you had been a European colonist arriving at Plymouth Rock in 1620, owning fine paintings would have been the last thing on your mind. Finding dinner and getting through the winter alive were a little more important! Although the indigenous peoples of the Americas—the Native American Indians—had highly sophisticated art, European colonists did not have professional painters until the eighteenth century, and they painted mainly portraits. We also did not have a tradition of religious art, our colonial parent culture being predominantly Protestant. Indeed, even as America progressed and prospered, there was a lingering suspicion that the fine arts are somehow useless or, worse, "elitist," since we also claim to be a classless society. Let the Europeans spend money on these luxury decorations; we would invent better light bulbs, cars, and airplanes. Even though Thomas Jefferson said, "I will be a soldier and a politician so that my son can be an architect and *his* son can be an artist," we never seemed to get around to that third generation until very recently. Our idea of beauty was pretty well confined to nature itself (which we had a lot of!). So our first successful artists were painters in the Hudson River valley who went out of their way to associate landscape painting with nature and God in order to make art more acceptable (and saleable) to religiously-minded Americans, who still had little use for "art for art's sake." As late as 1900, few rural Americans had ever seen an original work of art except their own quilts and furniture.

This attitude began to change in the late nineteenth century, when many urban Americans began to see the arts as the mark of a developed and civilized country. Our great museums, like the Metropolitan Museum in New York, the National Gallery in Washington, and the Chicago Art Institute, were specifically established to raise national standards of culture as well as the *moral* standards of the average working person (art was thought to be able to do this), and these goals were so stated in the museum charters. The British Museum, in contrast, was at first open only during working hours and never on weekends precisely so that the cultured elite would not have to rub shoulders with the working class!

The phenomenon called the "salon" illustrates how important the fine arts were in Europe. Every year between roughly 1660 and 1900, the King of France presided over the opening of the Paris Salon, an annual juried exhibition of several *thousand* new artworks. Crowds mobbed the galleries, eager to see what was up and make informed judgments, aided by over one hundred newspapers that reviewed and commented on the show. Artists who showed at these salons, or, better yet, won medals, were assured of commissions and fame (yes, they gave out awards—like our Oscars), and artists whose works were rejected had to start over next year (yes, they had a jury—like our Oscars). The important issue here is what we can call "shared experience." The French public went to the salons for the same reason that we go to movies, to keep up with contemporary culture and not be left out of conversations. They loved being critics, as we do, because making judgments about other people's efforts and opinions is one of our chief pleasures as human beings.

Today we have the idea that artists are members of some special race with unique powers and visions, "geniuses" who reveal these visions to the rest of us mortals—for a price. However, this concept of the artist is pretty recent. Before the Renaissance, artists were not considered intellectuals, but merely tradesmen or manual laborers in highly stratified societies where only members of the aristocracy (the upper or "leisure" classes) were deemed to have the capacity for higher knowledge or sensitive feelings. But Renaissance artists wanted to improve their income and social status, so they began to promote themselves by putting out the notion that they were not really doing manual labor at all—that art was about *thinking,* that artists had a special pipeline to beauty, and that a few extraordinary artists were geniuses blessed with a truly divine gift. By 1500, artists like Michelangelo had acquired superstar status and had the nobles eating out of their hands.

This brings us to the reason why art history was invented—

money. You can't buy and sell history or genius, but you can buy and sell artworks. Art and money have been close friends ever since the ancient Romans began buying and copying famous sculptures, and there has been a flourishing international art market since the Renaissance invented the idea of the celebrity artist and collectible art. That market is now worth several billion dollars a year. So, if you were a king or a pope, or had made a fortune selling coal, and now wanted to impress your rich friends and meet some of those interesting "Bohemian" artist-celebrities (people who were known to have a lot of fun when they weren't making masterpieces), it was natural for you to begin collecting art. However, you needed a professional to tell you *what* to buy, and that was not as easy as it sounds. There are millions of artworks floating around the world and most of them are just plain bad or, worse, fakes. They do not come with instructions or stamps of authenticity, and they rarely even had signatures before the eighteenth century. If the art world had decided that Michelangelo and Monet were artists worth buying, you needed to know if a particular artwork was indeed by Michelangelo or Monet—and what it was worth.

Enter the art historians. They studied documents, looked closely at the painters' brushwork, wrote the books, and were prepared (for a fee) to authenticate and evaluate a painting. (Even the IRS will not argue with a Ph.D. in art history!) Thus, the early efforts of the discipline of art history focused on defining the exact *body of work* of individual artists and on developing methods and tools for doing this. Now we have modern scientific techniques to date and authenticate artworks, but early art historians only had their eyes. So they developed the idea of "style."

Style is one of the most difficult and important concepts in the history of art, and the word "style" can mean many things. We use the word in everyday conversation to mean anything that is excellent or unique, as in "she's got style." In art history, a "style" means any *group of artworks* that look similar, and there can be very large categories of style, like "Impressionism" (Monet's *Haystacks*), "Northern Renaissance" (Van Eyck's *Wedding*), and "Pop Art" (Hamilton's collage). There may also be very small categories, like the style of *The Creation of Eve,* the fifth panel in Michelangelo's Sistine Chapel ceiling (which is in fact stylistically different than the sixth panel, or *The Creation of Adam,* because Michelangelo's style changed or "developed" between the two pictures. Trust me: you really can see the difference.) In fact, every artist and every work of art has a unique style or "handwriting," and the more individual that style, the better. The components of style are the *visual language of art*—quality of line, brushwork, color, space, light, composition, action, and "expression." Using the examples illustrated here, it is obvious that the works by Monet, Giotto, Leonardo, Van Eyck, Michelangelo, Hamilton, and Reinhardt exemplify different styles because they *look different.* People who specialize in recognizing styles are called *connoisseurs* (ka-no-sirs), and a talented one can recognize the smallest difference between, say, two paintings by Monet made in 1890 and 1891. One of the joys of art history is learning to recognize the various styles of artists and art movements and guessing who did a picture before you look at the label. You can develop that skill pretty quickly when you take an art history course.

But, beyond connoisseurship, the idea of style has a more important purpose. Art historians believe style is the expression of the deepest *values* of any culture, and we also believe that no style is inherently better than any other, in other words, that quality in art is *relative.* Thus you may personally prefer one style to another just as you may prefer strawberry to chocolate ice cream, but these are not *objective* judgments. For the art historian, the best example of any group of stylistically similar cultural artifacts is inherently as good as the best example of any other, no matter how far removed they are in time and space—although the *art market* may have different ideas.

Before about a hundred years ago, all paintings were representations or imitations of the "real world," and they often illustrated a *text* such as the Bible or an actual historical event. Both artists and critics considered these "history paintings" to be the highest and most difficult type of art—far more important and "elevated" than the other *genres* or types of painting such as portraiture, landscape, still life, or "low life." This hierarchy of subjects may seem silly to us, for whom landscape paintings are especially pleasing, but the art world of the past held to this ranking very strictly. Remember that earlier civilizations had greater need for art and higher purposes for it than we do, and art was especially important for religion. Most people in the Renaissance still could not read, so church interiors needed pictures of Bible stories. Indeed, Pope Gregory the Great had already said in the seventh century that the Catholic Church officially approved of images, "which can do for the illiterate what the Bible can do for those who can read," that is, *instruct, remind, and inspire* worshippers. So artists in Catholic countries—especially Italy, where churches featured murals (wall paintings) instead of stained glass windows—developed history painting into an effective method of communication, and the artist became a "professional visualizer"—something like a movie director.

Giotto's *Lamentation on the Death of Christ* in the Arena Chapel in Padua, painted about 1305 (figure 8), is rightly one of the most famous and original history paintings ever made. Looking at it today you might think it is nothing special, but Giotto has done several wonderful new things compared to the stiff, symmetrical, flat works that came before him. He has given the "actors" on his stage a shallow three-dimensional space to inhabit, and we can see that their bodies have mass, weight, and volume ("tactile values," as Bernard Berenson put it). They move, act, and relate to each other like human beings with real emotions. True, the landscape itself is pretty skimpy and there are some awkward places where the bodies don't bend or twist very well, but we can't ask Giotto to invent everything all at once! Above all, there is real human feeling in the picture, and this was totally new in 1305. Giotto clearly thought about this Bible story carefully, and dramatized and humanized it for maximum emotional impact. We feel as if we could step into the picture and be part of the action, and we can understand the pity and sorrow in the faces of St. Mary and St. John simply because we are human beings. (The next question that the art historian wants to ask is *why* this humanizing change in style happened at this particular time. Hint: have you heard of St. Francis of Assisi?)

If we compare Giotto's fresco to Leonardo's *Last Supper* (figure 4), it is obvious that Leonardo, who lived two centuries after Giotto, can handle the human form better. His figures have relatively more weight and muscular definition, move more gracefully and purposefully, and interact even more like real people. Leonardo also understands the action of *light* better: notice that in

Fig. 8.
Giotto di Bondone, *Lamentation on the Death of Christ,* fresco, c. 1305.
(Arena Chapel, Padua.) Art Resource.

the Giotto we're not quite sure where the light is coming from, while Leonardo's painting has a clear light source. Also, Leonardo's space is much more believable and exists even without the figures, which is not true in Giotto. This is achieved by the new "scientific perspective," which uses mathematics to make the architecture diminish to the single "vanishing point" at the head of Christ.

It certainly seems clear in hindsight that Italian Renaissance artists were moving toward greater accuracy in depicting nature, space, and the human figure. Does this mean that Leonardo was a better artist than Giotto? Italian Renaissance artists and patrons did not have our modern "historical" or relativistic attitude toward art. For them there were only two kinds of art—good and bad—and art was better the more it approached the perfect imitation of nature. But today we are inclined to say that not all things are possible at all times and, *considering when he painted,* Giotto was as good as he could possibly be. Leonardo only built on Giotto's achievements. We would say that it is unfair and pointless to rate the relative quality of these two artists because both reflected their times and their artistic environment, both were innovators, and both were part of a continuum. Naturally, *you* are free to choose which artist you prefer (personally, I prefer Giotto), but these are private judgments, not historical ones.

Let's take a more difficult case, Ad Reinhardt's *Abstract Painting* of 1961 (figure 9). Remember our toolbox containing the elements of art? It does not seem to be of much use here, does it? We cannot consider the text or story because it does not have any story. We cannot judge it in terms of its fidelity to visual reality because this painting clearly has no interest in imitating reality. We cannot make a "formal analysis" because it has no "form" in any traditional sense—no line, shape, or composition, and very little color. (In fact, there are actually nine smaller squares in this painting, each a slightly different shade of black—very difficult to see in the original, and almost impossible to reproduce in a book) This work, which we can call "nonrepresentational" or abstract, deliberately gives us almost nothing that we recognize as being part of a traditional painting except that it is flat, square, and hangs on a wall. It is as if the artist looked back through the whole history of art to identify everything a painting used to be—and then turned his back and walked away.

Many viewers like you may say that this picture is ridiculous, that it requires no "skill," that "anybody could do it," and that the painter is just trying to "fool the public." Well, Ad Reinhardt is clearly not trying to fool us in any traditional artistic sense, because, unlike Leonardo or Monet, he does not pretend that his painting is a hole in the wall or an illusion of three-dimensional space—that is *really* fooling, and artists had been doing it for 500 years. Reinhardt's painting is in fact absolutely and devastatingly *honest* because it doesn't try to be anything but what it is. It does not pose as literature, try to elicit any emotion from us, or make us believe anything, although it seems to have something to say about the psychology of perception. But I know what you mean if you say that the painter was trying to fool the public: you think that Reinhardt is just trying to make money by "conning" the art world when he is actually "laughing all the way to the bank." Indeed, if you had bought this painting when it was first shown in New York in 1961 for its then modest asking price of about $1,000, you could now sell it and retire. Well, if it is so easy to fool the public and get rich, I hope you will do the same—or tell me how so I can do it! The truth is that Reinhardt was just as dedicated and serious as any other professional artist. He just arrived at a different place—an art movement we call Minimalism. Thousands of other artists were trying just as hard to become famous and rich, but only this painting and a very few others have lived to become classics. And if you think the painting is upsetting today, you should have heard the reactions to it in 1961!

Like Giotto's fresco, Reinhardt's painting can be best understood in its historical context. If we now look back at *Abstract Painting* against the background of art before 1961, it makes perfect sense and seems to be the logical (if radical and terrifying) outcome of all that history. No artwork stands alone, and no great artist ever paints without looking over his shoulder at history. Reinhardt understood history, imagined where painting ought to go, and took it there. He believed painting ought to be purely about vision itself and had to be ruthlessly cleansed of everything that was not really proper to it—like literature and illusion. He had to see what he could *get rid of* and still have a painting. Obvi-

Fig. 9.
Ad Reinhardt, *Abstract Painting,* oil on canvas, 60 in. × 60 in., 1960–66.
*(Purchased with funds from The Lauder Foundation, Leonard and Evelyn
Lauder Fund 98.16.3. © 2001, Estate of Ad Reinhardt/Artists Rights Society
[ARS], New York)*

ously this painting is not about the "real" world but is rather *art about art* because the motivation and "content" of this work arise almost entirely from the "art world" itself, which is surely not the case with Giotto's *Lamentation*. What is the same is that both paintings mean a lot less without their historical context.

If Reinhardt's *Abstract Painting* is valuable, what is "value" in art and how do artworks acquire it? Is value aesthetic, historical, or commercial? There is no point in pretending that artworks are just "priceless" artifacts that are only interesting as sources of pleasure or historical information. We all instinctively want to know how much artworks are worth in hard cash, and we tend to adjust our estimate of an artwork's importance and quality to its price, which is the ultimate scale of value in our materialist age. If I tell you that the Leonardo da Vinci's *Mona Lisa* in the Louvre Museum is the most desirable portable artwork in the world, that even if the French Government ever decided to sell it the bidding would start at 200 million Euros, and that the apparently equally fine portrait of a court lady by Leonardo on the wall next to the Mona Lisa is probably worth only about 50 million Euros, are you supposed to think that the Mona Lisa is four times as good? It is hard to see the Mona Lisa any more as a historical artifact: all we see is the veil of money in front of it.

Today there are thousands of artworks for sale in studios, galleries, auction houses, and Web sites around the world, but the vast majority of these will finally be worth much less than their current asking price (especially the works of Thomas Kincaid). The few works by highly desirable "Old Masters" like Leonardo, Rembrandt, Monet, or Van Gogh fetch staggering prices because the art market functions on supply and demand and because works by these revered masters almost never come on the market. Bill Gates paid $30 million for a notebook by da Vinci, and a *drawing* by Michelangelo recently sold for over $10 million, not just because Michelangelo is *the* most revered old master, but also because works by him almost never come up for sale.

Ironically, many of these artists were destitute during their lives—Vincent Van Gogh, for example. Today you can go to the Van Gogh Museum in Amsterdam and see hundreds of his works displayed together simply because the poor man *sold only one painting in his entire short life* (he died in 1890 at age thirty-seven), and his brother's wife was sentimental enough to keep the worthless things around until Vincent became famous, which surprised her as much as it did everyone else. The very idea that Vincent would have an *entire museum* for his own works just down the block from the National Museum of Holland where the great Rembrandts hang would cause Van Gogh himself and all his contemporaries to spin in their graves. The last Van Gogh to sell at auction went for $88 million. Were Van Gogh's contemporaries so wrong, and is the current art market so right?

In fact, the "value" of art rises and falls over time like any commodity, and what is up today may be down tomorrow. For example, who would you say was the greater artist, Michelangelo or Raphael? Right: *who is Raphael?* Well, Raphael Sanzio decorated the papal apartments in the Vatican Palace at exactly the same time that Michelangelo was working next door in the Sistine Chapel. Today, the herds of visitors simply ignore the Raphael rooms on their way to see Michelangelo, but, strange as it may seem, Raphael was regarded as the greater artist for 400 of the past 500 years. It was only during the last century that Michelangelo's "stock" began to rise and Raphael's to fall. We like Michelangelo better because he seems to speak to *us*.

I say "seems" because we can never be sure we're reading Michelangelo "correctly." Maybe we value things in his work that he would have dismissed as unimportant or unintended. For example, many of Michelangelo's works are unfinished. We are pretty sure that he intended to finish them but just never got around to it, or got "blocked," or wasn't being paid, or had to leave town in a hurry. His early works like the *Pieta* in Rome and the great *David* in Florence are finished to a high polish, but many of his later works have only the suggestion of faces, arms, and legs. Some, like the so-called *Slave* or "Prisoner" (figure 10) in Florence, seem still "imprisoned" in their blocks of marble, emerging (or disintegrating) out of (or into) the stone. We in the modern world are attracted to these unfinished works because they seem to be metaphors for life in our own age—an age of uncertainty and anxiety. Such would be an "interpretation" of Michelangelo's late works, but might Michelangelo say we are all wrong? Does the artist have exclusive rights to interpretations of his own work? Much has been written on this subject, as you might guess. In fact, all the books and articles ever written about Michelangelo would easily fill the room where you are now sitting.

Great artworks always reward a close look with insights into the human condition, but we have to look *actively* because, unlike modern media like television, movies, and music, which keep running whether or not we pay attention, paintings just *sit there.* Viewers, before the advent of electronic media, could spend hours looking at and talking about paintings in the same way we hash over *The West Wing* or *Star Wars.* If they found an artwork that was worth a second look and kept on rewarding them with new insights, undiscovered relationships, and, above all, with *truth,* then that artwork would live and prosper. People would desire to see it, to talk and write about it, and it might become a classic or a masterpiece. Why do some movies, TV shows, songs, and books continue to be watched, played, and read while most sink into oblivion? For exactly the same reason that traditional artworks do: because they reward us at each encounter with new insights and truths about the human condition. However, nobody knows which artworks will survive to become masterpieces until "history" makes its ruthless judgments. For example, when director George Lucas showed the first rough cut of a movie called *Star Wars* to some of his friends, they thought it was absolutely *awful,* and nobody had any great hopes for a little movie called *Casablanca,* either.

As you can see, the history of art is a serious and difficult academic discipline with its own methods, vocabulary, and goals. Dedicated people spend their lives studying it. But even a general knowledge of art can give immense pleasure—even change your life. I have taught thousands of students, and I frequently receive postcards and e-mail from former students, who tell me that their courses in art history turned out to be much more valuable in later life than they expected. Almost all of you will eventually visit great museums like the National Gallery in Washington, the Louvre in Paris, the Vatican City, The Museum of Modern Art, or the hundreds of fine regional museums in America and abroad. Almost all of you will buy houses, clothes, cars, furniture, that require aesthetic—that is, artistic—decisions. Students who take some art history in college find that they begin to enjoy the arts and start to think about *quality* in their visual surroundings and in

Fig. 10.
Michelangelo Buonarroti, *Slave (Prisoner)*, marble, c. 1530. *(Academia, Florence.)* Archivi Alinari/Art Resource.

their lives. They tell me a new world has been opened for them, that they feel more connected to the past and the people of the past, and that friends they know and work with also enjoy the arts—without being elitist or snobbish. (*Reverse* snobbery—proud and willful ignorance—is much more common in America.) Moreover, if you aspire to enter one of the professions such as law, medicine, politics, engineering, finance, or teaching, you will find that some basic knowledge of the arts and art history is useful if not expected. To give a cruel example, if you are being interviewed for an important job and someone asks if you happened to see Monet at the Met, don't answer, "Did he score a goal"? or "Who's playing drums for him now"?

The global art world is a multi-billion dollar industry that requires thousands of professionals, so art history can also be a portal to numerous rewarding careers: art galleries, museums, auction houses, art publications, dot-coms, and art support organizations employ thousands, to say nothing of the many artists and teachers working in the field. If you are interested in a career in fashion, advertising, publication design, web design, or just about anything that involves images or aesthetic choices, some knowledge of art history is essential. None of these careers is easy, and the only reason to major in art history or a related field is because you really want to, but the careers are there for students with inclination and dedication. Finally, aside from its value as a basic social skill or a career portal, knowledge of the arts is rewarding and interesting in itself. Indeed, art is one of the chief pleasures of human beings—one of the things that *makes* us human—and knowing history makes the art much more rewarding, and more fun. There's a whole lifetime of art out there. Enjoy it!

WORKS CITED

Smith, Graham. *Source: Notes in the History of Art* 9 no. 4 (Summer 1990): 30–34.

WEB RESOURCES

The World Wide Web has revolutionized the teaching and study of art history because it is now possible to reach out in real time and bring almost every artwork ever made into the classroom or your computer screen. For examples of course outlines and Internet databases in art, see the homepage of any "webbified" art historian like Pippin Micheli, author of the legendary *Art History Browser* (http://www.ariadne.org/studio/michelli/), Chris Witcombe of Sweetbriar College (http://witcombe.sbc.edu/research resources/), or my personal course pages at http://puffin.creighton .edu/fapa/aikin/Web-files/aikins_courses.htm. There you will find links to huge art databases like Mark Hardin's *Artchive (http://www .artchive.com/), the Web Gallery of Art* (http://gallery.euroweb.hu), and to hundreds of museums around the world—almost all of which now have a significant web presence. You can find almost every artist who ever lived and every artwork ever made through *Artcyclopedia* (http://www.artcyclopedia.com), or use your search engine (I recommend the freeware at *Copernic.com*).

7

The Study of History

Robert M. Senkewicz

The Past, Present, and Future of History

The origins of the study of history are located deep within each one of us, in the human psyche. They are based on the ways in which we conceptualize our relationships to ourselves, each other, and our world. In this chapter, I would like to introduce you to the discipline and study of history. I will attempt to do that by describing first what "history" is and break it down into its two component parts. Then I will offer some reflections on both the theoretical and practical value of studying history.

I am sitting right now in front of a computer monitor as I write this chapter. While I am working here, I also have a picture in my mind of a classroom and of a student in that classroom asking me a very good question about an aspect of the American Revolution, which was the subject of the course. I know that the events of this picture actually occurred last year. While I am working here, I also have a picture in my mind of the Point Reyes National Seashore just north of San Francisco, where my wife and I are going to spend two days a week from now, during spring break. Right now I am related to the past (the class last year), the present (this chapter), and the future (our mini-vacation next week).

All of us have this triple focus to our lives. Connected to the past, we live in memory. Inhabiting the present, we live in experience. Looking toward what has not yet occurred, we live in anticipation. In a real sense, at every moment of our lives, we simultaneously dwell in the past, the present, and the future. The intellectual endeavor called "history" is the formal study of this multidimensional aspect of human existence.

In the popular mind, history is entirely about the past. While that is the truth, it is not the whole truth. To understand this, let's look at two history books that happen to be on my shelves and which I am using to prepare my classes. One is entitled *John Adams,* and it was written by noted historian and biographer David McCullough. It begins with an event on January 24, 1776. John Adams and a companion were starting out on their journey from Boston to Philadelphia, where Adams would attend the Second Continental Congress. The book itself was published in 2001. The second book is entitled *Theaters of Conversion,* and it was written by art historian Samuel Y. Edgerton. Its subtitle gives an indication of its content: *Religious Architecture and Indian Artisans in Colonial Mexico.* This volume is a study of various worship environments, especially mission churches, in Mexico during the sixteenth and seventeenth centuries. It was also published in 2001.

These books illustrate a simple yet important point about history, for both are explicitly related to two different eras. One is the time of the past, when the events they described occurred. The other is the time of the present, when they were written and published. The point is that "history" has an irreducibly double focus. It is concerned with memory, since history is the study of the past. But it is also very directly concerned with experience, since the act of engaging in the study of history is always done in the present.

HISTORY AND THE PAST

In considering these two aspects, let us begin with the past. We know that memory is complex and unstable. It "plays tricks" on us. We might think that something happened that did not occur, or we might remember it happening differently than it actually did. One person over time can remember things differently, and two or more people can remember the same event in radically variant fashions. The 1951 Japanese film *Roshomon* by Akira Kurosawa, in which a group of people remember a grisly murder in entirely different ways, is a brilliant examination of this deeply rooted human phenomenon. Another aspect of memory experienced by all is that memories often come to us emotionally "loaded." If I remember a time in my life when I was particularly happy or sad, chances are that I will find myself happy or sad in the present as I do this remembering.

We all know from our experience that the past comes to us in different ways. In the context of the study of history, the past also comes to a historian in many different ways. There are different types of sources through which historians try to recover the past. Some of these are archaeological. They might be sites such as the ruins of ancient cities and temples. They might be parts of buildings or walls. The book I mentioned earlier, *Theaters of Conversion,* contains many photographs of the exteriors and interiors of Mexican churches, and these structures are important sources for the history with which that volume is concerned. The discovery in the nineteenth century of Mayan ruins hidden beneath the dense jungle of the Yucatán peninsula fundamentally altered our understanding of ancient Central America. Even now, archaeological discoveries in Israel and Palestine are changing the way in which scholars are evaluating the narrative and historical sections of the Hebrew Scriptures.

Another set of sources comes to us from ancient papyrus and its subsequent successors, down to the present, acid-filled paper that we use today. These are texts, such as legal codes, royal decrees, documents about land ownership, commercial records, newspapers, government documents, and scores of other types of written or printed material. These texts are crucial to our understanding of many aspects of the past. For instance, in the sixteenth century, the Spanish *conquistadores* read a formal document (sometimes in Latin!) to groups of uncomprehending indigenous peoples they encountered. The document, called the *requerimiento,* told the Indians that the pope had decreed that they were now subjects of the Spanish monarch and had to submit to his rule. While some Spaniards regarded the document as ridiculous, even at the time it was being read, it helps us to understand the initial stages of European imperialism in the New World.

A further set of sources consists of personal texts. These can be letters, reminiscences, diaries, travel journals, and other types of writings. These documents can, in many instances, uniquely illuminate the past. For instance, the other book I mentioned earlier, *John Adams,* is largely based on Adams's correspondence, especially the long-running series of letters he wrote to and received from his wife and intellectual partner, Abigail. This correspondence enables the author to present a different picture of Adams than the currently accepted one. These sorts of texts, used carefully, can give us insight into the motivation of historical figures at important times in their lives.

In the Library of Congress, for instance, there is a letter that President Abraham Lincoln wrote to his cabinet in August of 1864 as he was running for re-election against a "peace" candidate, George McClellan. The letter demonstrates that Lincoln anticipated losing the election, and he genuinely believed that the result of his loss would be the permanent dissolution of the Union. He told his cabinet that after the election "it will be my duty to so cooperate with the President-elect, as to save the Union between the election and the inauguration; as he will have secured his election on such ground that he cannot possibly save it afterwards" (Fehrenbacher, 621). This document affords a privileged glimpse into Lincoln's famously anguished soul as he followed the progress of the war and calculated his own political fortunes.

There are two problems associated with historical sources. Paradoxically, historical sources are overwhelming in their numbers and, at the same time, there are too few of them. For example, a person who wanted to write a biography of Benjamin Franklin would find that Franklin's collected papers stretched to a hefty thirty-five volumes. That would account only for Franklin's writings. The writings of the people whom he knew, who influenced him, and whom he influenced, are equally daunting. George Washington's papers run to almost forty volumes, Alexander Hamilton's to almost thirty, and Thomas Jefferson's to over thirty. Even Franklin's thirty-five volumes would not include all the people in Pennsylvania and in England who knew Franklin and influenced him. Clearly, the would-be biographer of Franklin could spend eight hours a day reading Franklin's works and the works of all those with whom he shared ideas and not be finished with this task for decades! What is true in this example is also true for many other historical projects. In many cases, the number of existing historical sources far outstrips the capacity of the historian, or even groups of historians, to master them.

On the other hand, every source that we find makes us wish that we had another source to fill out the picture more completely. For instance, we can go the Ellis Island Immigration Museum in New York harbor and read the names of hundreds of thousands of European immigrants who entered the United States in the late nineteenth and early twentieth century. But when we confront the stark reality of these dense lists, we find ourselves wishing that we could know more: what were these people actually thinking when they stood before the first American official they encountered, an immigration officer who was trying to figure out how to spell their names? What were they looking at as they traveled toward Manhattan? Who was the first person to meet them? Where did they spend their first nights? These questions, and many like them, can never be answered because the extant sources do not provide the information.

What this means is that we can never fully reconstruct the past. In the nineteenth century, the German historian Leopold von Ranke wrote in his work *History of the Latin and German Peoples* that the object of the study of history should be to recover the past "as it really was" (*wie es eigentlic gewesen*) [cited by Stern, 57]. This ideal points to an essential part of historical study, for we need to be as accurate as we can in using our sources to study the past. If we use them creatively and imaginatively the sources allow us to reconstruct pieces of the past.

For instance, many women and men who traveled west over the Great Plains of the United States in the nineteenth century kept travel journals. They recorded natural landmarks, the places at which they met Indians, the shifts in the weather, the conditions of the rivers and streams they crossed, and the like. By reading hundreds of these diaries and journals, by cross referencing them with each other, and by comparing different accounts of what appear to be the same landscape features, historians have been able to reconstruct rather precisely the routes taken by generations of trappers, hunters, merchants, and settlers on the Oregon, California, and Santa Fe trails. At the same time, anthropologists and other researchers, by collecting the oral traditions of the indigenous peoples of these regions, have been able to reconstruct much more fully than ever before the varied histories of the American Indian groups who lived in the West centuries before the appearance of the first wagon train. By combining the results of all these researches, it is possible for us now to reconstruct the history of the American West in a fuller and more inclusive fashion than ever before. But that does not mean that we know the West "as it really was." We will never be able to know that, for the past was much more than a collection of events. It also consisted of the relationship among these events, the ways in which they affected each other.

We all know that human relationships are very tough to unravel, and the same is true for historical relationships. The most perceptive observers of human events have always known that. In his Second Inaugural Address, on March 4, 1865, President Lincoln reflected on the preceding four years of American history, a time of bloodshed and civil war. He remarked that the United States had been divided by slavery, and that "all knew that this interest [slavery] was, somehow, the cause of the war" (Fehrenbacher, 686). The vagueness of that word "somehow" points to the inevitable inadequacy of all our attempts fully to reconstruct the past.

HISTORY AND THE PRESENT

This aspect of the study of history leads us to its second focus: the present. The fact that we can never totally reconstruct the past means that we are always going to have to pick and choose what we want to study, what we want to try to reconstruct. We make choices, some conscious and some unconscious, every day. For instance, in the morning when we pick up the newspaper to read it we always have to pick and choose which section to read first. Some of us might go to the front page; others to the sports section; others to the business news; others to the comics. If someone asked us why we were reading that particular section first, we might say that we were interested in how our favorite team did last night, or in the latest dilemma of Dilbert, or in the President's news conference yesterday, and that was why we went to sports, or the comics, or the main section first. Or we might say that we always did it this way, that for no particular reason we had simply gotten into the habit of reading the paper in this way. But, whether we were aware of it or not, we did make a choice about where to begin.

In history, a similar process of choosing is always under way. In fact, the historian is always making choices. From the many sources that are available to study an event, the historian has to choose ones which he or she judges are the most crucial ones. Historians make their selections on the basis of a provisional interpretation they apply to the past. The fact of this provisional interpretation, which happens whenever any historian begins to research or compose any history, leads us to an important realization: history always and inevitably involves interpretation. There is no getting around that fact.

The earliest historians knew this very well. The study of history as we know it was more or less fashioned in the fifth century B.C. Athens by two men. The first, Herodotus, often referred to as the "father of history," wrote a history of the Persian invasions of Greece. Toward the end of the same century, the Athenian Thucydides composed the other great seminal historical work, his *History of the Peloponnesian War,* which concerned a long conflict between the city-states of Athens and Sparta. Herodotus and Thucydides began their works with their names. Herodotus began: "These are the researches of Herodotus of Halicarnassus, which he publishes, in the hope of thereby preserving from decay the remembrance of what men have done, and of preventing the great and wonderful actions of the Greeks and the Barbarians from losing their due meed of glory" (1). Thucydides began in the same fashion: "Thucydides, an Athenian, wrote the history of the war between the Peloponnesians and the Athenians, beginning at the moment that it broke out, and believing that it would be a great war and more worthy of relation than any that had preceded it" (Strassler, 1).

Soon after their personal introductions, Herodotus and Thucydides introduced the readers to their methods and interpretive frameworks. For Herodotus, the method of history involved interviewing those whom he thought best would be able to provide him with accurate accounts of various aspects of the war. So he plunged right in and began, "According to the Persians best informed in history, the Phoenicians began the quarrel." In the course of his work, Herodotus related many stories about the cus-

toms and habits of the peoples whom he interviewed for his
work. His own interpretive principle became clear close to the
beginning of the book. Long-standing customs and habits, he argued, largely determine the course of events. Thucydides, on the
other hand, approached matters with a different interpretive principle. For him, events were driven by considerations of power
and strategy and emotions. In the midst of a discussion over how
the war actually started in the late 430s, he distinguished between
the tactical maneuvers of Athens, Sparta, and their allies, which
began the conflict, and "the real cause" of the war, power. "The
growth of the power of Athens, and the alarm which this inspired
in Sparta, made war inevitable," he stated (Strassler, 16).

It is not my intention here to consider which of these two
interpretive principles might be more adequate to understanding
the human condition (although in the classes I have taught in
historiography—the study of the writing and practice of history—
students have had very spirited discussions on these two historians
and their ways of practicing history!). I simply want to point out
that in these two foundational classical works, interpretation was
taken to be an integral part of the writing of history.

Another way of appreciating the degree to which interpretation
is woven into the writing of history is to examine a part of the
Bible. Scholars sometimes refer to the individual who wove together the final version of the books of Joshua, Judges, 1 and 2
Samuel, and 1 and 2 Kings as "the Deuteronomic historian."
Even though the events from Joshua to 2 Kings covered centuries, the Deuteronomic historian was not interested in trying to
reconstruct the entire history of those years. Time and again, the
author impatiently tells readers that, if they are interested in more
detail, they can go look it up in another book. After considering
one of the kings of Israel, for instance, the author says, "Now the
rest of the acts of Jeroboam, how he warred and how he reigned,
are written in the Book of the Annals of the Kings of Israel" (1
Kings 14:19). These sorts of matters fell outside of his interpretive
framework. That framework was interested in only one question:
how could God's chosen people have been conquered by the
Assyrians and Babylonians? For the Deuteronomic historian, the
reason was that the rulers did not insist on the exclusive cult of
Yahweh, and proved too lenient in allowing other cults to co-

exist with his. After recounting the fall of the kingdom of Israel in 721, the author breaks off the narrative and makes his interpretation explicit: "This occurred because the people of Israel had sinned . . . they had worshiped other gods" (2 Kings 17:7). Regarded as a historian, the Deuteronomic writer demonstrates clearly that interpretation (in this case a theological interpretation, but an interpretation nonetheless) is an indispensable part of the fabric of writing history.

Interpretations can stem from many sources. They can stem from a theology, as we have just seen. They can also stem from a philosophy, as was the case with Marxian historians in the twentieth century. In that framework, the most important aspect of any human person or social reality was the relationship of that person or reality to the economic means of production. Whatever their origin, the crucial issue is how well interpretations correspond to the other focus of history which we considered earlier, namely the historical sources. Historical interpretation needs to be consistently related to the sources and to the evidence that the sources provide. Interpretation that simply ignores the evidence—such as interpretations that claim that the Holocaust never happened— are anti-historical, since they are not faithful to the irreducibly bipolar focus of history. Historical sources and evidence do not, by themselves, create an interpretation. Historical sources do not come to us in an already-existing pattern. In that sense there can never be a totally "objective" history, if by "objective" we refer to a meaning that is already "back there" in the past that the historian simply has to discover. Sources and evidence are more useful in determining that certain interpretations, such as the Holocaust denial interpretation, are invalid. But once certain interpretations are ruled out, a number of other ones are left as possible. It is usually not the case that one and only one interpretation is consistent with the evidence. The work of history is not done like the work of a researcher in a laboratory. History is more of an art than a science.

So history is a relationship. It is a relationship that stems from the deepest human impulses. It is a relationship between past and present, between memory and experience, between evidence and interpretation, between sources and historian. Like all relationships, history consistently defies easy categorization. And like all relationships, it is one that is best understood from the inside. The richness is only tasted once you plunge into it.

WHY STUDY HISTORY?

Why has this relationship exercised such a pull over humanity for centuries, and why is it still regarded as a cornerstone of liberal education? Why, in other words, should you study history?

There are two very common reasons that are often adduced in this context. The first concerns the last time frame with which we began this chapter, the future. History, it is often said, can help us prepare for, understand, and even predict, the future. This is the popular understanding of George Santayana's maxim, "Those who cannot remember the past are condemned to repeat it." This notion is rooted in the fact that many of the natural forces that surround us are, in fact, repetitive. The seasons, the tides, and the cycle of planting and harvesting all have a rhythmic character to them. It was often thought in the ancient world that history was endless repetition, a thought neatly encapsulated in the verse from Ecclesiastes, "What has been is what will be, and what has been done is what will be done; and there is nothing new under the sun" (Eccles. 1:9).

St. Augustine argued that such a view was incompatible with Christianity, and his view of history as a more linear process has suffused the culture of the West. But an informal version of the cyclical view always remained in circulation. The founders of the United States, for instance, passionately studied the history of the decline of the Roman republic. They believed that Roman history demonstrated that republics always degenerated into factional bickering, followed by chaos and a breakdown of order. In the face of this chaos, people would be susceptible to the wiles of a strong leader who would promise them security. The leader would inevitably evolve into a tyrant. The system of checks and balances devised at the Constitutional Convention of 1787 was designed in part to try to prevent the history of Rome from repeating itself in the new American nation.

But history does not repeat itself except in patterns so large that they have little predictive value. We don't need history to tell us that people can be aggressive and exploitative, and that they often seek to aggrandize their own power. We see that every day. If history could only confirm the obvious, it would not be very important.

The second reason often brought forward as an inducement to study history is that there are certain inevitable "laws" of history and that history has "lessons" to teach us. The trouble with that notion is that it is not too clear what these laws actually are. Also, the notion that history has lessons is belied by the fact that people don't seem to be too easily able to figure out what these lessons are. The field of military history tends to confirm that. The idea that generals often draw bogus lessons from history and too often fight the last war is a cliché, but it has more than a grain of truth. The tragic death toll of World War I, for example, resulted partly from the fact that the military tactics of the nineteenth century, dating all the way back to Napoleon, were applied to a situation radically changed by new technologies such as the machine gun. The result was that the "lessons" of history contributed to producing four horrifying years of brutal and bloody trench warfare.

Another instance of the misapplication of the so-called lessons of history was the United States' decision in the mid-1960s to send large numbers of troops to fight in Vietnam. American leaders said that we needed to do that to stem the tide of international Communism. Policy makers explicitly employed the "Munich analogy." This analogy argued that Western European leaders had refused to stem the tide of Nazism in the late 1930s (a refusal symbolized by the 1938 Munich agreement which condoned Hitler's takeover of Czechoslovakia), and because of this failure had to fight a larger and more costly war with Germany later. So, the argument went, the United States needed to draw the line against Communism in Vietnam, or else we would have to fight a larger and more costly war against that enemy later. As it actually turned out, we lost the war, and Communist governments took over all of Indochina in 1975. Yet fifteen years later, international Communism died as the Soviet Union imploded. Once again, the "lessons" of history proved to be elusive.

The reason that these two seductively simple reasons for studying history—that history repeats itself and that there are lessons to be drawn from it—is not persuasive is straightforward. Both concentrate too much on only one part of history's double focus, the past, and they ignore the interpretive side of history. It would be more accurate to claim, not that history repeats itself, but that historians do (for good and ill!). Similarly, history does not teach us anything; historians try to.

There are, however, four very good reasons to study history. The first one is that history, as we have seen, is rooted in one of the most basic human experiences, the experience of change. The past is always changing into the present, and the present is always changing into the future. History helps us understand change. And to try to understand change is to try to understand life itself. The study of history demonstrates that change is difficult, chaotic, and uncertain. In fact, it is so problematic that much human endeavor has been devoted to trying to resist it and roll it back. Many great historical movements were rooted in an attempt to recover what was thought to be a mythic golden age in the past. The Protestant Reformation, for instance, was partially an attempt to recover the allegedly wonderful simplicity of the primitive church. The Glorious Revolution in England, the American Revolution, the French Revolution of 1789 all involved, among other things, attempts to stem the advances and perceived corruptions of the modern world and return to an earlier and more placid time.

As mentioned earlier, history can be said to repeat itself only in very large patterns. One of those patterns is that the actions and projects of dynamic individuals and groups often produce consequences they did not intend. The rise of mass participatory democracy in the United States, for instance, was the last thing on the minds of the gentlemen elite who conceived and led the American Revolution. In this sense history is a brake on zealotry. Change is inevitable, and part of being human; but change is also complex and can rarely be reduced to simple or predictable formulas. This notion was clearly understood by one of the characters in Graham Swift's wonderful novel *Waterland,* when he reflected on the job of being a history teacher: "What is a history teacher? He's someone who teaches mistakes. While others say, here's how to do it, he says, and here's what goes wrong. While others tell you, this is the way, this is the path, he says, and here are a few bungles, botches, blunders, and fiascoes" (177–78).

Since there is no more constant aspect of human life than change, there is no more urgent endeavor than history, the study of change. Through the study of history we learn that change is necessary but unpredictable, fascinating yet dangerous. It can veer into surprisingly creative and surprisingly destructive directions. History thus underscores the fragility of human planning, and it emphasizes the need to protect the most vulnerable members of society from the unanticipated consequences of even the best intentions.

The volatility of change points to a second reason for studying history. History exposes us to another constant of the human condition, differences and variety. When I talk with students who have just returned from spending all or part of their junior year abroad, I am constantly struck by how their experiences of living outside their home culture has changed them. Living in another country has given them a new depth, as they realize that "family" is a much more extensive thing in the Mediterranean world than it is in the United States; that capitalism is not universally celebrated in our world; that Christianity is not everywhere regarded as a religion of peace and justice. The study of history makes this experience available even to those who have not had the opportunity to live in a foreign country. As the British writer L. P. Hartley has put it, "The past is another country." Immersing oneself in the customs of a fifteenth century pre-industrial French village and seeing how social life was organized there can open one's eyes in the same way that serious travel can. Studying the brutality of the African slave trade and realizing how the unbridled search for gain corrupted people living on five continents is a healthy antidote to perusing the advertisements in our glossy magazines. Studying the thirteenth and fourteenth century Sufi mystics of Persia can open our eyes to unsuspected possibilities deep within our own forms of spirituality. History can open our eyes to the richness and variety of the human experience, and it can expand our horizons in ways that little else can.

The fact that change and diversity are both complex and multi-faceted realities points to a third reason for studying history. Understanding complex phenomena demands a high degree of analytical skills. Studying history involves sorting through a mass of historical sources, devising interpretive hypotheses, and modifying or rejecting them in the light of further examination of yet more sources. As students of history learn to perform these tasks, they find that they are developing their abilities to think precisely, to reason logically, and to imagine creatively. Students of history discover, above all, that their discipline helps them (and their teachers force them!) to write clearly. They learn that clear writing is the surest path to clear thinking, and that sloppy writing is the clearest indicator of sloppy thinking. Students of history in college find that the study of this discipline helps them develop a series of skills which are important not only in history but in virtually any profession. The abilities to reason well and to write and present complex material clearly endows history college graduates with a strong background in history and a portfolio of skills which transfer well into business, the law, government, or public service, and any number of the helping professions.

One arena in which college students soon learn that they have to exercise their developing analytical skills is the Internet. They soon discover that, while the sheer volume of material on the World Wide Web is staggering, the amount of useful historical information on the Web is considerably less. In fact, there are probably fewer genuine historical sources on the entire Internet than on the shelves of any mid-sized college or university library. When you surf the Web for your history research, ask yourself two sets of questions. First, does the Web page you have found tell you where it obtained the information it is presenting? Are there references on the page to sources that you or any other surfer can independently check? Are there notes leading you to a reference work or a scholarly volume you can consult? If the answer to any of these inquiries is no, don't trust what is on this particular site. Second, if you have found some primary sources on the Web, can you trace the site on which you found them back to a reputable library or repository? Can you pare down the URL of the site to the home page of the Library of Congress, a major university or research library, or a state or regional historical society? If not, don't trust what you might find on this site.

There is a fourth reason to study history. The basic dynamic of human experience with which I began this chapter (memory, experience, anticipation) affects not only individuals, but groups as well. An especially important group in this regard is the nation.

As citizens of the United States, we have a shared past and present. Many of the holidays we celebrate, such as Thanksgiving, Independence Day, Presidents' Day, and Memorial Day, are rooted in that shared past. A number of other institutions and objects, such as museums, flags, historical markers on highways, and visitors centers at national or state parks also embody this national memory.

As we have seen, memory can "play tricks." In the case of a national memory, the danger is slightly different. That memory can easily be tricked and manipulated. The values of any present moment can provide an interpretive framework that can easily overwhelm and distort the past. In the late nineteenth and early twentieth centuries, for example, the prevalence of deeply rooted racism against African Americans nourished the historical judgment that the Civil War, which ended slavery, was a "needless" conflict that caused greater harm than good to the country. This view was carried, for instance, in the 1915 classic film *The Birth of a Nation*. In the 1950s, the presence of the Cold War, in which Americans were called on to close ranks against the Soviet Union, nourished a "consensus" approach to our past, which minimized and ignored deep-seated conflicts in our history. In some twentieth century totalitarian governments like the Soviet Union, the political imperatives of the day produced situations in which figures not favored by the current regime were excluded from history books and literally excised from historical photographs. If personal memory is unstable, then national memory is fragile and easily manipulated.

In this context, a historical sensitivity is an important component of mature and critical citizenship. In an age in which public policy debates are frequently conducted in paid political advertisements and thirty second sound bites, the importance of sober and clear-headed analysis based on a sophisticated understanding of our national past has never been greater. An informed citizenry with a deep understanding of the nature of history is necessary if museums are not to turn into uncritical shrines, and the commemoration of our national past is not to turn into an intolerant chauvinism. The ferocious 1995 controversy over how the Smithsonian should have organized an exhibit commemorating the fiftieth anniversary of the dropping of the atomic bomb and the end of the World War II demonstrated quite clearly that history can be a deeply contested field. We, and all countries, need citizens deeply grounded in the method of history and familiar with the always-provisional character of the historical enterprise. History is a voice of reason, and, as such, the enemy of absolute claims, whether those claims are for the complete rightness of one's country, the full justice of one's worldview, or the total perfection of one's religion.

Does all this mean that the study of history is the summit and end of a liberal education? Hardly. For one outcome of the study of history, when we reflect on the incredible dynamics of change and the unbelievable presence of so much variety and diversity (for good and ill) in our world, is awe and wonder. History ends in wonder, and that is precisely where Plato said that philosophy begins. History is the indispensable foundation for the liberal arts disciplines, which help you to ask the larger and really big questions in life, about human destiny, about justice, and about God.

WORKS CITED

Fehrenbacher, Don E., ed. *Abraham Lincoln: Speeches and Writings, 1859–1865*. New York: The Library of America, 1989.

Herodotus. *The Persian Wars*. Translated by George Rawlinson. New York: Modern Library, 1942.

Stern, Fritz, ed. *The Varieties of History: From Voltaire to the Present*. New York: Meridian, 1956.

Strassler, Robert B., ed. *The Landmark Thucydides: A Comprehensive Guide to the Peloponnesian War*. New York: Free Press, 1996.

Swift, Graham. *Waterland*. New York: Pocket Books, 1985.

8

The Study of Psychology

Scott VanderStoep

PSYCHOLOGY is the scientific study of people's thinking and behavior (Myers, *Psychology*). The great thing about being a psychologist is that if you are interested in the study of people, you can usually study them from a psychological perspective. As one professor I met in graduate school once said, "If you're interested in what people do, you should study psychology." Since so much of college involves learning about yourself and others, psychology is a crucial component of the liberal arts experience.

Lots of liberal arts disciplines study people's behavior. Psychology is not the only way of knowing about the human experience. Poets, historians, and philosophers all have interests in human behavior. What makes psychology unique is its approach. Traditional psychological inquiry has been grounded in the scientific method, more specifically the social-scientific method. A poet, a historian, and a psychologist may all be interested in the same human concern, for example, marriage. What will distinguish the analysis of these three scholars is that the psychologist will use scientific evidence in support of her claims. A poet may use personal experience and the experience of people he knows to craft verses about marriage. A historian may use archival evidence regarding marriage in a particular historical period. A psychologist may conduct large-scale surveys of married people to measure their marital satisfaction, or may conduct interviews and observations of married couples interacting with each other. All three scholars may come to similar conclusions about marriage, but their approaches will certainly differ.

When I say the scientific method, I don't mean to suggest the exact same approach as your ninth grade science teacher described. However, the approach is somewhat similar, as shown in figure 11. The approach is more complicated than this, and a course in psychological research methods (a course that will also do much to improve your critical thinking) will spend an entire semester going through all of the complexities imbedded in this simple diagram.

Most descriptions of the scientific method begin with theories—organized frameworks to describe people and events. Because psychology is the scientific study of people, theories are often easy to generate. Theories can come from observation, intuition, or reading previous research in psychology. Based on the development of this theoretical knowledge, a specific hypothesis (prediction) about human behavior is generated. For example, a theory may be that people want to appear to others as having a consistent set of beliefs and behaviors. That is, we want people to think that what we do is also what we say and vice versa. A specific hypothesis stemming from that theory might be that, when faced with a conflict between what we think (cognitions) and what we do (behavior), we will attempt to modify that behavior in order to appear that our cognitions are consistent with our behaviors. This well-known theory is called "cognitive dissonance" theory in social psychology (Myers, *Social Psychology*).

A specific test of this theory might be to set up a situation similar to one that I use in my introductory psychology class. I randomly assign students to one of two groups—one group is told to generate as many good arguments *in favor* of Issue A as possible (I usually pick a current hot topic on campus), and the other group is told to generate as many good arguments *against* Issue A. After the groups generate their lists, I have each student rate on a scale from 1 to 10 their agreement with Issue A—where 1 is strongly opposed to Issue A and 10 is strongly in favor of Issue A. If the group generating arguments in favor of Issue A scores higher than the group generating arguments against Issue A, then I would have evidence in support of my theory. My experience suggests that my hypothesis is almost always supported, lending support to cognitive dissonance theory.

This process is how research psychologists ply their trade—generating theories and hypotheses, putting these hypotheses to the test, analyzing the results of the research, and modifying/expanding theories based on the results of the research.

Fig. 11.
A Model of the Scientific Method

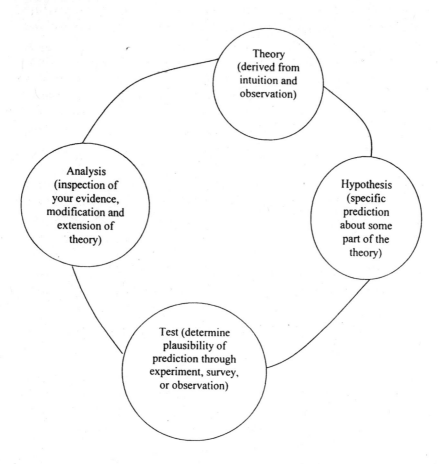

PSYCHOLOGY'S SUB-AREAS

I have noted that psychology differs from other fields, largely due to its methodology. Despite these differences, psychology has other points of contact with other disciplines. Some psychologists are interested in the brain, neurochemistry, and other physiological processes. These psychologists often have similarities to biologists. Other psychologists are interested in the study of people in a social context. These psychologists, called social psychologists, may be aligned with anthropologists or sociologists. Other psychologists may be interested in studying behavior in real-life settings, such as work (industrial psychologists) or school (educational psychologists). Industrial psychologists share interests with people who study management or finance, and educational psychologists share interests with educational scholars. Figure 12 shows the different sub-fields of psychology and their academic "cousins."

Many people are confused about what psychologists do. This is partly because of lack of information on their part, but also be-

Fig. 12.
Psychology's Sub-Disciplines

Area of Psychology	Topics Studied	Possible Related Academic Disciplines
Physiological Psychology	Brain and behavior, neurochemistry	Biology, Neuroscience
Cognitive Psychology	Study of learning, memory, and other mental activities	Artificial Intelligence, Philosophy, Biology
Educational Psychology	School learning, teaching	Education
Clinical Psychology	Diagnosis and treatment of mental illness	Social work, Biology, Neuroscience
Industrial Psychology	Work behavior	Management, Finance
Social Psychology	Individual in a social context	Anthropology, Sociology

cause psychology is such a broad field that it encompasses much more than people realize. When I was in college, I was often asked by a friend or family member, "What are you going to do with a major in psychology?" For those who gave me the benefit of the doubt and assumed I was employable, they usually presumed I was going to be a clinical psychologist or some other type of mental health worker. I still remember my grandmother, in the midst of the completion of my master's thesis in an area of experimental social psychology, asking, "Are you seeing clients?" I wasn't. I haven't, and I never will. In fact, my area of study within psychology at the time was about as far removed from clinical psychology as could be. Such a mistake is not uncommon, as many people's only exposure to psychology is via news and entertainment, where clinical psychology is usually highlighted.

Although clinical psychology is the most common form of psychology, figure 12 shows there are many areas of psychology (and several others are not listed). Furthermore, getting an undergraduate degree does not usually merit the title Psychologist. That term is usually reserved for someone with an advanced degree (master's or doctorate) in psychology, and refers to clinical psychologists as opposed to research psychologists. Thus, it is important to remember that there are several different areas of psychology, and they do not all involve working in mental health.

WHY STUDY PSYCHOLOGY?

In all the different sub-areas of psychology, the study of psychology will nurture your cognitive and emotional growth in several ways. Below I discuss three reasons why studying psychology will benefit you.

Critical Thinking

Many college students, after graduation, end up in careers for which they were not originally trained. Actual examples from my institution include a physical education major who works in a marketing department at a hospital, a psychology major who works in instructional computing, and a history major who became a dot-com millionaire. Given changing interests, changing job needs, and changing technology, it behooves students to learn general learning, thinking, and motivational strategies. Such general strategies will give you more flexibility after you graduate from college to move into different vocational areas. It is clear that specific vocational areas need specific vocational skills to be learned in college—for example, nursing, accounting, and engineering. But many liberal arts disciplines focus less on specific behavioral skills and more on fostering general learning and thinking skills. Consider some of the ways in which psychology promotes critical thinking.

1. Quantitative Reasoning: Law of Large Numbers

Psychology is a science, specifically a social science (as opposed to chemistry), and more specifically, a quantitative social science (as opposed to some areas of anthropology and education). One of the goals of taking psychology courses is to learn to reason about quantitative information. To do research, psychologists collect information on the aspect of human behavior in which they are interested. For example, imagine an educational psychologist interested in the effects of self-esteem on academic achievement. The psychologist first needs to construct valid measures of self-esteem and academic achievement among college students. Next, the psychologist would like to determine if there is a relationship between these two measures. At this point, the psychologist would desire to collect measures of self-esteem and academic achievement from as many college students as possible. Why not select only five or ten college students and measure their self-esteem and academic achievement? The reason rests on a fundamental law of quantitative science—the *law of large numbers*.

To understand this statistical principle, it is helpful to understand the difference between a *sample*—a group of people in a research study—and a *population*—the whole group of people from which a sample for the research study is drawn. In the example above, the sample is the group of college students in the research study, and the population is all college students. One goal of psychological research is to make inferences about populations based on samples used in research studies (ideally, sampling the entire population would be the way to do this, but this is almost never practical). The law of large numbers states that the larger the sample of people in the study, the more accurately the sample will reflect the population. So, why is a research study with only five or ten people undesirable? Because such a small sample of people will not as often reflect the population accurately. Thus, one benefit of studying psychology is that students learn to be cautious of claims made by small samples.

Consider some examples of effective critical thinking using the law of large numbers:

- Critically (but cordially) challenging a roommate who prefers Professor X to Professor Y, simply because she heard one or two testimonials from former students who were positive about the teaching of Professor X. A sample of one or two is too small and very unreliable.
- Rejecting advertising claims based on the anecdotal evidence of a few people. As an example, while I wrote this, the television was on in the other room. I overheard a claim that a breakfast cereal caused noticeable weight loss. The testimonials came from five or six people, hardly sufficient to satisfy the law of large numbers.

Now that you have had an introduction to the law of large numbers, consider a problem I often ask my introductory psychology students on the first exam (adapted from research by Nisbett and Ross; Kahneman and Tyversky):

Three hospitals have the following birth records: Hospital X delivers an average of ten babies a day. Hospital Y delivers an average of thirty babies per day. Hospital Z delivers an average of sixty babies per day. Assuming the percentage of boy babies born at each hospital is 50 percent during the course of a year, which hospital will have the most days when more than 60 percent of the babies born are boys?

A. Hospital X
B. Hospital Y
C. Hospital Z
D. All three are equally likely

The answer is A. The reason, according to the law of large numbers, is that small samples are the least likely to reflect accurately the population. Since we know the population value is supposed to be 50 percent (stated in the problem and knowable by common sense), we are more likely to find deviations in small samples. As an analogy, consider flipping a coin. Suppose you flip a coin ten times versus sixty times. Would you be surprised if six (60 percent) of the ten flips landed heads? Probably not. How about thirty-six (60 percent) out of sixty heads? You should be more surprised. What about one million flips? Should you expect 600,000 (60 percent) heads? Statistically speaking, it is impossible. This example shows that larger sample sizes give a better picture of what the sample really looks like (in this case, the population is 50 percent heads and 50 percent tails).

Just as with coin flips and birth records, the same is true in psychological research. More people in your survey or experiment will mean a more accurate picture of the population you are trying to study. In psychological research, more is almost always better. As you study psychology, you will be more effective in identifying weaknesses in claims based on small numbers of people.

2. Correlation Is Not Causation

Psychologists are interested in studying relationships between variables. In the example above, the relationship of interest was between self-esteem and academic achievement. Social scientists make a distinction between a relationship between two measures, and one measure being the cause of the other measure. If two variables are related (called a correlation), it does not necessarily mean that they are causally connected. In general, to show that one event caused another, three conditions must be met: (1) the two events must be correlated; (2) the proposed cause must precede the proposed effect in time (i.e., the cause must come first); and (3) all other possible causes must be eliminated.

In the example above, to show that high self-esteem causes improved academic achievement it must be shown that: (1) there is a correlation between self-esteem and academic achievement; (2) changes in self-esteem occur before changes in academic achievement; and (3) other causes that could explain improved academic achievement must be eliminated. To determine that one event caused another, psychologists conduct *experiments*—a methodological approach where the psychologist systematically alters the variable believed to be the cause and controls all variables to determine if the cause does indeed have its intended effect. Not all research questions in psychology are amenable to study by experiments, however. In those cases, psychologists must employ *correlational* strategies—methodological approaches that measure the variables as they occur in natural settings. Correlational research strategies establish that two variables are related—high self-esteem is related to higher academic achievement—but the relationship does not imply that the variables are causally connected.

One of the features of critical thinking that studying psychology will provide for students is an understanding of how to identify when two measures are causally connected and when they are only correlated. Consider one example from an exercise that I use in class to encourage students to think critically about correlation and causation (taken from Bolt, and Dietz and Gortmaker).

> According to medical research, increased television watching is related to obesity. In other words, the more TV watching a child does, the more likely the child will be obese. Does this mean that TV watching causes obesity? What explanations can you generate for this correlation?

In general, when two variables—say X and Y—are correlated, there are three possible explanations: X could cause Y, Y could cause X, or some third variable—Z—could cause both X and Y. In this example, it could be that TV watching causes obesity. TV watchers are less likely to be engaged in aerobic activity. TV shows also often contain commercials for high fat, high sugar foods, which may be consumed by the viewers. This seems to be the most plausible explanation for this correlation.

But critical thinking could also lead you to other explanations. It could also be that obesity causes TV watching, a somewhat less intuitive hypothesis. Perhaps those who are already obese may be more inclined toward sedentary activities such as TV watching. Evidence for this may come in the form of finding that obese people are more likely to play chess and musical instruments, and less likely to be involved in activities requiring aerobic activity. A third explanation is also possible: that some other variable, such as genetic predisposition to being overweight, could cause both increased TV watching and increased obesity.

The study of psychology, more than almost any other discipline, will provide students with vital thinking skills related to quantitative and methodological issues. The content of psychology is interesting in and of itself, but perhaps the feature of studying psychology that will have the most beneficial long-term impact is the improvement it can create in quantitative and methodological reasoning skills. (For more information on this improvement and other thinking strategies studying psychology impacts, see VanderStoep and Shaughnessy.)

Self-Discovery and Improvement

The study of psychology also helps you learn more about yourself. Most psychological research involves studying people. Learning fundamental principles about how humans behave and think quite obviously leads the student of psychology to better self-understanding. Furthermore, since much of psychology examines the factors that predict human flourishing, I believe that studying psychology also can lead to improved quality of life. Consider some examples:

- Psychologists have extensively studied learning and motivation in school. Research has revealed a variety of factors that will improve school learning. For example, research suggests that to do well in school you should: (1) space your studying for tests out over a several-day period rather than cram the night before; (2) set specific and difficult, yet attainable, goals for your learning; and (3) try to find personal meaning and value in your coursework. All of these strategies, research suggests, will result in better learning. These are just three simple examples of how studying psychology can improve your school learning. (VanderStoep and Pintrich have produced a book of learning and motivational strategies for college students based on psychological research. The book has several suggestions for using psychology to improve your learning.)
- Research in psychology has shown that happy people usually have, among other things: (1) meaningful employment or engaging tasks outside of work; (2) close relationships; and (3) an active religious faith. Age, gender, or wealth are not correlated with

happiness/life satisfaction (Myers, *Pursuit of Happiness*). What do you value in life? Are they things that predict life satisfaction? Can you use the study of psychology to learn more about yourself and identify ways in which you might want to change your values and life pursuits?

Vocation

As I alluded earlier, most students of psychology have encountered pragmatic friends and family who say, "What are you going to do with a psychology major?" As annoying as the question might be, it's a legitimate concern. When students and prospective students ask me this question, I provide two answers. First, studying psychology is not like specialized professional and pre-professional programs that train you for a particular field. For example, the study of nursing, accounting, or education will train you for those specific fields, but very little else. Psychology does not provide that degree of employment focus. However, it does provide *some* employment focus. The most common example of employment directly linked to the study of psychology is a career in mental health—such as a case manager for disabled adults or a program coordinator for troubled youth. The second response to that question is that in addition to focused employment opportunities, the study of psychology involves general and broad training such that highly qualified psychology students could find themselves in any number of vocational sectors. Examples include human resources, statistics, information technology, and criminal justice.

It is important to remember that to be a "psychologist" in the professional sense of the word requires a degree beyond undergraduate studies. Master's degrees are available in many areas of psychology, including industrial psychology, school psychology, and counseling/clinical psychology. Doctorates are available in all areas of psychology. The Ph.D. degree involves many years of schooling, independent research investigations, and (in the case of clinical psychology) many hours of field experience. The Ph.D. is usually best for those interested in teaching psychology at the university level, those interested in running their own research labs, or those who want to be private-practice psychotherapists.

For those interested in the helping professions, bachelor-level opportunities are available; however, anecdotal evidence suggests that these are lower-pay, higher-burnout positions. For those interested in graduate studies, some states make a distinction between a Licensed Psychologist (L.P.—a Ph.D. clinical or counseling psychologist who has passed state certification) and a Limited Licensed Psychologist (L.L.P.—a psychotherapist with a more limited degree of clinical privilege).

CHALLENGES TO THE STUDY OF PSYCHOLOGY: WHEN RESEARCH CONFRONTS CULTURE AND RELIGION

I conclude this chapter with a discussion of particular challenges that some students of psychology may encounter. These challenges are unlikely to be discussed in any other textbook, but they are based on experiences I have had with students during my ten years of teaching undergraduate psychology. Sometimes I encounter these dilemmas in students who have an enormously high regard for psychological research. Sometimes I encounter them in students who have a very low regard for psychological research. And sometimes I encounter them among students whose religious faith makes them skeptical of psychology.

Challenge 1: Does Psychology Always Speak the Truth?

Some students of psychology believe psychological research is infallible and free of bias. If a psychologist identifies a correlation between Variable X and Variable Y, then such students believe that this finding is factually correct, believable, and undeniable. Far be it from me to discount the authenticity of psychological research, but let me suggest two considerations students should have when evaluating psychological research. First, all research has assumptions underlying it, and psychological research is no exception. In psychology, one assumption of psychological research is that people's behavior can be measured numerically. We must ask if this is always the case. Consider research on childhood trauma. How does one measure childhood trauma, and how does one create a scale that will effectively discriminate different levels of trauma? Underlying most psychological research is an assumption that behaviors and thoughts can be assigned numeric values. In fact, I do believe one can study childhood trauma numerically, but it is still important to critique the research to determine if the claims are valid.

A second consideration when evaluating psychological research is the orientation and worldview of the research and the theory underlying the research. The study of psychology does not take place in a vacuum. Psychologists approach problems with certain values and beliefs about the world. It sounds cynical to call these values and beliefs "biases," but perhaps bias is not a bad word—it simply makes apparent what ideas a psychologist brings to her field. Consider two examples. First, consider psychologists who study the effects of day-care on children. How would one become interested in research on day-care? What values and beliefs about children and about day-care would inspire someone to find this area of psychology interesting? Whatever the motives, it seems at least possible, I would argue even likely, that those beliefs would influence the way in which the research was conducted.

As a second example, consider research on the effects of spanking on children. It is important to consider the same questions in this research as those in the above example. What are the researcher's beliefs about spanking? Does the researcher think that violent actions beget more violent actions? Does the researcher have particular interpretations of religious texts that make spanking permissible (or even preferred) as a mode of discipline? Has the researcher spent time working with violent youth who were abused by their parents, and did that abuse start as spanking? It seems clear that one's beliefs about children's capabilities and how to discipline wrongdoing are a valuable part of how to interpret research on spanking.

In summary, psychology is rarely value-free or objective. Therefore it does not present "the truth" about human behavior in an absolute sense. As stated at the beginning of the chapter, psychology provides one way to understand human behavior, but its approach brings with it values and beliefs that influence how psychology is studied and how psychological research gets interpreted. That psychology is value-laden is not necessarily a deficit, but simply an acknowledgement that psychology is motivated by human interests, and it is those same human interests that shape and inform the doing and interpreting of psychology.

Challenge 2: What if I Disagree with the Research?

This challenge often surfaces among students who espouse a deep religious faith and find, at least at first glance, that their faith clashes with psychology. Consider one common topic in psychology that is likely to produce this challenge: Research has shown that there are genetic, hormonal, and neurophysiological differences between heterosexual and homosexual people, mostly men (see, for example, Levay). As a student, what is your reaction to this finding?

I have had students respond to this research on biological differences in sexual orientation by simply stating that they "don't believe it." There are reasons to be skeptical of the research on the origins of sexual orientation, and Jones and Yarhouse have thoroughly critiqued the research and its possible methodological weaknesses. And if students are skeptical of the research on methodological grounds, then that is the kind of critical thinking we like to see in psychology students (as noted above). But that is not usually what happens, partly because, in fairness to introductory psychology students, they lack the background to offer such a methodological critique at that stage of their career.

But how should students respond to research in psychology that they find controversial? My view is clear: If students don't like what the research says, I don't think students can just say they "don't believe it." The finding is a part of the field of psychology, and students must address it.

As you probably guessed, this challenge is not problematic when the research findings are consistent with one's religious and cultural beliefs. So, for example, if students feel that homosexuality is immoral, they are more likely to find reasons not to accept the research. If students feel that homosexuality is a lifestyle that should not be condemned, then such research may validate their beliefs and they may embrace it. I find such a double standard unacceptable. And let me be clear: I am not singling out one side of the debate on sexuality as guilty of misinterpreting research.

My criticism is more general and my caution is to avoid selectively reading research that only comports with one's worldview.

Challenge 3: Psychology is Unimportant

People who see psychology as unimportant may accept the truthfulness of the research, but they will not find the claims particularly helpful for their lives. In other words, these critiques of psychology would hold findings from psychology in low esteem. I can think of three ways in which this could happen. First, this opinion of psychology can be found in people who feel that research in psychology does not add any unique contribution to their understanding of the world. In other words, psychology simply duplicates what could have been learned from philosophy, biology, or theology. Second, others might hold this view because psychology has no direct relevance or application to their lives. The second form of this challenge is often found among people with religious faith. For example, some Christians are critical of research on self-esteem. These people might not dispute the basic finding that those who feel good about themselves will have better psychological functioning. They are more likely to dispute, however, the implications of this research for their lives. Secular research on self-esteem is based on the idea that one's self-esteem is derived from past learning history, successes and failures, and estimates of self-worth. Thus, knowing about secular research on self-esteem may not be all that informative to Christians who derive their self-esteem from a very different source (Joosse).

A third version of this critique comes in the form of students who understand and affirm the research in psychology, but the research does not make a moral claim on their life. For example, students may accept the finding from neuropsychology that shows that gay men and straight men have different size cell clusters in a region of the brain (called the hypothalamus) that is implicated in sexuality. They may also understand and affirm that veracity of research that shows a genetic component to sexual orientation—identical twins are both gay at a much higher rate than fraternal twins or siblings (Bailey and Pillard; Hershberger). Some would argue that this research, while interesting and true, makes no claim about the moral legitimacy of homosexuality. Believing that sexual orientation has a genetic or physiological basis may inform one's view about the morality of homosexuality. However, others may view the research in the same way, but derive their moral beliefs about sexual orientation from a different source. Thus, it is important to realize that some people may use psychological research to guide ethical decision-making, whereas others may simply find it a descriptively interesting account of human action.

CONCLUSION

Psychology is the scientific study of what people do and think. It is an important window through which we are able to understand human beings. Psychology is perhaps less defined by its content than by its method of inquiry. Other academic disciplines explore human thought, action, and culture; you can also learn about human beings by studying theology, philosophy, and literature. I believe psychology's contribution is unique in that it offers a study of human events grounded in scientific methodology.

Occasionally, the method of inquiry in psychology creates challenges, perhaps particularly for people whose religious beliefs are central to their world and lifeview. For Christians, for example, faith is the window through which God's world gets understood. However, sometimes people are presented with research findings with which they don't agree. When faith beliefs run up against scientific knowledge, this creates a dilemma. People must sort out how they will come to grips with the dilemmas that a clash between psychology and their other beliefs—beliefs derived from their faith or their culture—might create.

WORKS CITED

Bailey, J. M., and R. C. Pillard. "Genetics of Human Sexual Orientation." *Annual Review of Sex Research* 6 (1995): 126–50.

Bolt, M. L. *Instructor's Manual to Accompany Myers' Psychology.* 6th ed. New York: Worth, 2001.

Dietz, W. H., and S. L. Gortmaker." Do We Fatten Children at the TV Set? Obesity and Television Watching in Children and Adolescents." *Pediatrics* 75 (1985): 807–12.

Hershberger, S. L. "A Twin Registry Study of Male and Female Sexual Orientation." *Journal of Sex Research* 34 (1997): 212–22.

Jones, S. L., and M. A. Yarhouse. "Science and the Ecclesiastical Homosexuality Debates." *Christian Scholar's Review* 24, no. 4 (1997): 446–77.

Joosse, W. "Has Self-esteem Gone Too Far?" *The Banner* 131 (1996): 12–15.

Kahneman, D., and A. Tversky. "Subjective Probability: A Judgment of Representativeness." *Cognitive Psychology* 3 (1972): 430–54.

Levay, S. "A Difference in Hypothalamic Structure Between Heterosexual and Homosexual Men." *Science* 253 (1991): 1034–37.

Myers, D. G. *The Pursuit of Happiness: Who is Happy and Why.* New York: William Morrow, 1992.

———. *Psychology.* 6th ed. New York: Worth, 2001.

———. *Social Psychology.* 6th ed. New York: McGraw-Hill, 2002.

Nisbett, R. E., and L. Ross. *Human Inference: Strategies and Shortcomings of Social Judgment.* Englewood Cliffs, NJ: Prentice Hall, 1980.

VanderStoep, S. W., and J. J. Shaughnessy. "Taking a Course in Research Methods Improves Reasoning about Real-Life Events." *Teaching of Psychology* 24 (1997): 122–24.

VanderStoep, S. W., and P. R. Pintrich. *Learning to Learn: The Skill and Will of College Success.* Upper Saddle River, NJ: Prentice Hall, 2003.

9

The Study of Sociology

Robert K. Moore Jr.

WHAT IS SOCIOLOGY?

FORMAL DEFINITIONS of academic disciplines are frequently dry and uninteresting. These sorts of definitions, with their precise terminology and technical jargon, sometimes seem intended to deter, rather than encourage, people from learning more about a subject. It is for these reasons that I hesitate to begin this chapter with such a definition; for me, sociology is anything but dry and uninteresting. Indeed, for anyone with a healthy sense of intellectual curiosity, sociology is exciting and fascinating. Are you interested in the causes of crime? How can we explain high divorce rates? What causes people to join cults? What are the reasons for high rates of teenage pregnancy? Why is poverty a continuing problem in our society? Why are there income disparities based on gender and race? All of these questions and many more are of concern to the sociologist, and the discipline of sociology can give us the tools to provide answers to these questions.

In general, sociology is the scientific study of human societies. According to Curran and Renzetti, "sociologists examine the collective interactions of social actors within a particular social structure and the collective meanings that these actors give to their interactions with one another" (2). In other words, sociology focuses on *group* properties as opposed to individual or psychological characteristics. Sociologists are certainly concerned about individuals, but we are interested in how they view themselves and others based on what they are taught through society and culture.

For example, the problem of teenage pregnancy obviously involves the decision-making of individuals, but the reasons why they make the decisions that they do can be understood as a result of social factors. Teenage girls who become pregnant typically have learned that having a baby is acceptable behavior within the social setting that they find themselves in. They often come from families where there is a history of pregnancies at a young age, and they frequently are not performing well in school. Having a baby seems like a legitimate way to gain respectability and the other presumed benefits of adulthood. All of this is not to say that this is the *correct* decision. But sociologists are interested in how the world appears from the perspective of the *social actor*. In a way, it is as if we are all actors in a play, and we are learning our lines and our roles as we go along.

The various positions that we hold (for example, husband, wife, boss, worker, student, professor) have certain behavioral expectations called *roles* associated with them, and we learn how to behave in a certain manner by gaining knowledge about these roles from our culture. The roles that individuals play can vary considerably both within and across cultures. For example, women in Islamic cultures are taught that they should cover their bodies and faces with clothing, and that they should not be in public places without the accompaniment of a father or husband. Women in the United States, on the other hand, have learned a whole different set of behavioral expectations from their culture, and many would find the expectations placed on the behavior of Islamic women to be overly restrictive.

Some of the positions we occupy are voluntary (for example, athlete), while others are involuntary. One's race, for example, is involuntary, and in racially discriminatory societies, individuals learn what is appropriate and inappropriate behavior based on their skin color. Prior to the civil rights movement in the United States, there were severe consequences for black citizens if they behaved in a way that was seen by whites to be offensive. As individuals, these persons felt the physical and emotional pain inflicted by the racial majority, but the "rules of the game" had been socially constructed and transmitted. It is this "social construction of reality" that is of interest to the sociologist, and the discipline of sociology provides us with terms, concepts, theories, and research tools that enable us to better understand the social world.

Sociology is a discipline with many specialties and sub-disciplines. A student could take courses in a wide variety of areas, including the following: Sociology of Sports, Sociology of Religion, Sociology of Work, Urban Sociology, Sociology of the Family, or Social Inequality. Each area focuses on a particular part of society and examines the groups and belief systems found therein.

WHY STUDY SOCIOLOGY?

There are many reasons to study sociology, the most obvious being simply to understand the social world in which we live. But, as one of the disciplines known as the liberal arts, the goal in studying sociology should be more than that. According to May, there are three good reasons to study any of the liberal arts. These are economic, personal, and social; or, stated differently, careerist, quality-of-life, and humanitarian.

Students are rightly concerned with the economic or careerist elements in choosing a field of study. Regardless of the intangible benefits that might accrue to educating "the whole person," the fact is that students will be entering the world of work upon graduation, and they have every reason to be concerned about what salable skills they will be taking into that arena. Unfortunately, often times a false choice is offered: either study or major in a more vocationally-oriented field that teaches job-specific skills, or study in the broader liberal arts and hope for the best. This places the student in an unnecessary predicament for several reasons. First, liberal arts subjects teach a breadth of skills that will serve the student in his or her career long after narrowly defined job specific skills are rendered obsolete. Knowing how to think, write, and communicate in a critical and effective way is central to leadership in almost any organizational context. The discipline of sociology focuses on these skills, as students are encouraged to critically examine a number of social issues and problems. Because the subject matter that comprises sociology does not lend itself to easy and obvious conclusions, students are forced to consider a number of different theoretical and political perspectives. If the questions presented in any given course in sociology are considered seriously and conscientiously, the result will be the development of critical thinking and analysis skills that will serve the student well throughout his or her lifetime, and in any number of different settings.

Beyond these general critical thinking skills, sociology also provides students with very marketable skills in various forms of research and analysis. In a general sense, the research methods that sociologists use can be divided into those that are quantitative and others that are more qualitative. The quantitative methods focus on survey and other forms of data that must be collected, organized, inputted, and ultimately analyzed. Qualitative methods may focus more on interviews with subjects, or analysis of other forms of information, but the process is fundamentally the same as for quantitative data: the data must be collected, organized, and analyzed. The value of the skills obtained in doing sociological research cannot be underestimated. Students who master these skills find readily available work upon graduation in a number of different government, non-profit, and business settings. Given the overwhelming reach of computer technology into all aspects of society, a firm grounding in the skills obtained through sociological research will prove invaluable to students over a lifetime, and in any number of employment settings.

May's second reason for studying liberal arts subjects such as sociology is to enhance one's personal quality of life. At its best, sociology can perform the central mission of liberal arts: to *liberate* the mind from ignorance and narrow thinking. It forces us to ask fundamental questions about society and encourages us to reconsider the "world taken for granted." In this way, we become more enlightened as citizens and more understanding of the human condition in the general sense. This benefit to studying sociology may not be readily apparent in terms of career advancement, but the advantages to such a perspective are enormous. One of the current catch phrases in the world of business and politics is "thinking outside of the box." Sociology does not just encourage this way of thinking; it demands it. This type of liberation in thought is both exciting and challenging, and encourages us to grow as human beings. In other words, it enhances our human abilities to question the world around us.

Finally, May writes about the social or humanitarian benefits of studying the liberal arts. It is in this realm that sociology can play a most significant role. Within the discipline, sociologists speak of the abstract distinction between "pure" and "applied" research. Yet any serious analysis of a social issue contains an applied component. If one is studying the causes of racism, then it should be clear that there are policy implications for dealing with this problem. The same is true if a sociologist is studying welfare reform, voter participation rates, domestic violence, or the role of religion in human societies: all of these inquiries will give rise to policy implications that can have real world consequences for large numbers of human beings. To the extent that sociological research informs policy decisions, sociologists can contribute much to advancing humanitarian causes and enhancing social life more generally.

Thus, there are numerous reasons why a student might want to study sociology. Whether the objective is to enhance career prospects, enlighten one's thinking, or help to build a better society, students of sociology will find a wealth of opportunities in their discipline. Perhaps the best aspect of these opportunities is that they allow the pursuit of the above objectives in a way that need not be mutually exclusive.

STUDYING SOCIOLOGY SUCCESSFULLY

The successful study of sociology requires the mastery of traditional study skills as well as an openness to engage with new sources of information made possible through the technological revolution that we have witnessed in recent years. The benefits of traditional study skills may seem obvious, but the pace of life and the expectations that have grown up around computer technology threaten the mastery of the more basic tools of learning. Given instant access to all sorts of material on the Internet, one is easily tempted to utilize it for any and all kinds of study tasks. But the Internet, while an incredibly valuable tool, has serious limitations. While very helpful in a number of areas, there are certain things that the Internet cannot do. The Internet cannot get inside a person's brain and make the connections that are necessary for true learning. The Internet can provide mountains of information, but it cannot do your reading assignments for you.

In short, there is no substitute in sociology, or any other field, for fundamental reading and library skills.

Careful reading takes time and focus. Skimming textbooks for the terms in bold print might work at some level for passing multiple-choice tests, but ultimately the student is shortchanging him or herself. Time-consuming and studious reading is necessary if the depth of any writing is to be fully appreciated, and this is certainly true in the field of sociology. The various theoretical perspectives are complex and involved, and only by careful consideration and attentive reading can the student successfully master the subject matter. Perhaps it would be nice, but there is simply no shortcut for putting in the necessary time required to truly engage in academic learning. This pertains not only to reading, but also to becoming familiar with the library resources that are central to doing sociological research of any kind.

The great benefit of the Internet is that it can allow us to access all sorts of information from any number of devices in a variety of locations. And it is certainly true, as discussed below, that the Internet contains a virtual treasure trove of data and information for wonderful sociological research. But the ease with which we can access information via the Internet can also deceive us into thinking that it is the only source of information that we will ever need, and nothing could be further from the truth. Books, articles, journals, and other forms of writing exist that have not been digitized and placed on a Web site. If the material is not available in digital form, you can search the Internet forever, and not find it. In other words, if students assume that they have exhausted all possibilities because they have done an extensive Web search, they will be mistaken. While there is much of value on the Internet, it is but one source of information. Consequently, the mastery of sociological subject matter requires that Web research be supplemented with more traditional library research.

As with careful reading, traditional library research can be time-consuming. And compared with Internet access from the comfort of one's home, spending time in the library can be inconvenient. But, as with the ultimate benefits of attentive and in-depth reading, the mastery of library research skills can be very rewarding. Of course, the benefits of these skills are not limited to any one field of study. With good library research skills, for the student of sociology or any of the other liberal arts, a more comprehensive learning takes place. Without good library skills, students will only see a partial picture at best.

Having cautioned about the limits of the Internet for sociologically-based research, it is now time to sing its praises. The Internet has brought online an astonishing amount of information that allows sociologists to do research that was either impossible just a few years ago or would have taken considerably longer to accomplish. The most important area of advancement involves the collection and dissemination of data sets collected by the government. If the student of sociology is interested in studying changes in the occupational structure and the composition of the labor force, the U.S. Department of Labor and the Bureau of Labor Statistics have hundreds of comprehensive data sets that will facilitate this sort of research. If the student of urban sociology wants to review changing housing and residential patterns in a particular area in an effort to understand neighborhood racial integration, the U.S. Bureau of the Census has the data necessary to pursue this study. If the student of criminology is interested in differential crime rates between the city and the suburbs, the FBI Uniform Crime Report is available online for his or her analysis. In addition, there are hundreds of online databases from both governmental and private sources related to alcohol use, domestic violence, and countless other topics. These databases allow researchers to study sociological phenomena without actually collecting the data themselves, and allow for ease of reformatting for asking creative questions that might not have been explored by the original researchers who collected the data. The Internet makes sophisticated sociological research possible for more individuals than ever before.

In addition to being the source of complex data sets, the Internet can also be very helpful in the initial collection of data. Online surveys can replace the old pencil and paper variety and allow for instant tabulation of the results without the tedious process of entering data for every completed survey. Likewise, in-depth interviews can be conducted online. In the case of surveys and interviews, it may well be the case that face-to-face interaction between the researcher and the subject is the most preferable method. Nonetheless, the Internet provides numerous prospects for conducting all kinds of sociological research in creative and exciting ways. Overall, the successful study of sociology requires openness to both traditional research methods as well as those made possible by the technological revolution.

SOCIOLOGY AND THE LIBERAL ARTS

Just as important as being open to research methods, however, is keeping an open mind when it comes to the subject matter of the discipline. If your mind is already made up regarding a particular issue such as welfare reform or teenage pregnancy, then sociology will probably be of little value to you. But if you are willing to engage the wide range of subject matters and issues with an open mind, then you are well on your way to being a successful student in the discipline.

Of course this general advice applies to other liberal arts disciplines besides sociology. Students of history, political science, economics, literature, philosophy, and other subjects are well advised to approach their studies with an open mind. If these subjects are to enable a student to be "liberated" from ignorance and narrow thinking, a willingness to examine new ideas is central to academic success. With respect to these other disciplines, I believe that sociology is uniquely situated to allow for connections that can highlight the linkages between what are often seen as separate and discrete subject matter areas.

Sociologists, for example, may be concerned with the division of labor in any given human society. That is, what kinds of jobs are available and who does what kind of job? This is a classic question in sociology, but it immediately raises questions that connect it to other disciplines. Most obvious, perhaps, is the relationship to economics because of the job issue. But there is also a connection to political science because politics play a central role in shaping economic policy and dealing with questions such as the minimum wage and occupational safety and health. The study of work also raises some fundamental questions about philosophy and the meaning of life. Is work something to be endured, or is it a means of achieving human happiness? With respect to psychology, how does one's work life affect psychological wellbeing and interaction with family and friends? Lyrics about work and social class find their way into many forms of music. Essays and novels frequently have themes associated with work. The list could easily go on because sociology is a discipline that can lead you directly or indirectly to questions that are central to most other disciplines in the liberal arts.

In fact, sociology is considered by some of its proponents to be the "master discipline" because it is so comprehensive and multifaceted in terms of its subject matter. No doubt practitioners of other disciplines would question this assertion, and it is clearly a presumptuous exaggeration for any discipline to proclaim its "master" status. Yet sociology does allow us to make sense of a variety of areas of social life within one framework, and as a result, it invites us to see the various connections between seemingly separate disciplines. In reality, life is wonderfully complex and multidimensional. While in theory one can separate economics from politics, in the real world they are substantially intertwined.

Another example of intertwined disciplines can be taken from philosophy and political theory. What is the model of the ideal citizen? Indeed, what does citizenship itself mean? These are questions that implicate both disciplines in addition to others. We could also look at the research of sociologists of religion and quickly learn that they are concerned with some of the same issues as theologians and students of religious studies. There are other examples that are just too numerous to list, but the basic point is clear: sociology, as a discipline, is very broad in terms of its subject matter, providing an opportune vantage point from which to ob-serve and make linkages with other disciplines in the liberal arts.

Sociology Outside the Classroom

Sociology is somewhat unique in that its "laboratory" is virtually all around us at any given time. We are living in society just as surely as fish live in water, but this does not necessarily make it obvious to those of us living our day-to-day lives. In fact, sociologists are fond of saying that humans in culture are like fish in water; the fish doesn't appreciate the value of water until it finds itself on dry land. Likewise, we humans can be largely ignorant about our immersion in society and culture until we find our-selves out of our accustomed environment. When, for example, we travel in a foreign country, we are reminded of the many customs and practices that we might take for granted in our own culture. Like a fish out of water, we suddenly realize how much we had assumed was "normal," only to find out that it is a prod-uct of local culture. For this reason, many sociologists are in-volved in studying sociological phenomena in other cultures and societies. Because many things in a different culture will appear new to us, we can often identify and ask questions about things that the native people will take for granted. Such is the benefit of the "sociological imagination." It encourages us to question the world taken for granted, and therefore shed light on things that others don't see.

Because the sociological perspective can easily be practiced in societies and cultures not our own, sociology departments fre-quently endorse a variety of study abroad programs that provide students with wonderful opportunities to study while visiting other parts of the world. Whether it involves studying Aboriginal art in Australia or sweatshop clothing plants in El Salvador, sociol-ogy is particularly well suited to asking questions that allow for comprehensive and insightful analysis. But one does not need to travel to the other side of the world to experience a different culture; in many cases, such an environment can be found within a few miles from campus.

If your campus is in an urban or suburban area, most likely you are protected from such things as crime and poverty by physical boundaries and security forces. But if you venture off campus, you probably won't have to travel much geographically in order to find yourself in another world in terms of culture. Sociology has a strong tradition of studying those that live on the "margins" of society. Since the late nineteenth century, when the so-called Chicago School of sociology was emerging within the infant dis-cipline, practitioners were studying the poor and the homeless, prostitutes and criminals, and others who seemed to inhabit a world of "social problems." The purpose in studying these groups was not just academic in nature; rather, the goal was to understand why these groups experienced problems so that a solution could be proposed and policy enacted to improve the situation. This is very much in keeping with the humanitarian or social component of liberal arts study discussed above. While sociologists over the past one hundred years have sometimes differed in terms of their commitment to an applied social science with the goal of changing society, there has always been a critical mass of sociologists who saw this as their primary mission. According to their view, this commitment to social change was central to the discipline; they viewed their objective, social scientific work, as a means to an end, and not an end in itself.

While other sociologists have expressed concerns about the objectivity of this kind of research, there continues today a commitment on the part of many in the discipline to use their research to enhance the quality of life for those on the margins. This can be done in a number of different ways. For example, it is possible to study illegal drug use and the spread of AIDS to reach conclusions that the two are connected, and to propose policy changes that might lessen the problem. Sociologists have a long tradition of this sort of research, and this is just one way that students can study sociology beyond the bounds of the classroom.

Another way to study sociology outside of the classroom is to participate in "service-learning" courses. These courses are specifically designed to connect community service with academic learning in the classroom. Service-learning courses are offered in a wide variety of liberal arts disciplines and are increasing in popularity in both private and public colleges and universities across the country.

One example of such a course in the field of sociology involves looking at the effects of changes in welfare. In a course entitled "Law and Social Policy," students examine the changes in laws that have recently taken place in the United States. These laws were designed to "end welfare as we know it," and put in place far-reaching changes in terms of eligibility for benefits and other areas. Armed with the academic background on this debate, students are then required to perform three hours of service per week at a selected site that allows them to see first hand the impact of changes in law and social policy. In this case, students could choose from serving in a soup kitchen, a charter school, a men's homeless shelter, or a shelter for mentally ill homeless women. Through this experience, students will have a first hand look at the issues that are central to welfare reform. They will be able to compare their service experiences with their academic background and assess the advantages and disadvantages of welfare reform legislation. Of course, there is another benefit to this type of experience: students are directly involved in seeing how other people live their lives and are giving of themselves in the process of learning. These sorts of service-learning classes in sociology and other liberal arts classes provide wonderful opportunities for learning elements of the discipline that cannot be fully communicated in the classroom.

Yet another opportunity for sociological education outside the classroom is found in the form of internships. Most departments of sociology have internship programs that allow the student to work a limited number of hours per week for academic credit at a site that is linked to the student's primary areas of interest. Internships can be in any number of areas, but the main requirement is that the experience provide something of academic value. For example, if a student is interested in the sociology of work, he or she might arrange an internship with a labor union. If a student is interested in criminal justice, an internship might be arranged with the district attorney's office, or with the office of probation or parole. If a student is interested in problems related to domestic violence, an internship at a women's shelter might be appropriate.

The possibilities for internships are very wide-ranging, and sociology departments encourage them for a number of reasons. First is the "real world" component of the experience. No matter how much a student reads on the topic of probation and parole, there is no better way to complete an understanding of this topic than to actually sit behind the desk at the probation office and listen to intake interviews. The same is true for understanding domestic violence. It is one thing to read about it in a book, and another to actually see and talk to the victims.

Another reason that sociology departments encourage internships is career related. In one sense, an internship allows the student an opportunity to determine whether or not an occupation in a given area is something he or she would like to pursue. This is a valuable lesson regardless of the determination. If a student feels this is a good career path to pursue, then that is a positive outcome. But even if the student determines that this would not be a good career path, it is still a positive outcome because he or she can now direct career energies in another direction. Yet another career-related benefit to internships is the establishment of both formal and informal contacts that can lead to actual jobs upon graduation.

CONCLUSION

Whatever type of study one pursues in sociology, it is a subject that encourages continuous learning. Once one approaches issues with sociological curiosity, it is difficult to stop thinking about the world in a new and exciting way. As with other liberal arts, sociology presupposes a vision of the future that involves purposeful action by citizens who are critical thinkers and who understand how the flow of history shapes the lives and opportunities of groups and individuals. If, as May argues, the central tasks of the liberal arts involve the furtherance of understanding, interpretation, and criticism, then sociology is a discipline that can help students achieve these ends for a lifetime of effective citizenship.

WORKS CITED

Curran, Daniel, and Claire Renzetti. *Living Sociology*. Boston: Allyn and Bacon, 1998.

May, William F. "A Public Justification for the Liberal Arts." *Liberal Education* 68, no. 4 (1982).

10

The Study of Political Science

Philip A. Dynia

What is "Political Science"?

As THE NAME "political science" should suggest, students who pursue this particular major will be studying politics and political phenomena in a systematic, coherent, and ordered way. But to better understand what students encounter in the discipline today, we must say more about three key concepts—politics, science, and government. Much confusion has resulted from failure to precisely define and understand each and how they are related. "Government" does not mean "politics." Nor does "politics" mean "government." And neither should be equated with "political science."

Let us begin with some basic observations on the word "government." The verb "govern" means to command, to control, to direct. Government may be defined as the form or system of administration by which a community is managed, and typically includes (but is not limited to) the executive, legislative, and judicial bodies of a state or nation.

As a colleague (Stan Makielski) pointed out to me in his comments on an earlier draft of this chapter (and I now shamelessly borrow his valuable insight), it is helpful, in thinking about the major social science disciplines, to understand that each one centers on a primary question. For history, what happened? For psychology, how do we think? For anthropology, how do people live? Economics, how are resources allocated among people? Political science asks the question: Who governs?

Government is the society's final arbiter, like the umpire in a baseball game. Government decides who gets what resources the society possesses, resolves conflicts between individuals or social groups, and brings together the elements of society that are needed to pursue social goals; for example, those that individuals are incapable of accomplishing (providing for police, fire, and military protection are classic examples). Unlike the umpire, however, the government doesn't just apply the rules; it also is responsible for making "the rules of the game" that apply within a particular territory.

Governments are found in every human society, but they vary a great deal in size and complexity (as will the societies themselves). Most industrialized nations will have the three basic components, as noted above—executive, legislative, and judicial—as well as a complex bureaucracy. A tribal society may be led by a chieftain or small group of elders. Only government has the right to make authoritative rules; for example, rules that are considered legitimate and that may involve some form of punishment for those who transgress those rules. As one classic formulation puts it, government is that entity that possesses a monopoly on the legitimate use of force within a community.

"Politics" derives from the Greek word, *polis* (which might be translated as "community") and signifies, as will be explained below, a particular way of accomplishing the task of governing. But before considering the present author's understanding of politics, a cautionary note. Put twenty political scientists in a room and ask them for a definition of politics, and you may well get close to thirty definitions. The concept is, of course, fundamental, and how it should be understood is perhaps the most contested question in the discipline. Some of the complexities will become evident once the student has taken a few introductory courses. What follows is adequate for our present purposes.

Politics is one answer to what is arguably the oldest problem in human history: how do human beings create and sustain an ordered society? Put somewhat differently, it is the question of how the society should be governed and who should participate in that governing process. Several centuries before the birth of Christ, Plato, and later his pupil Aristotle, sought to answer this question and gave us the first attempts in Western history to create political science. Aristotle's insights remain especially useful even today. Aristotle understood that there were many ways to govern a society, and that one way, fairly common in his own time and not that uncommon today, involved tyranny (the rule of one strong man in his own interest) or oligarchy (the rule of one small group in their own interest).

But politics is an entirely different (and for Aristotle, preferable) phenomenon. Politics is associated with complex societies with many different members, interests, customs, traditions, and religions. Politics involves "accepting the fact of the simultaneous existence of different groups, hence different interests and different traditions, within a territorial unit under a common rule." It does not matter how that unit came into existence. What matters is that its social structure is complex, and that there is tolerance of these differences, and beyond mere tolerance, encouragement of "the open canvassing of rival interests" as the basis of government (Crick, 18). Politics is very much about conflict because it encourages competition among interested groups for things they want. Thus understood, politics also involves freedom—the groups must be able to articulate their interests to the rulers. They must be tolerated; they must have a legal position and sense of security that will enable them to contribute to the process of governing.

Certain common usages of the adjective *political* may cause the student to misunderstand precisely what the political scientist means by politics. Many people use the adjective to refer to any kind of governmental action, or the activities of individuals or groups (for example, political parties) that seek to influence the government's decisions. Certainly these are matters included in what political scientists study. But "politics" is perhaps best understood as a unique solution to the problem of order in society. Not the only solution, as noted above; Aristotle was familiar with order imposed by tyrants and order that reflected the interests of only a small part of the community. Politics, at its best, strives to make it possible for all the interests in society to contribute to the essential business of government—the maintenance of an ordered society. Political governance is different from other forms of government, because the "who" that governs includes the active and meaningful participation of those who are being governed.

The "science" component of contemporary political science can also be traced to Plato and Aristotle. The word "science" tends to conjure up images of laboratories, technicians in white coats, and various experiments in the physical world—the work of physicists, chemists, or biologists. While these are indeed important elements of science, the term can also be used in a more general sense to indicate a systematic way of gathering and organizing knowledge. That knowledge may be about the physical world, but it can also involve, as Plato and Aristotle understood, the social world of human interaction and behavior. In either case, science is primarily about method. Essential components of the scientific method include selecting problems to study, formulating hypotheses about what the scientist might expect to discover, actually accumulating data (facts), testing the hypotheses against the data, and verifying the results (Murphy, 3). The systematic method of gathering and organizing knowledge about voting behavior, lawmaking, judicial decision-making, civil rights policy—to cite only a few examples of a list that might cover several pages and not be exhausted—constitutes the scientific dimension of political science.

As with other social sciences, political science cannot hope to achieve the degree of precision and predictability that is found in the physical sciences. Human behavior—its roots and causes—is simply too complex and to some degree unknowable (perhaps even to the actors themselves) to allow for such precision. But the goal—systematic knowledge about that which can be studied—remains.

From the time of the ancients until well into the twentieth century, political science scholarship involved primarily the study of philosophy, law, and history. In the twentieth century—and largely through the efforts of scholars in the United States—political science expanded to encompass the systematic analysis of political behavior and political decision-making. Economic and mathematical modelling and policy analysis are now important components of the discipline, and the methods pioneered by Americans—along with European scholars such as Hannah Arendt and Paul Lazarsfeld, who came to America between the two world wars—are now used by political scientists throughout the world. Their goal remains the same as that of Plato and Aristotle centuries before: describing and explaining governments, politics, political behavior, and public policies with the greatest accuracy achievable, utilizing the most rigorous standards of investigation and proof.

A few years after its founding in 1909, the American Political Science Association recognized only four subdivisions of the discipline—American government, comparative government (the analysis of different kinds of government around the world), political theory, and public law. Today, those major fields include international politics, methodology and political philosophy (two distinct components of what was formerly political theory), public policy, and public administration. There are nearly seventy-five subfields of the discipline, ranging from advanced industrial societies through developing nations, feminist theory, international political economy, literature and politics, political psychology, religion and politics, urban politics, and women and politics.

Today, the ranks of political scientists are diverse not only in terms of subfields, but in terms of gender and ethnicity. Recent decades have seen growing numbers of women and minorities joining the discipline.

Students should note that, depending on the size of the political science department at their school, not all of these specialized subfields may be offered. At the very outset of their academic career, students should meet with the chairperson of the department to discuss the political science curriculum at that particular institution in an effort to understand the rationale, philosophy, and design underlying the courses that are required and the electives that are offered. Students should also be prepared to work closely with their academic advisor in choosing courses needed for their major and any particular area of specialization that may be of interest. And while students certainly should expect that a good political science department will offer basic courses in all or most of the major fields of the discipline, they should also realize that even the very best department is unlikely to be so well-staffed as to be able to offer courses in all of the subfields.

Finally, it is likely that students entering college probably studied "current events" or "social studies" in high school, and may be wondering how political science at the college level is different. Certainly, current events, including a wide variety of political developments at home and abroad, are important to political scientists. And political scientists freely borrow methods and insights from other social sciences. But high school often centers on familiarizing students with key political actors and political and social issues, and understanding basic concepts and processes (think of the probably-familiar textbook chart showing "How a Bill Becomes a Law"). While basic political science courses at the college level will review many of these topics and spend time defining basic concepts, the larger concern is to teach students to think critically, analytically, and systematically about all of these events and processes and to discover enduring principles underlying the often confusing and seemingly random and unrelated swirl of "current events." Moreover, a good political science curriculum will involve an integrated course of study where knowledge acquired in one course is developed and broadened in subsequent courses. By the time of graduation, the political science major should not only know *what* is happening in the political arena, but also understand *why* and *how*.

WHY STUDY POLITICAL SCIENCE?

There was a time when government was the concern of only a few—monarchs, their advisors, generals, and warlords. Ordinary people had little to say about how they were governed, and knew very little about how government worked. The "age of democratic revolutions," which began with the American experience in 1776 and France in 1789, changed the world forever and brought to many nations a degree of participation in public affairs that had not been seen since Athens in the time of Pericles. Today the industrialized democracies are still relatively few compared to the number of autocratic governments, but it is true to say that democracy remains perhaps the greatest political aspiration throughout the world.

American citizens enjoy remarkable opportunities for participation in public affairs and civic life, running the gamut from voting to striving for appointed or elected office. Obviously, political science gives citizens the knowledge and skills to become effective members of the polity and to shape the debate about public problems and the allocation of society's scarce resources. Political science gives the student the tools to further the values and preferences that one considers most important. In fact, there is ample research to indicate that higher levels of education and knowledge about politics translate into greater interest and participation in government and public affairs.

Given the greater role of government in our lives, the decisions government makes can very directly impact our wealth and well being. Taxes are an obvious example. Protection of the environment is another. And if one is of draft age, whether and with whom we may go to war is an even more striking example. The decisions range from those that have national and international implications to those as mundane as local zoning ordinances. Political science students are in an especially good position to volunteer in community organizations and organize at the "grass roots" level where so many issues—education, public health, the environment—are shaped as much by local and state actions as by decisions made at the national level.

Quite apart from these benefits associated with studying political science, there are a variety of career opportunities open to political science majors. These include (but are hardly limited to) careers in government (employment in either the federal, state, or local civil service), non-profit organizations, law, business (both domestic and international), journalism, political campaigning and polling, education (from elementary to graduate), and (last, but not least) public service (elected or appointed office, or employment with organizations—for example, League of Women Voters, the American Civil Liberties Union—that seek to shape public policy).

And even if one does not pursue a career with so obvious a connection to the world of politics, the fact is that majoring in political science develops certain skills that are useful to anyone whatever they do in life. Your political science major should enhance: communication skills (for example, by teaching you to listen critically, to present ideas clearly either orally or in writing, to interpret data); research and methodological skills (for example, interpreting and analyzing data, understanding statistics, designing research projects, developing advanced library skills); analytical skills (for example, understanding the elements of a complex problem, seeing the elements from a variety of perspectives, assessing the implications of one policy decision as opposed to others); planning and development skills (for example, organizing information, determining strategies, making effective decisions); and group and leadership skills (for example, working on team research, developing consensus, taking initiatives). For elaboration on and further examples of each of these, see *Careers and the Study of Political Science* or visit www.apsanet.org.

How Does One Study Political Science Successfully?

In many instances, the techniques needed to study political science successfully are not dramatically different from those needed to do well in any other liberal arts major. Reading skills (including the ability to read critically and to outline readings) and classroom skills (effective listening and the ability to take meaningful notes in class) are essential. Students should discover at the outset of their academic careers what kinds of resources their school provides to assist them in developing these abilities. Learning how to read a book or listen to a lecture, and how to study what one has mastered from these sources, are absolutely essential. These matters should be discussed at some length in the very first meeting with one's academic advisor, but also touched upon regularly thereafter.

Perhaps the other great key to studying political science successfully (and again this point could be made of any other liberal arts major) is to understand what is being required in any particular course and to communicate regularly with the professor teaching the course. Starting on day one, make certain you understand the syllabus and course requirements. If anything is unclear, ask the professor to clarify the matter. Different courses may employ different techniques. Often, even the same course being taught by different professors will involve significant differences in how the professor approaches the course, what the professor expects the students to accomplish, and how the professor expects the students to perform. Given the pervasiveness of e-mail or special programs like Blackboard, contacting your professor is very easy. But there is no substitute for regularly stopping by the professor's office and chatting, however briefly, about your progress in the course and how you can best meet the professor's expectations.

The variety of Internet sources that can help the student master political science courses is quite literally mind-boggling. It would be futile to attempt to list them all (though I have included a few starting points—and I must emphasize "starting"—at the end of this chapter). Here, again, rather than spending hours surfing the Web and trying to weed out what is worthwhile from what is not, look to the particular course, the professor, and the syllabus. If the professor has Internet source suggestions, they will be on the syllabus, discussed in class, or found in your textbook(s). If not there, ask your professor for suggestions. The Internet is a powerful educational tool, but it should be used very selectively.

HOW DOES POLITICAL SCIENCE RELATE TO OTHER DISCIPLINES IN THE LIBERAL ARTS?

Political science has always been a very eclectic discipline. Plato and Aristotle were arguably the first political scientists, and they brought to the study a philosophic perspective that endures to the present day. After philosophy, perhaps the most important of the liberal arts that contributed to political science was history, and then law (this as early as the Roman Republic). These remained the bedrock of the discipline well into the late nineteenth century. As noted above, beginning in the early decades of the twentieth century, political scientists—while continuing to pursue the fairly broad normative questions that these disciplines typically dealt with—also began to look to the behavioral sciences (sociology, psychology) to try to understand the actions taken by individuals involved in political affairs, and also to mathematics, in order to process and evaluate the vast amounts of data collected using this approach. Today, it is fair to say that there are few subfields in the discipline that do not have some connections to, and do not draw insights from, one or more of the liberal arts discussed in this book. One need only look to the list of subfields provided by the American Political Science Association to see some of the more obvious connections: history and politics, life sciences and politics, literature and politics, normative political theory (also known as political philosophy), political behavior, political communication, political economy, political psychology, religion and politics, and science and technology.

While the discipline's name may not appear in one of these "official" subfields, the fact is, all may be used by individual professors in individual courses or in pursuit of specific research interests. Several years ago, I taught (along with a colleague from the College of Music), a course that examined the interconnections between music and political regimes, based on the premise that at certain times in Western history, all of the arts (including music) were manipulated by the ruling powers for their specific purposes.

At present, the ability to interconnect liberal arts disciplines, and the opportunities for each to enrich the discourse of the others, is limited only by the imagination of the professors involved. A student majoring in political science today should also be grounded in the basics of each of these liberal arts disciplines—at the minimum, an introductory course in each, but possibly more courses in some, depending on what the student hopes to accomplish by majoring in political science. Here again, working closely with one's academic advisor is extremely important.

How Can One Study Political Science Outside the Classroom?

There are myriad opportunities for the student of political science to pursue the discipline outside of the university classroom and library. Consider a very simple fact—government institutions are pervasive in our society. Even in the smallest college town, there is likely to be a mayor and city council, police, and courts. Much of their work is open to the public. And students may discover that many public officials are more than willing to talk with students about what they do as public servants. If you are at a state school, it may be located in the state capital, in which case you also have within fairly easy reach the state legislature, state appellate courts, and various state executive agencies. It is also likely that there will be some kind of federal agencies located there or nearby—there are, for example, hundreds of federal district courts throughout the United States and likely, if not on your doorstep, to be within a fairly easy driving distance.

Students will also discover rather quickly that many of these government agencies are understaffed and welcome student interns. It is unlikely, if you get an internship in one of these offices (and your chances are quite good), that it will be a paid internship. But an internship is a tremendous opportunity—an opportunity to learn, certainly, but also an opportunity to make contacts and to gain experiences that will make you very attractive to a future employer. And most schools, even if they may not be affiliated with some highly formalized national internship program (for example, the Washington Semester program at American University in Washington, D.C.), will encourage students to find internship opportunities and will structure the work experience in such a way that the student can also receive academic credit for the internship. Many colleges and universities require students to perform community service, for which they receive academic credit while also gaining valuable experience in and understanding of "the real world." This is another one of those areas where serious, early discussion with a department chairperson or your academic advisor is vital.

Students should also seriously consider a semester abroad program. In a world of sovereign nation-states interacting with each other in a wide variety of ways, it is important to learn to think globally. The political science curriculum will offer a variety of courses dealing with international politics, but here too, firsthand experience is a powerful way to learn about the politics and culture of other nations.

Politics is an extremely dynamic process. Every day the evening news is filled with stories that have political connections and ramifications. Students can learn a great deal by regularly keeping abreast of current events. At a minimum, the serious political science student should watch a good news broadcast and read a good newspaper every day. Excellent broadcast sources include PBS, CNN, CSPAN, and the major networks. One of the best newspapers, *The New York Times,* is readily available. Again, speaking with one's advisor (or with one's professor in a particular course) is an excellent source to discover what news is worth following. The more one does so, the more one sees how vital are the connections between the abstractions and analyses in the classrooms, and the day-to-day reality of the larger world. (A cautionary note:

All media have certain biases, and they may not always be evident. Political science majors should consider including in their non-major electives a course—probably offered by the Communication Department—that centers on critical understanding of contemporary media sources.)

I hope that I can be allowed to indulge in a final personal example. In the fall 2000 semester, I taught a course on the American presidency. In the early weeks of the course, I spent a great deal of time on the mechanics of the Electoral College, as well as on close and disputed presidential elections, the variety of state and federal laws that govern aspects of the presidential electoral process, and the many ways in which crucial outcomes can hinge on the votes in a single state. By the end of the discussion, most of my students were quite bored with the topic and far more eager to discuss the unfolding campaign and the strategies of [Governor] Bush and [Vice President] Gore. By election night, that part of the course was, for most of the students, a dim memory happily left behind . . . until the next day, which dawned with no clear winner because of uncertainties and irregularities centered on the vote in Florida. The evening before, the networks had called Florida's electoral votes for Gore. Then they reversed their call. Eventually they predicted Bush would carry Florida, but by a very narrow margin. Gore, on his way to concede the election to Bush, reversed course when told of ballot irregularities in some counties and allegations of discrimination against likely Gore voters in others.

In the days and weeks that followed, the country was fixated with events in Florida, including: legal challenges by both Bush and Gore to each others' votes; more or less successful attempts by various Florida counties to re-count the ballots cast on election day; threats by both the state legislature and Congress to intervene in the process; controversial decisions by the Florida courts, some of which favored Bush, others of which favored Gore, and which culminated in the matter being decided by five Justices of the U.S. Supreme Court, who in effect elected George Bush president by halting the recounting of ballots that, it was thought, would give Gore the edge in Florida. While not claiming to have anticipated any of the specifics that transpired in Florida, I am pleased that my students were in a better position than many

Americans to understand the complex political and legal background of these events.

WHAT IS THE VALUE OF POLITICAL SCIENCE FOR A LIFETIME OF LEARNING AND LIVING?

Perhaps that last personal example is particularly apt in answering this final question, what is the value of political science for a lifetime of learning and living? Politics and governing are processes that involve, on a daily basis, changes and challenges that are sometimes dramatic and unexpected. There are underlying principles, rules, and regularities that allow for some measure of stability, but there are also myriad opportunities for the unanticipated and the unpredictable to occur. (No pundit could have foreseen the events of September 11, 2001, in New York and Washington, and we will be discovering and grappling with the consequences of those events for our nation and the world for many years to come.) Sometimes the world of politics seems quite overwhelming. Sometimes politicians say one thing and do something else. Sometimes politicians seem more interested in their own interests than those of the public. Undoubtedly, these are some of the reasons many Americans denigrate politics and politicians (if it hasn't happened to you yet, it certainly will—a good friend staring at you with utter astonishment when you tell him or her that you are majoring in political science. What's a nice kid like you doing in a place like that?).

But every one of your political science professors hopes that you will also come to learn about the good that politics can do, and come to understand, as suggested in the very opening paragraphs of this chapter, that political governance, as opposed to rule by one thug or a group of thugs, is one of the greatest accomplishments of civilization. And every one of those professors hopes that you will graduate with an understanding of how politics works, what constitutes its working well and/or badly, and what the governed—who are in reality the ultimate governors—can do to set things right. Those are important things to know and undoubtedly provide for a lifetime of learning and understanding, and should you so choose, a lifetime of intelligent and informed (and perhaps even sympathetic) involvement in public affairs and public life.

WORKS CITED

Careers and the Study of Political Science. 6th ed. Washington, D.C.: American Political Science Association, 2001.

Crick, Bernard. *In Defense of Politics*. 2nd ed. Middlesex, England: Penguin Books, 1964.

Murphy, Robert E. *The Style and Study of Political Science*. Glenview, Illinois: Scott, Foresman and Company, 1970.

SELECTED WEB SITES

The following sites contain much valuable information, as well as many links to equally fascinating sites. They are not listed in any particular order.

http://web.gsuc.cuny.edu/clags/home.htm
http://www.lib.umich.edu/govdocs/polisci.html
http://www.rvc.cc.il.us/faclink/pruckman/PSLinks.htm
http://www.vanderbilt.edu/~rtucker/polisci/miscpol.html
http://www.vanderbilt.edu/~rtucker/polisci/
http://vax.wcsu.edu/socialsci/polscres.html
http://www.psr.keele.ac.uk/
http://www.libarts.ucok.edu/political/links/poliscilinks.html

11

The Study of Philosophy

Joseph W. Koterski, S.J.

THE GREEK ROOTS of the word "philosophy" mean "the love of wisdom." At its best, the study of philosophy will involve the pursuit of wisdom about the most basic and important questions, including the meaning of human life, the nature of our universe, and our proper relation to God. For this reason, the formal study of philosophy has long held a central place in a liberal arts education and continues to be of high value within a college curriculum.

But the great variety of philosophical schools can make it difficult for the beginner to grasp just what is actually being studied in this discipline. There often seems to be more disagreement than agreement. In some respects, philosophy can appear to be a mode of relentless questioning in search of fundamental principles rather than a developed body of knowledge that one might systematically acquire. Further, it is certainly legitimate to speak of the possibility of a philosophical approach in virtually any other field of learning. A philosophical approach requires having sufficient distance from the material under study in order to reflect on what that discipline considers to be its fundamental principles and to evaluate how well the discipline is doing. A philosophical approach to that discipline will involve a review of the types of assumptions, evidence, and arguments that it uses and an assessment of the certainty accorded to the truth-claims that are typically made for whatever counts as knowledge in that field. The value of getting such a bird's eye view of the whole field is obvious. Yet, this is by no means all that we mean by *philosophy*.

One of the persistent vestiges of the medieval origins of the modern university is the custom of getting a "Ph.D." in subjects as diverse as chemistry and sociology. Why should someone who

has done advanced work in these subjects, or in history, or literature, be awarded the degree of "doctor of philosophy?" When
the institutions that today we know of as colleges and universities
were first developed during the middle ages, there were separate
professional faculties of Law, Medicine, and Theology, each with
its own distinctive subject-matter and method. The pursuit of
knowledge about nearly everything else was directed by an Arts
faculty (hence the tradition of having a "College of Arts and Sciences"), whose governing discipline was Philosophy (see Southern). In this sense the word *philosophy* is being used collectively
and with a generous hospitality for many fellow travelers, much
in the spirit of its etymological origins as "the love of wisdom."

With appropriate development of professional methods over
the course of time, many other disciplines besides medicine, law,
and theology have matured into distinct disciplines. Whether still
others will branch off, and whether some of those that have
branched off may wither away (one thinks, for instance, of the
decision by Yale University to close its sociology department for
lack of a sufficiently distinctive and rigorous methodology), only
time will tell. But philosophy continues to play a unifying role
for a curriculum, both as a way to understand the place of different kinds of specialized research within the whole body of human
learning and as a discipline in its own right for reflecting on the
highest level of principles, the sort of principles that are fundamental to every other kind of inquiry but are not the focus of
any one of those particular disciplines, such as the principles of
contradiction, identity, causality, and sufficient reason.

When considered as regards its distinctive content, the field
of philosophy may be legitimately divided into three domains:
reflection on *thinking and knowing,* on *being and its kinds,* and on
making and doing. Among the branches of philosophy concerned
with *thought and knowledge* are disciplines such as logic, epistemology, and the philosophy of science. Those that deal with *being,*
and the kinds of being, include not only the part of philosophy
with the greatest breadth, metaphysics, but also the philosophy of
nature, philosophical anthropology, and the philosophy of God
and of religion. The philosophical disciplines that study *making*
and *doing* can be exemplified by ethics, politics, and aesthetics.

For the purposes of this guide to the liberal arts, it will prove helpful to consider each of these in turn.

THE PHILOSOPHY OF THINKING AND KNOWING

Among the areas that have enduringly been regarded as philosophy in the technical sense of the word, we find the study of the principles of sound reasoning (logic) and the understanding of knowledge itself (epistemology, a term derived from the Greek word for scientific knowledge, *episteme*). Like fishing, one often learns how to reason well by simply doing it and having the results tested by experience and critiqued by others. But over the course of time, a number of basic rules of reliable thinking and critical reasoning have been articulated. Some of the advanced areas of study in this sphere include hermeneutics (the study of principles and strategies for the interpretation of texts), the philosophy of science (reflection on the principles, methods, assumptions, and results of scientific inquiry and demonstration), philosophical psychology, and cognitive science (philosophical study of the ways in which human beings think and feel and know). But the basic areas are logic and epistemology.

Informal logic is the study of such topics as the typical fallacies one finds in a wide range of ordinary cases of reasoning and persuasion (see Engel). *Hasty generalization,* for instance, is the fallacy of jumping too quickly to a broad-statement without sufficient evidence. An *argument from authority* refers to a claim that does not disclose sufficient grounds for its truth but invites belief simply because of our respect for someone who holds it. *Ad hominem* arguments divert our attention from the actual truth or falsity of a position to the unsavory reputation of the person holding the position.

Formal logic, on the other hand, is the study of the forms or structures of argument (independent of the content) in order to determine the validity of the reasoning (see Copi). Abstract symbols, such as letters of the alphabet, are often used to stand for the content when we are trying to test the validity of the argument-patterns. By distinguishing among the types of *syllogism* (the technical name for a unit of argumentation that links together two *premises* in order to yield some *conclusion*), the appropriate rules for sound reasoning can then be easily stated in highly general form. *Categorical* syllogisms, for instance, are those in which the propositions are straightforward assertions, whether affirmative or negative and whether universal in scope (*all x is y* or *no x is y*) or restricted (*some x is y* or *some x is not y*). Those syllogisms that contain *if . . . then . . .* statements are called *hypothetical* syllogisms, while those that depend on alternatives (such as *either . . . or . . .*) are called *disjunctive* syllogisms. In each case the appropriate rules must be met for the reasoning (on any subject whatsoever) to be valid. No valid conclusion may be drawn, for instance, if both premises are negative; and no universal conclusion may be drawn if both premises are particular.

As in mathematics, skill in logical analysis can only be obtained by steady practice in the use of these rules. But the formal study of this discipline, in either its classical form (Aristotelian logic) or its modern version (symbolic logic), provides a very powerful set of tools for checking the rigor of reasoning. One of the key lessons to remember is simply that if one dislikes a conclusion, it is not enough just to disagree. That would simply amount to being arbitrary, not being reasonable, and whatever is arbitrarily asserted may equally well be arbitrarily denied. It is necessary to attack either the validity of reasoning or the truth of premises used in the argument; success by either approach will mean that one has genuine reason to disagree.

The crucial distinction being made here is between two pairs of evaluative categories in logic: *valid/invalid* and *true/false*. In any formal discipline (or in any conversation over the backyard fence!), the reasoning someone is using could be perfectly valid by having observed all the rules, and yet the conclusion will be unacceptable if one of the premises used in that reasoning is false and does not accurately reflect reality. On the other hand, all the premises could be perfectly true, but if they are not put together well in the chain of argument, they will not prove what the person using them wants to prove. Now, to know the truth of those premises requires more than logic, but to be logical in our agreement or our disagreement with any argument, we must insist on truthful propositions and on valid reasoning.

The related discipline of *epistemology* puts a further question.

How do we know whether a given assertion is true and how sure are we? To say that a proposition is *true* usually means that the content of a given statement accurately represents reality (whether by affirming something about reality that is actually the case, or by denying something that is genuinely not the case). But questions about the *truth* are different from questions about the *certitude* of a person holding that proposition. I may, for instance, be very sure of myself on a given point, and yet be dead wrong! Or I might be uncertain for some reason and yet turn out to be right. Assessing the grounds that a person has for maintaining a particular view is a matter of measuring both the *objective* situation and the *subjective* state of the person making a claim. Confusion about this important distinction has led to all sorts of errors in philosophy and elsewhere, for instance, among those who hold that an idea must be true if we are certain about it. In fact, a host of questions about knowledge arise once we start trying to develop a theory about how knowledge itself works.

The tremendous amounts of data that a person may need to penetrate and reconcile in trying to claim that one actually *knows* something (and not just has *an opinion* on the subject) can be vast, but the principle of knowledge is always *unity*: It is a matter of seeing what is recurrently the same, the common structural feature, amid the variety of appearances, however complex or even conflicting. Philosophers in the realist tradition like to define knowledge as *justified true belief*. That is, we can claim really to *know* something (1) when we have an account of it in which we really do believe what we are asserting; (2) when what we are asserting is actually true; and (3) when we are justified in believing it to be true. If we weren't sure, or if what we were so sure of turns out not to be true, or if we were not justified in believing something to be true even though it is true, we would not yet have achieved knowledge.

There are many related questions here. How high are we setting the bar with respect to justification? What evidence do we need? What counts as good evidence in any particular discipline? The sort of evidence required in a court of law, for instance, in order to have certainty "beyond a reasonable doubt" is different from the sort of evidence required, say, in physics or in literature. How much, for instance, do we need to be able to explain in order to claim even that the earth revolves around the sun? Most of us "know" this to be a fact and yet would have a hard time providing a justification for our true belief about the subject. In order to learn the evidence and arguments that constitute the justification for this belief, we will need to head to another part of the curriculum. But among the projects important to philosophy is the appreciation of *what it is to know something* in any discipline. And for this appreciation, some healthy *skepticism* may well be in order—not the complete skepticism that denies the very possibility of knowing anything, but enough mature skepticism to be able to mount a reasonable challenge to opinions too hastily delivered and to belief too hastily offered.

THE PHILOSOPHY OF BEING AND ITS KINDS

For the sake of clear exposition, we have discussed logic and epistemology first, but ultimately the rules for *sound thinking* and for *claiming* that we *know* anything rests on the way things *are,* and this means the study of *metaphysics* and the *philosophy of nature.* Among the more important specializations within this area of thought we find *philosophical anthropology* (the philosophy of the person and of human nature) and *philosophical theology* (reflection on the nature of God and on attempts to prove the existence of God by reason without presupposing things like religious faith or divine revelation).

At the core of metaphysics one finds questions about *essence* (*what* any given thing is) and *existence* (*that* it is), as well as about *being* (reality) and *becoming* (change) (see Clarke). In the history of philosophy, the investigation of these concerns has often taken the form of the problem of the One and the Many. What is at issue here is providing a reliable account of *sameness* and *difference.*

In our experience, we invariably encounter many different objects, but we also experience recurrent *types* or *kinds.* That is, there are *many* distinct instances that belong to any *one* kind, and the kind can be identified over and over again because all the beings of this kind have the same *essence.* But (looking more broadly) there is also something that beings of different kinds share (whatever the distinctive traits they possess in common only with members of their own kind), namely, the fact that they actually *exist*. Further, things of one kind can be changed into something of a wholly different kind (when food is digested, for instance, it becomes part of us and ceases to be what it was). And to complicate the account a little more, it is not enough to consider the way in which individual things appear at any one moment. One has to recall that individual beings of certain kinds grow and develop over the course of time and yet remain the same individual being and remain the same in kind. Perhaps a thought-experiment can help here: When you were younger, were you the same person you are now? When precisely did you come into existence, such that through all the time since then you can truthfully be called the same being, however many the differences in size, shape, appearance, and experiences over the course of time in which you have been growing and developing?

Metaphysicians have come up with quite different ways to provide a reliable account of being and becoming, and for this reason it will be important to study the history of philosophy and to see how taking a stance on one problem has an effect on other problems. Figures like Socrates and Plato, for example, have emphasized the importance of the *form* that is at the root of all the beings of any one kind. They tend to hold that these forms (sometimes called Ideas) exist eternally in a sphere separate from any of the physical instances of that form in the world. By comparing the multiple, changing objects of this world with such stable beings as the Ideas, the Idealists seem to have a reliable way to know what kind of thing it is. But, in regarding the changing, material world of our experience as somehow less real than the unchanging world of the Ideas, the philosophers of this school must then face the difficult problem of *participation* in order to explain just how it is that multiple individual beings share in the reality of the single Idea.

By contrast, figures like Aristotle preferred a more empirical approach and emphasized a pair of co-principles, matter and form, that are present in all the objects within this world as the basis for explaining the various kinds of being as well as the changes that beings undergo. Having the forms inside of objects as their structures makes it unnecessary to face the problem of participation; but since the form that is intrinsic to one being is not the form that is inherent in some other being, a new problem arises: how to account for our knowledge of these kinds. With the coming of Christianity, figures like Augustine found ways to appropriate the basic Platonic scheme in a fashion that was compatible with faith, namely, by locating the Ideas in the mind of God, and thinkers like Aquinas developed a creative synthesis of the Augustinian tradition with Aristotelianism. In the modern period, there have been such diverse approaches as the rationalism of Descartes, the empiricism of Locke, the skepticism of Hume, and the idealism of Kant. Although the presentation of their philosophies in any detail is beyond the scope of this chapter, there are many reliable histories of philosophy and of its periods (for example, Copleston).

In the course of exploring metaphysics, philosophers have developed such notions as *actuality* and *potency* and have wrestled with the perennial problem of *universals*. It is important not to let the diversity of approaches put one off. Philosophy is like a map, and there are different kinds of maps for different purposes. A flat map of an area, with all the streets labeled, will help one figure out how to get to a particular address, but it may not give one much appreciation of the topography. A topographical map will help a hiker, but it may well bring in unnecessary complexity for someone trying to get driving directions. And neither one will provide much sense of the curvature of the earth in the way that a globe does. Just as different maps serve quite different purposes, so too with philosophy, for each of the diverse approaches taken has quite distinct advantages for appreciating the unity, complexity, and diversity of being. One needs to get accustomed to using a certain map long enough in order to see just what it has to teach about the lay of the land. Once we have come to see how it works, we will be able to employ maps that are reliable with great advantage and to dispense with maps that are either inaccurate in some important respects or not as useful as others for guiding us on some particular type of quest.

One of the most fruitful, if not controversial, philosophical categories has been the notion of *nature*. When philosophers use this term, they are usually not discussing the great outdoors, but rather the inner principles of a being's growth, development, and typical activities. Some philosophers now think that this concept is outmoded or hold that it is impossible for human minds ever to know the natures of things. And yet the penchant of chemists, for instance, to talk about the way that a given substance typically reacts, or for biologists to describe the way the members of a given species usually hunt or build nests or associate is an outgrowth of thinking in terms of the *natures* of things. The beginning student may well meet this idea in a course that is increasingly being used as the introduction to philosophy, *the philosophy of human nature* (sometimes called *philosophical anthropology* or *philosophy of the human person*).

Now, philosophers have regularly disagreed about what human nature consists in, and some (like the Existentialists) have even disputed the notion that there is such a thing as a common human nature. The irreducible uniqueness of being a person makes this an excellent topic for investigation, and yet it seems undeniable that there is some sort of natural kind to which all human beings belong, even if our power to make free choices and to have personal histories means that the common nature we humans share is significantly different from the highly deterministic nature found in other species. In the philosophical study of human nature, we meet not only questions about distinctively human traits (like *rationality* and *freedom*), but also the more basic question about the legitimacy of thinking in terms of natures and kinds. As a general rule, it is helpful to remember that for distinctions to be real and not just verbal, there must be some real difference objectively present in the beings under comparison. Further, the sort of difference required to assert *a difference in kind* is this: all the beings of one kind must possess some trait or property (albeit in varying degrees according to their stage of development or their circumstances) that is totally lacking in beings not of that kind. With careful rubrics like this in mind, there can be extremely profitable discussion in philosophical anthropology about such topics as the relation of human beings to other kinds of animals and to artificially intelligent machines, and then explorations of the ethical implications that can be grounded on differences of kind, for only a true difference of kind can justify a difference in the way things are treated.

Another application of the philosophical notion of *nature* comes in courses about the nature of God and about the various kinds of proof for the existence of God that have been attempted. For many people, the reality of God is a matter of faith, but ever since the beginning of philosophy among the Greeks there have regularly been attempts to establish a rational basis for such belief. Some of these attempts argue that certain facts about the natural world stand in need of a cause that transcends this world, while others start from facets of human existence, such as morality, and argue that there is need of a God in order to guarantee the moral order and to remedy injustices that would otherwise go unrequited.

Besides examining the cogency of proofs for God's existence, courses in the philosophy of God also tend to treat the question of God's nature. The limits of our imagination can easily crib, cabin, and confine our ideas of God in ways that are ultimately incompatible with the demands of divine nature, and so philosophers have tried various ways of conceiving the infinity and the spirituality of God. These efforts not only entail the purification of human language as applied to a being that is in principle outside our direct experience; they also require great flexibility of mind in trying to hold together positions that can easily seem incompatible. How, for instance, can human beings be free in their choices if God really knows everything? Doesn't knowing something (such as a free choice we are going to make someday in the future) mean that the decision in question is already determined and not free? The solutions that have been proposed for questions like these often involve the interesting position that God does not dwell in time but in eternity, and that the paradoxes implied are not real contradictions but come from our situatedness within time.

PHILOSOPHY OF DOING AND MAKING

A third area that is frequently recognized to be a part of philosophy concerns questions of ethics and value. On the assumption that we are only responsible for what we do and make, and not for just what happens to us without our consent or involvement, the main subjects here are ethics, politics, and social theory. But this sphere also includes such advanced disciplines as the specialized areas in ethics (like *bioethics, business ethics,* and *the ethics of the professions*) as well as *aesthetics* and *philosophy of law.*

Moral relativism is extremely common today in all these areas, and its proponents tend to assert the importance of individuals (or cultures) in deciding what is to be held as right and wrong, as good and bad. In opposition to such relativism, there have been various attempts to defend moral objectivity while simultaneously defending human freedom against various forms of determinism. As a general rule, the moral theory that a given philosopher proposes will be directly related to the vision of the human person that the philosopher champions (see Baker). Those who emphasize freedom and autonomy as the source of human dignity often have a moral theory in which things are right or wrong because they are consistent or inconsistent with human freedom and rationality. On the other hand, philosophers who see human dignity as an inalienable implication of the common nature that all human beings share will tend to measure the moral value of our actions precisely by whether our choices respect that dignity or not. In both cases, these ethical theories are honoring the sort of freedom and rationality that is specifically characteristic of human existence and a necessary condition for moral responsibility. However, they differ with regard to the basis for objectivity in morality, and they give different weight to moral consideration of factors such as the motives, circumstances, and the consequences of our actions.

The poles around which ethics courses operate are several. Questions about good and bad, about right and wrong, as well as about what is permissible, obligatory, and forbidden all have their place in the discussion (see Pojman). Besides interesting logical questions about how one moves from descriptions of the situation as it is to prescriptive statements about how it ought to be, there are also important epistemological questions, including whether there are moral truths or whether all value-talk is relative to individual or cultural preference. For some theorists, the very idea of moral truths to which one ought to conform would be alienating, but others urge that human freedom is not adequately understood if we treat it as an arbitrary license to choose as one likes. Rather, freedom is the subjective condition of self-determination that makes us responsible for our actions; but it is only because there are moral truths that there can be authentic and inauthentic uses of one's freedom.

Among the prominent ethical theories that one is likely to encounter in basic ethics courses are the virtue ethics associated with Aristotle, the natural law theory developed by the Stoics and Thomas Aquinas, the utilitarianism usually linked to Jeremy Bentham and John Stuart Mill, and the duty-ethics (technically called *deontology*) of Immanuel Kant. It is easy to mistake the plurality of theories for the sort of choices one encounters in a supermarket, as if selecting an ethics were like deciding what one wants to buy. And yet there is no doubt that there are some significant differences among the main alternatives.

Aristotelian virtue ethics stresses the structure common to all the moral virtues, for he regards *virtue* (human excellence) to be a well-developed *habit of choosing the mean between extremes* in regard to our actions and feelings. The demands of courage, for instance, may well vary from one person to another and even within the same person from one situation to another, but in all cases this virtue will consist of finding the right response to perceived danger as a mean between cowardice and foolhardy recklessness.

Natural law theorists usually subscribe heartily to Aristotelian virtue theory but add the idea that there is a moral law that has been placed within us by the designer of our nature. This law is somewhat like the basic operating principle in animals (their "natures"), in that there are natural inclinations within us to act for things that are good for members of our species; but it is also quite different, precisely because we are creatures of reason and freedom. For natural law theory, we need to use our minds to reflect on whether any given inclination, especially in light of our personal and communal experiences, will genuinely fulfill the potentialities of our existence or in some way frustrate it. Further, by appealing to the idea of justice, natural law theory also claims to have a standard for measuring the moral status of existing political institutions, humanly made laws, and customs that have arisen in one culture or another. It is easy to see the forcefulness of this approach by asking what made a practice like slavery morally wrong even when it was permitted by law and custom; natural law theory points to the common nature of every human person as something that is, at least in principle, able to be understood sufficiently to apply the standard that beings of the same kind or nature may not arbitrarily be treated differently.

Utilitarianism has a rather different picture of human existence when it advocates that the proper standard for morality is the *maximization of pleasure* and the *minimizing of pain* (understanding these terms, of course, in a sophisticated way and not merely in terms of crass hedonism). Operating from a strong sense of the role of pleasure and pain in human life, utilitarians see *reason* not as a vehicle for *discovering* ideal moral values but as an *instrument* for figuring out how to engineer the greatest good for the greatest number. The stress here is on practicality.

In direct opposition to this utilitarian emphasis on the calculation of value in terms of the likely consequences of our actions, *Kantian duty-ethics* stresses the demands of rationality. As free and rational agents, reflective human beings will recognize these demands as crucial to maintaining the dignity that comes from being autonomous, from choosing in a way that preserves their freedom and autonomy. Somewhat like the Golden Rule (do unto others as you would have them do unto you), Kantians urge that the *categorical imperative* is the main rule for morality: whatever you wish to permit yourself, you must permit to others; whatever you wish to forbid to others, you must forbid to yourself. By making the rule by which you intend to operate universal, you can more adequately reflect on whether the rule really honors one's rationality or somehow contradicts the very rationality and freedom that are at the basis of one's own moral status.

Thus far we have, for the most part, been discussing morality as it applies to the individual, but this branch of philosophy also considers questions of politics and society as well as the many questions that arise in the technical and professional spheres of human life. Political philosophy, for instance, includes the discussion of the nature and ends of government, the source and limits of authority, the merits of various forms of organization, and the sorts of virtues that are required by one or another kind of regime. Specialized forms of ethics, such as business ethics or medical ethics or bioethics or jurisprudence take up the general principles of morality and apply them to the problems specific to one or another field. Another whole range of inquiry treats questions of aesthetics, including such topics as beauty, art, and taste.

SOME ADVICE FOR STUDYING PHILOSOPHY

Since the study of philosophy is a matter of insight and argument, with wisdom as its goal, there is need to grow in certain virtues in order to be successful. First, perhaps, there is the virtue of *docility*—an attitude of receptivity in which one will be ready to give ideas, however new or different, an open-minded hearing. Yet the flexibility of perspective that is needed here should not be confused with a vacuous indifference. A willingness always to give a hearing does not mean accepting everything or anything, but a readiness to put what one hears to the test of rigorous reasoning in order to assess its truth. As one makes progress, there will be more and more of a framework from which to appreciate and to criticize. Such a person will display a sympathetic inclination to understand accurately and fairly even positions with which one is likely to disagree. In this way one will always be ready to learn something. When one still finds the need to disagree with a position, one will at least do it the honor of presenting the position fairly and of meeting with reasons of one's own the strongest arguments that position has, and not merely some straw figure that is easy to knock down.

A second crucial virtue for the study of philosophy is *discipline*. Philosophers have long struggled both against sloppy reasoning and against devious cunning designed to produce persuasion merely by rhetoric and appeal to the emotions rather than by reasoned argument. But the necessary discipline does not come all at once. Time needs to be spent on exercises in logic in order to become practiced at expressing arguments in correct form, at constructing valid arguments, and at spotting logical errors. Discipline is also needed for understanding the content of arguments and for appreciating the significance of distinctions toward which undisciplined minds often feel only impatience.

My own favorite technique in this regard applies more broadly than just to philosophy, but it is simply crucial for progress in this discipline. I recommend doing some writing whenever one is reading a philosophical text. This writing needs to be of various sorts. It can be as simple a matter as making a list of the key terms and their definitions, for precise definitions are indispensable for conducting rigorous argument. But it can also be a matter of tracing the pattern of an argument as it extends over paragraphs and pages and even chapters into its full form. For this I recommend that a reader stop every few paragraphs and write out in just a sentence or two what the text has said. Then, when one finishes some natural unit, one should look back and see if the summary composed by these sentences really follows as it moves step by step, and if there has been sufficient evidence at each step to justify whatever claim has been made. It may also help to number the steps and perhaps even to label each step in terms of the role it has played, whether as providing a part of the reasoning, as supplying part of the evidence, as raising or answering some objective, or as drawing the conclusion.

The value of this sort of exercise, of course, consists not only in better understanding of difficult texts, but in having more well-defined questions in class for any part of the text that was unclear. One will have a better chance of knowing what one knows and what one doesn't know. And if we really force ourselves to put these matters into our own words rather than just copying words from the text or merely highlighting words in the text, we will be far more likely to remember the matter precisely for having made a far more active use of the mind than we normally do. Needless to say, this is a slower process than many other types of reading, but the goal is understanding deeply: *non multa, sed multum*—not many things, but much!

With time, this discipline will come. What may have seemed a chore will become second nature to us. But all one's life, the virtue of a real *love for wisdom* will be most important. Wonder at being, and at its various kinds, and at value are crucial to philosophizing. One can see this wonder and this love shine in various forms. One will meet it every time one returns to the figure of Socrates in the dialogues of Plato. One will see it in a different way in the luminous clarity of an Aristotle or an Aquinas. One will see it when pondering on the paradoxes presented by the likes of Hegel or the Stoics. And one will experience it in the reversals of the usual perspective required by Hume or Kant. Entering into the give-and-take of argument, the patient appreciation of the history of ideas, the creative labors of devising distinctions and demonstrations, the search for insights and the struggle to record them accurately—all these activities are typical of philosophy and can be a way to wisdom.

WORKS CITED

Baker, Herschel. *The Image of Man: A Study of the Idea of Human Dignity in Classical Antiquity, the Middle Ages, and the Renaissance.* New York: Harper Torchbacks, 1947.

Clarke, W. Norris. *The One and the Many.* Notre Dame: University of Notre Dame Press, 2001.

Copi, Irving M. *Introduction to Logic.* Upper Saddle River, N.J.: Prentice Hall, 2002.

Copleston, Frederick. *A History of Philosophy.* 9 vols. Westminster, Maryland: Newman Press, 1946.

Engel, S. Morris. *With Good Reasons: An Introduction to Informal Fallacies.* New York: St. Martin's Press, 2000.

Pojman, Louis. *Ethics: Discerning Right and Wrong.* Belmont, CA: Wadsworth, 2002.

Southern, R.W. *Scholastic Humanism and the Unification of Europe: Foundations.* Oxford: Blackwell, 1995.

12

The Study of Religion

Kathleen S. Nash

WHENEVER I TEACH the introductory course in the academic study of religion, I tell my students about Plato's (c. 428–347 B.C.) dialogue *Euthyphro*. In the dialogue, Socrates (c. 469–399 B.C.) encounters the title character on his way to court to prosecute his father for an act of impiety. This interests Socrates because he also faces a charge of impiety for denying the old gods of Athens and creating new ones. Euthyphro claims that he knows he is acting piously by bringing his father to court. Socrates is eager to acquire such knowledge. Euthyphro first offers his own experience along with examples drawn from myth. These Socrates dismisses; he requires a general standard against which to determine whether an act is pious and impious. Euthyphro then claims that piety is whatever the gods favor. But there are many gods, Socrates says, and what one favors another rejects. Euthyphro then narrows his definition: piety is what all the gods approve of. Socrates locates more problems: Since what is "divinely approved" is determined by what the gods approve, while what the gods approve is determined by what is pious, "what is divinely approved" cannot have the same meaning as "what is holy."

Somewhat impatiently, Euthyphro tries another tactic: piety is knowing how to pray and sacrifice in a way that pleases the gods. Socrates takes this to mean that holiness is knowledge about what will benefit the gods and is curious to know how the gods benefit from prayer and sacrifice. Euthyphro retreats and admits that the gods receive gratification, not benefit, from human service. Socrates points out that they have arrived back at their starting point: to explain piety as an action that gratifies the gods is similar to explaining it as an action that wins their approval. He wants to begin the conversation again, but Euthyphro remembers an urgent engagement and quickly departs. Socrates regrets that the conversation has not made him "wise in religion."

I tell my introductory class that we could arrive at the end of the semester no wiser in religion than Socrates was because, like piety or impiety, religion is a difficult term to define. To attempt it is to risk pulling a "Euthyphro." Two things, I think, constitute this difficulty. First, religion is an ambiguous term; it means different things to different people. To some students in my introductory course on religion, "religion" means specific beliefs, considered personal and beyond question or analysis. Once, when I suggested that Eve from Genesis 3 of the Hebrew or Jewish Bible—the Christian Old Testament—could be more hero than villain for laying claim to "the knowledge of good and evil" that would make her like the gods, one young woman warned me that I was interfering with her religion. She thought I was attacking Christianity. She saw my alternate reading of Genesis 3 as a declaration that Christianity was irrelevant, even meaningless, since Christianity, in her view, solved the problem of "original sin" created in Genesis 3. Intellectually and emotionally, she identified religion with Christianity and was concerned that there could be other ways of interpreting a narrative she considered essential to that understanding.

Other students in the same class took a negative view: religion is a collection of laws that impede personal freedom; it appeals to people who cannot or will not take personal responsibility for their lives; it is an archaic system of beliefs about mysterious phenomena that science can now explain. They would agree with Karl Marx (1818–1883) that religion legitimates economic structures that privilege some groups and disenfranchise others. Another group distinguished between religion and spirituality. Religion, they maintained, is synonymous with "the church." There they have learned that God is a punishing judge who views believers as guilty and unworthy sinners who must earn his approval, a nearly impossible task, at the expense of their personal happiness. On the other hand, they claim spirituality offers an unconditional personal relationship with a loving, forgiving Jesus Christ; this Jesus has a personal plan for each of us that guarantees everlasting happiness, now and after death, if we can learn "to want what He wants for us."

A second difficulty with defining religion, at least from an academic perspective, has to do with the origins of the modern study of religion in the seventeenth- and eighteenth-century philosophical movement known as the Enlightenment. This movement celebrated rational inquiry as the source of truth and knowledge. People were encouraged to think for themselves and to question the validity of traditions handed down by the previous generation. The scientific method, that is, critical inquiry and analysis of empirical data, created a body of knowledge that challenged the truth content of what Christianity had been teaching. The knowledge produced by rational inquiry was called "Science." By default, "Religion" came to represent what had passed for knowledge before the Enlightenment. Religion and science were set against each other and regarded as promoting conflicting notions of truth.

THE CONTENT OR SUBSTANCE OF RELIGION

Along with the scientific study of religion during the Enlightenment came attempts to define religion, that is, to distinguish it from other aspects of culture. An early attempt to define religion in terms of intellectual content is found in the work of Immanuel Kant (1724–1804). He distinguished between "natural religion" and "revealed religion." Kant identified natural religion as a sensibility common to all people, an aspect of the human spirit, and revealed religion as a set of doctrines and practices, valued and passed on from one generation to another by a community because they had come from God. Later scholars continued to chase after the intellectual or substantive content of religion.

F. Max Müller (1823–1900), considered one of the founders of modern religious studies, described religion as "the natural and transcultural awareness that some Other is responsible for one's own existence and that of the world" (cited in Arnal, 22). For E. B. Taylor (1832–1917), the content of religion is a belief in spiritual beings; like magic, it is an inferior way of thinking about nature. J. B. Frazier (1854–1941) identified magic, religion, and science as progressive stages in the evolution of human intelligence, and saw religion as the attempt to pacify powers believed to be superior to human beings. True to the Enlightenment spirit, these three definitions connect religion with revealed knowledge, "doctrine" (how else could we know about the existence of spiritual beings outside our world?), and contrast it with more "accurate" scientific knowledge. More recent definitions echo these earlier concerns: for example, religion is "a system of beliefs and practices relative to superhuman beings" (see Smith, 935).

Other substantive definitions assert that we can identify at least two essential aspects of religion that distinguish it from non-religions and from philosophy: a belief in the holy and the conviction that if we seek to be fully human we must surrender to what we experience to be holy. Christian theologian and philosopher Rudolf Otto (1869–1937) defines religion as "the experience of the Holy." As a young student of theology, Otto had studied the life of the Protestant reformer, Martin Luther (1483–1546), and had become intrigued with the human response to what he called the *mysterium tremendum et fascinans,* the "awe-inspiring and attracting (appealing/enchanting) mystery." Luther, of course, saw himself standing before an awe-inspiring and fascinating mystery, which he called God. Otto speculated that in other traditions, there were comparable objects. In his writings he referred to them as "the numinous," the "wholly other," the "transcendent," or, his preferred term, "the Holy."

According to Alfred North Whitehead (1861–1947), "Religion is the vision of something which stands beyond, behind, and within the passing flux of immediate things; something which is real, and yet waiting to be realized; something which is a remote possibility, and yet the greatest of present facts; something that gives meaning to all that passes and yet eludes apprehension. . . ." (191). Surrender to this evolving reality brings the order and harmony for which we yearn. For William James (1842–1910), religion is the belief "that there is an unseen order, and that our supreme good lies in harmoniously adjusting ourselves" to it (48).

Unlike functionalist definitions (see below), these definitions assert that religion has an essential nature; it does more than give life meaning and provide solidarity with others. Paul Tillich (1886–1965), in fact, considered human needs and the focus of those needs, the "ultimate," to constitute the religious situation: Religion, in the largest and most basic sense of the word, is ultimate concern. And ultimate concern is manifest in all creative functions of the human spirit (7–8). We fashion religious worlds of meaning in response to our experience of the holy.

The historian of religions, Mircea Eliade (1907–1986), identifies the sacred as a structure or modality of human consciousness. That is, he sees the sacred as one mode of human awareness, a mode that lays hold to a transformative power of life. Eliade contrasts this modality with another, which he calls the profane. By profane ("prior to the temple"), he means that which is not yet sacred, not yet aware of the transformative power of life. For Eliade, religion is the process in which the sacred erupts into the profane and transforms it, making it holy or powerful, filling it with true life.

THE FUNCTION OF RELIGION

Other scholars ask about the function of religion: what human needs do religions meet? What is the role of belief in the life of an individual and in society? Does religion help people to lead happy and generous lives? Does it stifle their creativity or generate excessive guilt? These scholars are called "functionalists." For them, religion originates from our emotional, social, and intellectual needs and from the difficulties inherent in the human situation, especially the problem of suffering and death. Religion, then, is our effort to invest our lives with meaning and significance. The functionalist approach recognizes that religion involves emotions and actions that result in purposeful behavior and explains why religious belief survives alongside science. It satisfies the human need for meaning and order.

Since the September 11, 2001 terrorist attacks on the World Trade Center, the Pentagon, and the aborted attack on the White House, the ways in which people use religion to provide significance and meaning have generated a great deal of interest. Kenneth I. Pargament suggests that in response to crises, people turn to religion because it preserves those practices and relationships that were once meaningful to them. It persuades us to change hurtful behaviors in order to regain a sense of direction and trust that God is with us. It offers rituals that address feelings of isolation and grief and encourages us to reinterpret the crisis in ways that reaffirm basic values. In the months since September 11, for example, many people have re-evaluated their commitment to family and responded more generously to the needs of strangers. Rescue workers at "Ground Zero" found steel beams in the shape of a cross and derived strength and comfort from its presence. We gathered for candlelight vigils, created sidewalk shrines, and comforted strangers. President George W. Bush called for a day of prayer and remembrance and interpreted the terrorist attack as the beginning of a struggle between good and evil, which the United States would lead and win.

Pargament's analysis of the function of religion is a good demonstration of the ways in which religion fulfills our need to be part of a community and to feel connected. It also shows how we endow national symbols with particular meaning and power when crises threaten national identity. For weeks after September 11, factories could not keep up with the demand for U.S. flags. Flags appeared in store windows, on car bumpers, and billboards; they decorated lapel pins and tie clasps. A flag recovered from the ruins of the World Trade Center flew over the military base at Kandahar, Afghanistan, and was given a place of honor at the 2002 Winter Olympics in Salt Lake City. "Let's roll!", Todd Beamer's rallying cry to fellow passengers to move against the hijackers on United Flight 93 in the skies above Pennsylvania, has echoed through presidential speeches and heralded the opening of the Winter Olympics in Salt Lake City, Utah. In the midst of great tragedy, we find symbols and stories, both religious and political, with which to reinterpret our national identity.

THE ACADEMIC STUDY OF RELIGION

You may be taking "religion" courses taught by professors from a variety of academic departments: Theology, Religious Studies, Philosophy, Philosophy and Theology, Anthropology, History, and even Women's Studies! In the next section, we will examine connections between the study of religion and other disciplines in the liberal arts and the social sciences. First, however, let me describe two general approaches to the academic study of religion in a liberal arts setting: Religious Studies and Theology.

Traditionally, theology, the "study of God," has focused on explaining the divine revelation believed to be contained in the religious texts and doctrines, the "received traditions" of Judaism, Christianity, and Islam. Its first home is, then, within educational institutions affiliated with the synagogue, the church, and the mosque. Today, theology, understood more broadly, also has a place in academia. It is a rational inquiry concerned with evidence and logical argument. Academic theologians are in dialogue with a faith tradition and with its cultural and historical contexts. They provide a rational defense of religious faith that conserves and revitalizes traditional beliefs by reinterpreting them in relevant and intelligible language. At the same time, many academic theologians recast traditional beliefs in new metaphors and configurations of meanings that honor developments in the natural and the social sciences and that take seriously the experiences of groups marginalized by most traditional theologies. Liberation theologians, for example, contend that a preferential option for the poor is a basic theme of Christianity. Such an option requires Christians to observe oppressive poverty through the eyes of the men, women, and children who must endure it and to participate with the poor in their quest for liberation (for sources on liberation theology see http://www.paxchristiusa.org/).

Theology is often used as a synonym for a collection of traditional beliefs, rules, and practices that contemporary believers must drag behind them. Theology, however, is much more dynamic and creative. Theologians think critically about the ways members of a particular religious tradition can live faithfully within that tradition. They study the origin, development, and meaning of religious beliefs, morality, rituals, and practices. They also explore how the religious traditions should be expressed and reshaped in today's world. Theology, then, is the result of thinking critically about the significance of a religious tradition for human living.

At one time or another, each believer thinks critically about her tradition. Here are two examples. During the semester that Susan was a work-study student for my department, her grandmother was hospitalized for dementia. Her behavior had become more and more violent, and she often did not recognize Susan when she went to visit her. Susan believed that God was good and loving. This belief had given her a sense of safety and protection before, but now her questions outnumbered her professions of faith. Why wasn't God preventing the disintegration of "Gram Liz's" personality? How could her father be so angry and her mother so silent? They had stopped going to Sunday Mass. Should she? A second example: Miriam often attended Sabbath services with her parents, while Greg attended a neighborhood Lutheran Church after their marriage. As they prepared for the birth of their first child, dinner conversations often revolved around what they would do in the future. Just how committed were they to their respective traditions? Would it be confusing or enriching to observe both Jewish and Christian holy days? Susan, Miriam, and Greg are theologizing, struggling to shape their lives in light of their religious traditions.

In colleges and universities, theology makes its judgments and defends it conclusions by employing tools used in other academic disciplines (History, Philosophy, Psychology, Sociology, etc.) and by proposing rational, logical arguments. Since the Enlightenment, the hard sciences have demanded that any statement about our world can be regarded as factual knowledge only if we can verify it empirically or reproduce the phenomenon in a laboratory. Supernatural phenomena, things or events that go beyond the natural realm of our sense experience, are therefore not capable of being verified as real in this way. Thus it has become increasingly difficult since the seventeenth century for people living in scientific cultures to acknowledge the reality of God or a transcendent Mystery.

Theology's purpose is not exhausted in understanding the basic content of a religious tradition. It also includes explaining the significance of that religious tradition for human living. Like the human sciences, theology is generally concerned not only with understanding the various facets of human culture, but also with enriching human existence by bringing the results of that understanding to bear upon the questions or problems we confront in life; it also highlights the relevance of that tradition for living well.

Theology tries to bring together two points: human experience and the religious tradition. The religious tradition includes both written and unwritten sources: rituals, moral norms, common religious practices, hymns and prayers, doctrines, explanations of significant religious texts, and the Scripture of the tradition. Human experience is as important as the religious traditions. Theology has value and relevance only insofar as it shows how its religious tradition helps people to make sense of life and enables them to transform themselves and their world for the better. Theological questions arise from everyday human experiences. Theology tries to relate the whole of our religious tradition in a concrete way to life as we experience it. Simply repeating the religious convictions of a past age is not theology.

Some contemporary theologians are thinking about the task of theology in new ways. Judith Plaskow, Sallie McFague, and Elizabeth A. Johnson, for example, view the scriptures and traditions of Judaism and Christianity as records of past religious experiences and use them as reference points for the construction of God images and metaphors appropriate to the contemporary world. Out of the experiences of unjust suffering, sexism, economic oppression, and racism, theologians in a variety of cultures are formulating new images of God that do not legitimate current configurations of social power (for sources on women and theology see http://www.earlham.edu/~libr/acrlwss/wsstheo.html). In the next section, I discuss the influence of Women's Studies on the study of religion in greater detail.

THE STUDY OF RELIGION AND OTHER ACADEMIC DISCIPLINES

Religious studies, unlike theology, is a broadly-based category whose aim is description and analysis. It studies religion and religious traditions by using the methodologies of many disciplines: Anthropology, History, Literary Theory, Philosophy, Psychology, and Sociology (see Creel, 10–32). Religious studies, strictly speaking, is neither an academic subject nor an academic discipline. It has been described as "a subject field," which uses a variety of methodologies and which treats a growing range of issues and topics (see Capps, xv–xvi), most recently, for example, politics, race, gender, and science.

Religion and Anthropology

Anthropologists study existing religions in their cultural contexts. During fieldwork, they live within the culture they are studying, and out of their observations produce detailed descriptions of the ways in which the members of that culture create and acknowledge meaning and significance in their lives. Clifford Geertz's account of the activities surrounding the birth of a child in Java is an excellent example of the contribution of anthropology to the study of religion:

> The baby is washed, and then the mother; and there are spells for both of these performances, too. The umbilical cord and afterbirth are wrapped in white muslin, put into a jug, salted, and buried outside the house. . . . A little wicker fence is erected around the spot or a broken earthenware pot is inverted over it to keep dogs or other animals from digging it up, and a small candle is kept burning over it for thirty-five days in order to prevent evil spirits from disturbing it. (325)

Field reports, called ethnographies, explain the significance of such rituals to the people who perform them. Geertz relates that one woman blamed the death of her child on the midwife's failure to put enough salt on the umbilical cord when she buried it; as a result, the cord "came up" and killed the child.

Religion and Sociology

Some sociologists study the functions that religion and religious institutions serve in a given society, as well as the unique functions religions and religious institutions serve in all or most societies. Others study the social structures within religious organizations, as well as the particular problems and strengths of these structures. A third group of sociologists study religion and conflict. Some explore the causes and consequences of conflict within a given religion. Others study the conflict between religions to determine the nature of the conflict and the degree to which religious leaders help to solve or to exacerbate the conflict. Others look at the ways in which religion and society interrelate, how they modify, challenge, or reinforce each other.

A second approach to the sociological study of religion is the social construction of reality method. This approach assumes that the way we think and act, as well as the way in which society is organized, is a product of our interaction with our social environment. Sociologists who use this approach study the processes through which a particular interpretation of reality becomes reality for an individual: how does a religion maintain its view of reality in the everyday life of believers? How does it deal with doubt? How does it keep its members in line? How does it present competing views of reality as false or unappealing?

An excellent Internet resource for information on this aspect of the study of religion is the Virtual Religion Index, Anthropology and Sociology, available at http://religion.rutgers.edu/vri/anthro.html.

Religion and Psychology

Scholars who study religion from the perspective of psychology describe the effects that religious beliefs have on the human personality. Sigmund Freud (1856–1939), for example, claimed that religion is a type of neurotic immaturity; people create an image of God as father in order to fulfill infantile needs of being protected and being told what to do. Through psychoanalysis, we can overcome the desire for such an authority figure and accept the fact that the only meaning our lives have is the meaning we create for them; we are alone in a universe that, like us, will eventually disappear.

On the other hand, Carl Jung (1875–1961) reported that in his opinion, clients over thirty-five were ill because they had lost their religious understanding of the world; they recovered their mental health once they recovered that outlook. This religious understanding or deeper meaning is imprinted on the unconscious of each person. We cannot access this deeper meaning through our intellect or reason alone. We need symbols and myths to mediate this meaning, which Jung called the Self, a part of us and, at the same time, greater than we are. Despite his antagonism toward organized religion, Jung thought that religion offered the most effective constellation of myths and symbols through which we can experience and discover this Self and achieve psychological health and maturity.

Abraham Maslow (1908–1970) also argues that before we can become self-actualizing, we need "core religious experiences" or "peak experiences." Through these experiences, we acquire a sense of purpose and value for our lives, a sense of solidarity with others and with the world, a sense of self-worth and selflessness. Art, love, and nature provide contexts for these peak experiences, and they are also available in world religions. Psychological therapy, in Maslow's view, should enable and encourage openness to core religious or peak experiences.

For Internet resources, consult the Virtual Religion Index, Psychology and Religion, available at http://religion.rutgers.edu/vri/psych.html.

Religion and Philosophy

Philosophers of religion use critical inquiry to explore religious beliefs and the morality of religious codes of behavior. They pursue questions like: Is there such a thing as absolute right and wrong? What does God have to do with morality? Do the claims of religion make sense? What kind of meaning does it have? Is that meaning true or false?

For extensive resources, consult the Virtual Religion Index, Philosophy and Religion, available at http://religion.rutgers.edu/vri/phil.html.

Religion and Women's Studies

The "Declaration of Sentiments and Resolutions," written by Lucretia Mott and Elizabeth Cady Stanton and adopted by participants in the 1848 Seneca Falls (New York) Convention, the formal beginning of the women's movement in the United States, declared that "woman has too long rested satisfied in the circumscribed limits which corrupt customs and a perverted interpretation of the scriptures has marked out for her" (Schneir, 76–82). In 1895 Stanton's *The Woman's Bible,* a collection of commentaries on biblical passages about women, asserted that most of these passages describe cultural stereotypes; they are not divine revelations about the nature or role of woman.

These views found little support among feminists until they

reappeared in the 1960s during the second phase of the women's movement. Many women in Judaism and Christianity began to protest the exclusion of women, the mainstay of most traditional religious groups in the U.S., from full participation in these traditions. This protest produced varying degrees of change in the practice of religion. Some Protestant religious denominations now welcome women into the ordained ministry; in Reform Judaism, women rabbis and cantors lead synagogue worship. Women are also well represented on the faculties and among the student body of many Conservative and Reform rabbinical schools, seminaries, divinity schools, and Roman Catholic colleges and universities, even though Catholicism presently excludes women from all forms of ordained ministry. For sources dealing with women in a variety of religious traditions, see http://www.shc.edu/theolibrary/womenrel.html.

The women's movement has also begun to transform both the methods and the content of the academic study of religion (http://www.unisa.ac.za/dept/press/rt/22/theol1.html). New Testament scholar Elisabeth Schüssler Fiorenza, for example, argues that the Bible is a "root-model," rather than an absolute authority for life and faith. The process of analyzing cultural systems like religion, naming the ways in which these systems oppress and silence women and men because of gender, race, ethnicity, and sexual orientation, and overcoming this oppression is, she claims, a continuing source of revelation (14–22, 159). Islamic scholar Riffat Hassan demonstrates that popular views about male dominance and female subordination are not supported by the Qur'an, but are based on interpretations that support a patriarchal worldview. Rita Gross's study of Buddhism highlights the disconnection between theory and practice in that tradition. While Buddhist teachings prescribe gender equality and do not use male symbolism for ultimate reality, Buddhist women seldom have access to the same spiritual resources that are available to men. In separate analyses of the racism and classism in most Christian feminist spiritualities and theologies, Dolores Williams and Kelly Brown Douglas describe the religious experiences of African-American women and their struggles for liberation and autonomy. Many scholars emphasize the positive role of women in certain Native American and African religions. Others abandon the "East/West"

distinction and discuss world religions thematically in order to highlight the experiences of women in these traditions: the presence or
absence of female deities, focus on family or individual, acceptance
of male dominance or female power, etc. (see http://www.unisa.
ac.za/dept/press/rt/31/king.html). Feminist scholars continue the
work of reclaiming, reconstructing, and reforming their religious
traditions, finding in them resources to empower women in every
aspect of life (see http://www.religiousconsultation.org/liberation.
html).

The scholars I have just mentioned represent women and men
who remain within their religious traditions, despite the sexist and
misogynist attitudes and practices they encounter, in an effort to
transform them. Others, like Mary Daly and Carol Christ, conclude that patriarchal values and symbols are so essential and central to religions like Christianity and Judaism that woman can
never experience wholeness or autonomy within them. Daly rejects Christianity and calls for "the death of God the Father in the
rising woman consciousness and the consequent breakthrough to
conscious, communal participation in God the Verb" (10–12).
Christ dismisses Christianity because the "effect of repeated [mas-
culine] symbolism on the conscious and unconscious mind nor-
malizes and legitimates male authority" and female subordination
in society, the family, and religion. Women need the Goddess,
Christ explains, because the idea that women can be saved only
by men harms their sense of self (117–32).

This summary about studying religion from a Women's Studies
perspective is necessarily limited. An Internet resource for additional information is http://www.pinn.net/~sunshine/book-sum/
booksum.html.

STUDYING RELIGION OUTSIDE THE CLASSROOM

There are numerous ways to push back the classroom walls and
take the study of religion into your community. Many religious
traditions welcome guests at their worship services. You can often
find information about the time and place of these services in the
religion section of local newspapers. Take a look at these offerings
and plan to attend a service or information session that interests

you. You may want to call ahead and explain the purpose of your visit. Some groups will arrange to have a member of the community, often someone close to you in age, greet you when you arrive, introduce you around, and answer your questions. Ask a few friends to accompany you. These opportunities offer rich experiences of religious traditions not your own.

In museums you can often find exhibits of religious art, paintings, and sculpture that depict scenes from religious texts or images of religious heroes, as well as ritual objects, garments, and specially decorated manuscripts of religious scriptures. This artwork represents interpretations of religious scenes using the manner of dress, architecture, and room furnishings of the historical period in which the work was created. If a nearby museum has exhibits on art from Africa, Asia, Central and South America, or the Pacific Rim, for example, you have the opportunity to study artifacts that may have played important roles in rituals honoring ancestors or in ceremonies acknowledging a tribe's specific relationship to the animals on which they depended for food. You can also visit virtual museums on the Internet: New York City's Metropolitan Museum of Art (http://www.metmuseum.org/collections/index.asp), the National Museum of the American Indian (http://www.si.edu/activity/exhibits/nmai.html), the Anacostia Museum and Center for African American History and Culture (http://www.si.edu/anacostia/speak/start.html), the Smithsonian Museum of African Art (http://www.nmafa.si.edu/exhibits/currexhb.html), the Lourve in Paris, France (http://www.louvre.fr/louvrea.html), the African Art Museum (http://www.zyama.com/index.html), the University of Pennsylvania's Archaeological Museum with artifacts from Canaan and ancient Israel (http://www.museum.upenn.edu/Canaan/index.html), Duke University's Religion and Sacred Art (http://www.ackland.org/fivefaiths/06_00_00.html), the Art of Tibet (http://www.tibetart.org/choose.cfm), and the Islamic Gallery (www.al-islam.org/gallery/).

Interview family members about customs surrounding the celebration of religious holidays, about changing attitudes toward religion in your family, the influence of religion on decisions about reproductive freedoms, the right to die, sexuality, sexual orientation, etc.

Explore how religious groups in your community put their religious beliefs into practice by working in jail ministry, organizing social action programs, and working alongside the poor and the homeless to bring about economic and political change.

EFFECTIVE WAYS TO STUDY RELIGION

Some of you may grudgingly take a course in religion to fulfill a general education requirement; others may welcome the course as an opportunity to deal with personal religious concerns. Some of you may bring curiosity about customs and practices from other cultures but little or no interest in the claims that religion makes. Not only do we hold varied opinions about the truth and value of religion, religious traditions themselves differ dramatically in the claims they make and the practices they commend. Mix in cultural conditioning, language, family background, and personal eccentricities, and we have constructed the series of lenses through which we simultaneously see and interpret what we are looking at. Unlike corrective lenses that compensate for nearsightedness or farsightedness, these lenses distort what we are studying in order to fit the preconceptions we have about the world.

In order to address this interpretive problem, the nineteenth century German philosopher Edmund Husserl (1859–1938) developed phenomenology, a method we can use to bracket our habitual way of understanding the world so that whatever we are studying or observing can present itself to us relatively free of distortion. As we uncover the assumptions and biases we have in regard to a specific religion, we are able to put those distortions aside. Then we can begin to understand that religion from the inside. We make the effort to appreciate the meaning of the relationships, the objects, and the actions of the social world of the members of that religious tradition; we begin to see that world through their lens. According to Huston Smith,

> . . . being ourselves of a different cast of mind, we shall never quite understand the religions that are not our own . . . we need not fail miserably . . . [if we] take them seriously . . . we need to see their adherents as men and women who faced problems much like our own . . . we must rid our minds of all preconceptions that could

dull our sensitivity or alertness to fresh insights. If we . . . [can see] each [religion] as forged by people who were struggling to see something that would give help and meaning to their lives; and if we then try without prejudice to see ourselves what they saw . . . the veil that separates us from them can turn to gauze" (11).

To become insiders, we learn the skills required by "the hermeneutics of affection," the ability to hear views expressed by people from different traditions as if their loves might be or might become our loves. Alongside our critical analysis, we strive to develop a growing appreciation for the values of these traditions and their contributions to the task of creating a meaningful and significant human life (see Wiggins). For Internet resources on major religious traditions see http://religion.rutgers.edu/vri/index.html.

In the academic study of religion, we are both insiders and outsiders. As outsiders, we learn and practice "the hermeneutics of suspicion." We doubt and question every aspect of religion and religions. We uncover their strengths and weaknesses, their contributions to the human community from one historical era to the next. We also consider the destructions and divisions they promote, the hostilities they encourage, and the fanaticisms they breed (see Religion, Religions, Religious Studies homepage at http://www.clas.ufl.edu/users/gthursby/rel/).

WHY STUDY RELIGION?

The economist Michael Novak provides an excellent reason for including the study of religion in a college or university curriculum: ". . . religion is not outside of life, or above it, but within it, at the heart of everyday activities" (99). Religion, at times, seems the reverse side of the political coin. In the United States, for example, Christian moral principles inform much public policy. We live in a multicultural world; our colleagues often hold different worldviews that determine their approach to life and affect us in matters great and small. A study of these worldviews enriches our own perspectives about the larger issues of life; it invites us to stretch our imaginations and provides opportunities for dialogue and discussion.

Religion also plays a role in the process of globalization. If you are studying international management, for example, you already know that a course on Buddhism is an important part of your curriculum because it can untangle the intricacies of Japanese business protocol. Furthermore, while the influence of religion on family structures and governmental organizations is well documented, less attention is paid to the effects of new modes of production and delivery services on religion. In areas like Africa and the Middle East, economic development often means industrialization financed by corporations and conglomerates located in First World countries. Corporate representatives sometimes promote their own cultural values and customs as if they were as essential to increasing the gross national product as a strategic plan or state-of-the-art technology. Local religious traditions may be disparaged as "backward" and "dangerous" in order to marginalize supporters who resist change on religious grounds. A knowledge of these traditions and an active commitment to religious diversity prevent such polarization and encourage interactions that empower rather than demean.

Finally, religion is a product of culture that represents and celebrates the efforts of women and men like you and me to find meaning and significance for their lives. As a cultural artifact, religion offers us insight into ourselves as human beings—from it we learn the amazing goodness and the horrific evil that we can visit upon ourselves and others. A critical study of religion promises no single answer to the riddle of being human. Instead, it proposes a myriad of possibilities and invites us to question each one; at the same time, it challenges us to respect and defend this diversity.

WORKS CITED

Arnal, William E. "Definition." *Guide to the Study of Religion.* Edited by Willi Braun and Russell T. McCutcheon. London and New York: Cassell, 2000.

Capps, Walter H. *Religious Studies: The Making of a Discipline.* Minneapolis: Fortress Press, 1995.

Christ, Carol. *Rebirth of the Goddess: Finding Meaning in Feminist Spirituality.* New York: Routledge, 1997.

Creel, Richard E. *Religion and Doubt: Toward a Faith of Your Own.* 2d ed. Englewood Cliffs, N.J.: Prentice Hall, 1991.

Daly, Mary. *Beyond God the Father.* Boston: Beacon Press, 1973.

Douglas, Kelly Brown. *The Black Christ.* Maryknoll, N.Y.: Orbis, 1994.

Eliade, Mircea. *The Sacred and the Profane.* Translated by Willard R. Trask. New York: Harcourt, Brace and World, 1959.

Geertz, Clifford. *The Religion of Java.* Glencoe, IL: Free Press, 1960.

Gross, Rita. *Buddhism after Patriarchy: Feminist History, Analysis, and Reconstruction of Buddhism.* Albany: State University of New York Press, 1993.

Hassan, Riffat. "Muslim Women in Postpatriarchal Islam." In *After Patriarchy: Feminist Transformations of the World Religions,* edited by Paula M. Cooey, William R. Eakin, Jay B. McDaniel. Maryknoll, N.Y.: Orbis Books, 1991.

James, William. *The Varieties of Religious Experience.* New York: Mentor Books, 1958.

Johnson, Elizabeth A. *Friends of God and Prophets: A Feminist Theological Reading of the Communion of Saints.* New York: Continuum, 1998.

———. *She Who Is: The Mystery of God in Feminist Theological Discourse.* New York: Crossroads, 1991.

Maslow, Abraham H. *Religions, Values, and Peak Experiences.* Columbus: Ohio State University Press, 1964.

McFague, Sallie. *Models of God: Theology for an Ecological, Nuclear Age.* Philadelphia: Fortress Press, 1987.

Novak, Michael. "Religion and Political Economy." *The Religion Factor: An Introduction to How Religion Matters.* Edited by William Scott Green and Jacob Neusner. Louisville: Westminister/ John Knox, 1996.

Otto, Rudolf. *The Idea of the Holy.* Translated by John W. Harvey. London: Oxford University Press, 1923.

Pargament, Kenneth I. *The Psychology of Religion and Coping.* New York: Guilford Press, 2001.

Plaskow, Judith. *Standing Again at Sinai.* San Francisco: Harper and Row, 1990.

Schneir, Miriam. *Feminism: The Essential Historical Writings.* New York: Vintage Books, 1972.

Schüssler Fiorenza, Elisabeth. *Bread, Not Stone: The Challenge of Feminist Biblical Interpretation*. Boston: Beacon Press, 1984.

Smith, Huston. *The World's Religions*. San Francisco: HarperCollins, 1991.

Smith, J. Z., ed. *The Harper Collins Dictionary of Religion*. San Francisco: HarperCollins, 1995.

Tillich, Paul. *The Pattern of Culture*. New York: Oxford University Press, 1959.

Whitehead, Alfred North. *Science and the Modern World*. New York: Free Press, 1967.

Wiggins, James. "The Status of the Field of the Study of Religion." Address delivered at Syracuse University, Syracuse, New York, 1996.

Williams, Delores. *Sisters in the Wilderness: The Challenge of Womanist God-talk*. Maryknoll, N.Y.: Orbis, 1993.

13

The Study of Mathematics

W. James Bradley

WHAT HAS STUDYING MATHEMATICS been like for you? For some students, mathematics is an enjoyable and pleasant challenge, often intriguing. If you are one of these students, you probably enjoy solving problems and like the fact that most mathematics problems have a right and wrong answer. For others, mathematics is frustrating and discouraging, even a source of considerable anxiety. If this has been your experience, you would probably rather go to the dentist than do a mathematics problem. Also, you don't like the fact that mathematics problems have one right answer.

Why do people respond to mathematics so differently? Prior experiences in school, home environment, and personality all play a role. For example, many students liked mathematics until they had a particular teacher they couldn't relate to; since mathematical knowledge is cumulative, these students missed critical pieces of knowledge and could not get back on track. Others say that they liked it until they encountered algebra or geometry—often these students were required to take it before their thinking had matured enough to feel comfortable with the formal, abstract quality of these subjects and so found themselves continually frustrated. Some female students believe it's a male subject and not for them. However, many students find themselves slipping into mathematics as easily as a hand slips into a glove; they find it hard to understand why other students don't enjoy it as much as they do.

Such individual differences reflect our culture's experience of mathematics more broadly. On the one hand, our culture values mathematics highly. Children are required to spend many years in elementary and high school studying it; SAT and ACT tests have mathematics as a major component. At my college, for example, all students are expected to meet a mathematics requirement, and about half of the majors available require students to take a specific mathematics course or courses. For many colleges and universities, the percentage is even higher. A recent doctoral thesis compared newspaper editorials in Spanish speaking countries with those in the United States. The researcher observed that in Spanish speaking countries, when editorial writers want to emphasize a major point, they quote famous writers or poets. In the United States, when editorial writers want to emphasize a major point, they cite data. In American culture, numbers have a great deal of credibility. On the other hand, high school students often describe mathematics as "irrelevant." Many adults take pride in their inability to do mathematics and will say with an almost smug tone, "Since I graduated, I've never used any of the math I learned in school."

How can one subject simultaneously be seen as having the highest credibility and as irrelevant? In the next several pages, we will try to resolve this paradox. Our quest for resolution will take us on a journey. We will visit ancient Greece and seventeenth and eighteenth century Europe. We will look at the nature of mathematics, at what scholars have hoped it could accomplish, and at how it has come to occupy such a prominent role in Western education. And we will examine why its role is being questioned today.

HISTORY

We begin in Greece in the sixth century B.C., because the foundations that were laid there have shaped much of the world we know today. To the followers of Pythagoras, number was the source and meaning of everything. One of the origins of this notion was their experience of music. Suppose one takes two strings made of identical material and applies the same tension to each. If the length of the longer is an integer multiple of the shorter, the resulting sounds harmonize.

In the early fourth century B.C., Plato expanded on the idea that number is so basic. From his perspective, mathematics provided necessary, eternal truths; contemplation of these truths prepared one for further understanding, as well as for virtuous living.

Hundreds of years later, Plato's writings influenced early Christian thinkers who saw these eternal truths as residing in the mind of God at the time of creation. These mathematical truths provided the patterns upon which the natural world was founded and, furthermore, were planted by God in the minds of human beings as seeds of knowledge.

Euclid's *Elements* was completed about 300 B.C. This was an extraordinary work consisting of thirteen books on geometry and number theory. It starts with a very simple set of axioms and proceeds in a lucid and carefully organized manner to deduce a large number of facts about geometric objects and numbers, many of which are far from obvious. It became a model for scholars hundreds of years later for how knowledge should be organized and justified. Aristotle's works exemplify the same ideal. He saw human beings as having an intuition that enabled them to identify universally valid first principles about the natural world. Scientific knowledge, then, proceeded from these first principles by a chain of logical deduction. Seen in this way, science yields absolutely certain truths about the world.

Aristotle did not see the world as being organized on the basis of mathematical principles. Rather he saw physics, biology, mathematics, and other disciplines each as having its own unique principles. The principles of mathematics were truths about numbers and geometric objects and nothing more. Many centuries later, however, Galileo saw the natural world as mathematical. In 1623, he explained his perspective:

> Philosophy is written in this grand book, the universe, which stands continually open to our gaze. But the book cannot be understood unless one first learns to comprehend the language and read the letters in which it is composed. It is written in the language of mathematics, and its characters are triangles, circles, and geometric figures without which it is humanly impossible to understand a single word of it; without these, one wanders about in a dark labyrinth (cited by Drake, 237–38).

A generation later, Descartes envisioned a mechanical universe susceptible to mathematical analysis and proposed a method for analyzing it. Following him, Leibniz envisioned a rational, universal calculus that could be used to formulate and solve problems in all areas of human activity. In 1677, he wrote:

All inquiries that depend on reason would be performed . . . by a kind of calculus . . . And if someone would doubt what I advanced I should say to him: Let us count, sir; and thus by taking pen and ink, we should soon settle the question (cited by Crombie, 1009).

Thus the foundations were being laid for a view of the world that saw it as rational, mechanical, and capable of being described by mathematics. But the main event that advanced this perspective was Isaac Newton's discovery of the laws of gravitation. His *Philosophia Naturalis Principia Mathematica,* which expounded this work, was published in 1687. In the *Principia,* Newton showed how mathematical ideas that could be very simply and briefly expressed (such as the inverse square law for gravitation) could account for planetary motion. That is, from the point of view of his contemporaries, Newton's mathematics had solved a problem that had puzzled the best minds for millennia, namely, that of human beings' place in the universe. This work captured the imagination of many of the best thinkers of his time.

By the mid-eighteenth century, "Enlightenment" scholars were convinced that all science and technical arts could be pursued by the same rational method. They promoted this view in their grand publication project, the *Encyclopedie.* Many thinkers of this era were optimistic that comparable laws could be found for all dimensions of the natural world, including human society. That is, it would be possible to develop a rational science of society and a rational social order that would avoid war and greatly improve human well being. Although there have been critics of this perspective (such as the Romantics in the late eighteenth century), beliefs such as these dominated Western intellectual life from roughly 1700 until perhaps the 1960s. They are still highly influential today. For example, Auguste Comte worked in the mid-nineteenth century; many regard him as the founder of the social sciences. His dream, and that of others after him, was that the social sciences would become as empirically and mathematically rigorous as physics.

In summary, then, for the past three hundred years, the "Enlightenment perspective" has dominated Western intellectual life. This perspective is characterized by a desire for reliable knowledge that would provide a sure foundation on which to build human societies. It was also characterized by a belief in the existence of natural laws that underlie both the physical and social worlds. These laws were believed discoverable by empirical investigation. Mathematics was seen both as the language in which we can best express these laws and as a principal means to advance our understanding of them.

Today however, many people are skeptical of the Enlightenment perspective. In fact, many claim that we have moved from the Enlightenment (or "modern") era to a "post-modern" era characterized by a very different way of thinking than what I have just described. So, we need to ask, "Is mathematics capable of doing what Enlightenment scholars hoped for or not? If so, why? If not, why, and what can it do?" To address these questions, we need to look more carefully at what mathematics is all about.

WHAT IS MATHEMATICS?

Thomas Hobbes was a philosopher who lived from 1588–1679. A biographer, John Aubrey, described Hobbes's first encounter with geometry:

> He was 40 yeares old before he looked on Geometry; which happened accidentally. Being in a Gentleman's Library, Euclid's Elements lay open, and 'twas the *47 E. libri 1*. He read the proposition. By G__, sayd he (he would now and then sweare and Emphatical oath by way of emphasis) *this is impossible!* So he reads the Demonstration of it, which referred him back to such a Proposition; which proposition he read. That referred him back to another, which he also read. *Et sic diencaps* (and so on) that at last he was demonstrably convinced of the trueth. That made him in love with Geometry (cited in Davis and Hersch, 149).

Geometry became for Hobbes the model of how all knowledge should be organized. But Hobbes was not alone in this reaction. As we saw earlier, the greatest of the Greek thinkers, Plato and Aristotle, were inspired by geometry, as were many others since them. Because geometry is probably somewhat familiar to you, let's use it as an example to describe mathematics. But note that I am not going to try to "define" mathematics. Many writers have tried to do this, and the typical reaction of mathematicians to their definitions is "Well, everything here is true. But mathematics is more than this." That is, mathematics seems remarkably elusive and hard to pin down. So rather than try to define it, I'm going to sketch a few characteristics of it, rather like a sidewalk artist might sketch your profile. Anyone who looks at the sketch would recognize it as you, but there is much left out!

Let's begin by briefly recalling a few characteristics of geometry. It studies geometric objects—things like lines, circles, and triangles. Note that these objects don't exist in nature in the same way that trees, good friends, and colleges do. Rather they are idealizations of patterns that exist in nature—the edge of a desk if extended infinitely in both directions would be like a line, and the outline of the sun is roughly a circle. In spite of their abstractness, though, these patterns are easily recognizable even by very young children.

Euclidean geometry organized knowledge about these objects in a particular way. It began by stating five basic principles called axioms and five more called postulates (although today we would call them all axioms). These were intended to express a small collection of basic truths that everyone can easily agree on. For instance, two of these axioms are "If equals are added to equals, the wholes are equal," and "All right angles are equal to one another." One of them, the "parallel postulate," though, was not quite as easily agreed upon as the others and has been the source of considerable controversy. There are many ways to state it, but the simplest is, "Given a line and a point not on the line, one and only one line can be drawn through the point parallel to the line."

After the axioms are stated, definitions of new terms are allowed. For example, a circle is defined as "The collection of points equidistant from a given point." Geometers then proceed to discover new truths about circles and other objects they define. Such discoveries involve a mysterious process of intuition, reasoning by analogy, and deduction. However, in their presentation of these discoveries, geometers follow a formal process of deducing new truths from the axioms, definitions, and previously established results (theorems). No information other than these axioms, definitions, and theorems is allowed! Thus in its presentation, geometry is somewhat like a board game played with rules—only the moves specified by the rules are allowed.

Of course, this process completely depends on the reliability of deductive reasoning. However, philosophers and logicians have studied this process carefully for over two thousand years, and principles of reasoning have been laid out in which virtually everyone is very confident. The result is a system for organizing knowledge that spells out clearly what its most basic assumptions are and what its methods are for moving from the basic assumptions to further conclusions. There is much more to mathematics than geometry. However, all branches are similar to geometry in important ways.

Mathematics is about things that really exist. Mathematics is about abstract things, namely patterns. But patterns are no less real than concrete things. We have all encountered situations that involve patterns. For example, consider waves crashing on a beach, systematic discrimination in urban housing, the motion of molecules, the shape of a galaxy, the process of matching job applicants to open positions, and counting referendum votes in an election. All of these diverse situations involve patterns, and all have been studied mathematically. Consider the art historian who examines hundreds of paintings and looks for principles as to what characterizes paintings that are widely regarded as beautiful. In her search for patterns, she is engaging in the same kind of thinking as mathematicians engage in.

The connection between mathematics and concrete reality is genuine, but subtle and mysterious. What is the connection between our concept of a wave and an actual wave? Why is a crude circle with a few lines radiating from it on a child's drawing immediately recognizable as the sun? How did manipulating symbols on a sheet of paper enable Einstein to predict correctly that light rays would bend when they passed near the sun, a phenomenon that no one had ever observed? Mathematicians are concerned with ideas that originate in patterns we observe and experience. Pure mathematicians investigate the consequences of these ideas and the interplay among them. Applied mathematicians are more concerned with the implications of these ideas for our understanding of concrete realities. But both pure and applied mathematicians are often astonished at the unanticipated connections their ideas have to the concrete world.

Mathematics uses language in a special way. The poet, John Donne, wrote an epigram titled "A Lame Beggar." It reads:

> I am unable, yonder beggar cries,
> To stand, or move; if he say true, he lies.

The joke in Donne's piece rests in the ambiguity of the word "lies." While most mathematicians have a sense of humor, their professional language does not permit such ambiguity. That is, in mathematical language, words should ideally have univocal meanings—one and only one correct interpretation. In fact, mathematicians do occasionally use the same word to mean two different things, but only when it is clear from the context which meaning is intended. This precision is often a stumbling block for students—in ordinary usage, people rarely speak this precisely! But using language precisely serves two important purposes for mathematics—it ensures that in deductive reasoning, there are never two valid paths to different conclusions, and it makes it possible for two people to share exactly the same meaning.

Precision of language is an important feature of mathematics; many post-modern thinkers assert that because no two people's experiences are identical, we can never be sure that the meanings of our words are the same. The more unlike the experiences of communities are, the less they are able to understand each other. Mathematics implicitly acknowledges this problem but addresses it by carefully constructing definitions that give words univocal meanings. It is not easy to take terminology that is unfamiliar and think one's way into a definition formulated by someone else so thoroughly that his or her meaning becomes your own. But the benefit is great! It reduces controversy, and it makes it possible for people to genuinely understand each other, even across widely different cultures.

The use of symbolic notation. Mathematical symbols are often another stumbling block for students. But the use of symbols is closely associated with mathematicians' concern for non-ambiguity. Although it seems awkward at first, once one gets used to it, symbolic notation makes ideas clearer and simpler rather than more difficult. Consider the Pythagorean Theorem, that in a right triangle:

$$z^2 = x^2 + y^2$$

Now consider the same statement in words:

> If one multiplies the length of the hypotenuse by itself, the numerical value that results is the same as the numerical value one gets by taking the length of one of the sides, multiplying it by itself, then taking the length of the other side, again multiplying it by itself and adding that result to the previous product.

Verbal statements of mathematical ideas are typically lengthier, more complex, and more subject to misinterpretation than symbolic statements of the same idea.

The use of axioms. We saw earlier that the axioms of geometry serve as the starting points in a carefully organized hierarchy of knowledge. However, in any branch of mathematics, axioms serve another important role—they are explicit, publicly visible statements of the mathematician's assumptions. They are part of an ideal of "open knowledge"—subject to scrutiny or critique by any reader. The ideal of openness that characterizes mathematics prevents assumptions from being "slipped in" whether for ideological reasons or inadvertently. Near the beginning of this chapter, I pointed out the high level of credibility that mathematics often enjoys. Mathematics' insistence on open, precise statements of assumptions accounts for a lot of its credibility.

Proof as a standard of persuasiveness. What is the standard of persuasiveness in your major? That is, when someone puts forth a claim that such and such is true, how do scholars in your major judge whether that claim should be regarded as convincing? In natural science, the standard is the controlled experiment. In history, it is the compelling interpretation—the explanation of a historical event that takes all known data into account and has strong intuitive appeal. In mathematics, the standard is *proof*—a convincing argument that reasons from premises to conclusions, using only axioms, definitions, or previously proven theorems at each step and that respects the rules of logic. Proofs are another component of mathematics' ideal of openness—namely, that arguments are explicitly laid out for anyone to critique and are accepted only under careful scrutiny by experts in the field.

But even then, mathematicians remain open to the possibility that an error has been missed. Mathematicians' requirements that all claims be proven have tended to become stronger in the 2,600 years or so since Pythagoras. For example, in the seventeenth century, proofs were less heavily emphasized and were less rigorous than today. But in the new field of calculus that was developing at the time, many apparent contradictions arose. These were resolved by means of more careful definitions and more rigorous proofs. Mathematicians' insistence on proof is another reason for the high level of credibility that mathematics enjoys.

We can now begin to see what mathematics can do. It provides a language we can use to describe patterns precisely. It can enable us to explore properties of these patterns apart from their concrete sources and to prove the correctness or falsity of claims about these patterns. Once properties of patterns are established, they can increase our understanding of concrete situations where such patterns arise. Mathematics also establishes an ideal of openness about assumptions and analyses that encourages carefulness of thought and discourages unwarranted claims.

But we can also begin to see the sources of the paradox we cited near the beginning of this chapter. Mathematics values preciseness, careful reasoning, abstraction, and certainty. But postmodern popular culture today values experience, intimacy, emotion, and diversity. So it's not hard to see why mathematics might be regarded as irrelevant. Nevertheless, mathematics has been a part of human culture for over 4,000 years and has made an enormous contribution to it. So it would be easy to dismiss the perspective of those who regard mathematics as irrelevant. However, the situation is more complex than this. There are several critiques that post-modern thought has made of scientific thinking that are legitimate; many of these apply to mathematical thinking as well. So before we can resolve our paradox, we need to consider these.

CRITIQUES OF MATHEMATICAL THINKING

Perhaps the most important critique of scientific thought by post-Enlightenment scholars has been that its practitioners have been arrogant. This, of course, is not a critique of science per se but of how it has been done. Specifically, critics argue, scientists have claimed that scientific thinking is the only valid means of discerning truth. Further, scientists have excessively focused on the cognitive, rational, analytic side of human beings and have neglected the imaginative, intuitive, emotional, spiritual, and relational sides. Many of these critics argue that scientists have tried to squeeze all human experience into their mold, have exploited the environment rather than living in harmony with it, and have used claims of objective knowledge as a means to exercise power over others.

The fact that many scientists and mathematicians have claimed superiority for their methods is unarguable—its roots extend at least as far back as Descartes's *Discourse on Method* (1637), in which he argued that the certainty of mathematics should make it a model for all other branches of study. In fact, much of the conflict between science and religion of the past two hundred years has revolved around claims of superiority by one side or the other. The notion that science has neglected important dimensions of human personality is also not unique to our era—it was cogently argued by Romantics such as William Blake over two hundred years ago. But the Enlightenment belief in the power of science to create progress was too strong to be overcome at that time. Furthermore, examples of environmental exploitation are common today. Lastly, feminist scholars have perhaps been the most visible proponents of the criticism that claims of objective knowledge are often accompanied by exercises of power. They argue persuasively that such claims disenfranchise other ways of knowing that are more intuitive, interpersonal, and unique to an individual's experience and perspective.

Another critique is that science and mathematics do not provide the neutrality that has historically been claimed for them. For example, imagine a pleasant spring day and a gardener heading out into his yard with shovel and hoe in hand. Along the way, he passes his garage door that needs some paint. He notices it out of the corner of his eye, but ignores it. Then he spots a dandelion and 100 percent of his attention is focused on it. The point is that the tools we bring to a situation strongly influence both what we see and what we choose to consider. Thus a person who approaches a situation with a scientific or mathematical framework will tend to look for factors that can be measured, for data that can be collected, and for relationships that can be expressed as equations. In the process, she may neglect aspects of the situation that cannot be quantified or features that she judges could not be replicated in another study. That is, her commitment to science has so shaped her perception that she is not neutral.

A related critique is that in attempting to focus on facts, scientists and mathematicians have neglected values (principles that help us decide what is important) and norms (principles that help us decide what is right and wrong). For example, consider mathematical economics. Its objective is to help scholars understand economic phenomena such as economic growth, inflation, supply, demand, and prices. One of the key features of its methods is modeling a person's preferences. This is often done by an ordered list (first preference, second preference, etc.). It may also be done numerically, for example, by awarding a strongest preference 100 points, a weakest preference zero points, and other preferences different numbers between zero and 100 that reflect the strength of the person's preferences. Such models are often helpful, but if a scholar restricts himself solely to the use of this mathematical description of preferences, he has no means to critique the preferences. Thus, if a homebuyer's preference for location of his new house is on (say) an environmentally sensitive sand dune, the economist has no tools with which to critique that choice—it is simply a preference. Thus a consequence of this critique is that science and mathematics, particularly when applied to human affairs, cannot be separated from consideration of norms and values.

There are many further critiques, but I'll give one more before we move on. Jacques Ellul, a French scholar, has identified a significant way in which mathematical-type thinking has altered the "inner life" of our culture, that is, has shaped the patterns in which people think. He calls this pattern "technique," referring to a process of reducing human activities to routines that can be optimized for efficiency and productivity. (Ellul distinguishes "technique" as a way of thinking from "technology," the production of artifacts.) It is easy to cite examples to show how widespread the application of technique has become in Western culture. Assembly lines in manufacturing, systematic methods of accounting in business, standardized procedures for computing taxes, the use of bar codes to enhance grocery store check-out and keep track of inventory, the use of systems analysis to model the flow of information through a corporation, the use of *Roberts' Rules of Order* to govern a deliberative body, and the standardized procedures that large bureaucracies use to manage their activities are all examples. In fact, any computerized process is an application of technique.

One of the clearest illustrations Ellul gives of "technique" is the way in which economists at Cornell University in the early part of the twentieth century altered the design of American home kitchens. Their idea was to design kitchens that would optimize the process of food preparation; for instance, by minimizing the walking distance of a person preparing food. Thus, one of the principal recommendations of these home economists was to organize the kitchen around three distinct centers focused on the activities of preparation, cooking, and cleaning. The centers were placed to allow efficient flow of food and utensils from one to another. Nineteenth century kitchens typically had a table in the center of the kitchen. Hence, another recommendation was to remove the table.

Ellul is not suggesting that inefficiency is better than efficiency or that unproductivity is better than productivity. Rather, he is saying that secondary values (ones that exist to serve higher ends) have been made primary. That is, in their zeal to be scientific, many analysts consciously set aside values such as human dignity. As a result, productivity and efficiency became the only values recognized in their methods and hence became ends in themselves. Note that technique is not explicitly mathematics. However, it incorporates several of the values and ideals of mathematics—open knowledge, precision, abstraction, and impersonality—and is a consequence of Enlightenment thinking. So Ellul's critique is applicable to our considerations here.

RESOLUTION OF THE PARADOX

Now that we have seen a bit of what mathematics is and how it (along with science) has been criticized by post-Enlightenment scholars, we are in a position to attempt a resolution of the paradox we discussed earlier—that mathematics is simultaneously viewed as irrelevant and as having the highest credibility. Why is mathematics seen as having such high credibility? There seem to be two principal reasons. First, mathematics has set a high standard in its insistence that all claims be proven and all assumptions be made explicit. This standard has largely protected it from some of the controversies and failings that might have damaged its credibility over its long history. Second, mathematics has been extraordinarily successful in helping scholars understand both the physical and social worlds.

Why is mathematics seen as irrelevant? Again there seem to be two main reasons. First, what mathematics tries to accomplish does not comport well with the values and goals of contemporary society. Mathematics is primarily concerned with matters such as precise definitions, careful reasoning, avoiding ambiguity, and proving its claims. Contemporary society is more concerned with matters such as sharing feelings, experiencing intimacy, understanding unique individual experiences, and exploring the role of culture in how we perceive reality. That is, the type of understanding sought is quite different. Second, some of the most unpleasant aspects of life in the early twenty-first century, such as the threat of nuclear weapons and widespread pollution, are closely tied to technology and hence to science and mathematics. These unpleasant facts, when combined with the arrogance and neglect of the human dimensions of life characteristic of the Enlightenment perspective for the past three hundred years, have produced an aversion to science and mathematics in parts of Western culture.

Both perspectives—the one that sees mathematics as highly credible and the one that sees it as irrelevant—have validity. Is there any way to reconcile these in our thinking? I think so. But it means that both perspectives have to become broader. Those who tend toward the credibility perspective need to adopt a more humble approach, acknowledging that the Enlightenment perspective on mathematics and science has been arrogant and insensitive to human values. This means recognizing that other ways of knowing can be valid and that mathematics has important limits, such as the inability to provide a basis for choosing among competing norms and values. Those who tend toward the irrelevancy perspective also need to broaden. They need to acknowledge the enormous social benefits that mathematics has produced and recognize that there is considerably more to mathematics than simply manipulating algebraic symbols and proving geometric theorems that seem obvious without proof. They need to recognize that many features of mathematical thinking, such as clarity of language, seeking to understand patterns, careful thinking, and avoiding inconsistencies are part of everyday life. And they need to acknowledge that the values of openness and shared understanding that are so fundamental in mathematics are a positive example to every field of study.

What Does Mathematics Have to Offer You?

We have seen that our paradox is resolvable, although the resolution will require holders of both perspectives to give a little. Nevertheless, the roles vary widely that mathematics plays among college students. For many of you, specific mathematical skills will be needed. Natural scientists and engineers will need to understand calculus as well as more advanced mathematics. Anyone who has to deal with data—social scientists, business majors, nurses, natural scientists, and education students—will need statistics. Computer students will need discrete mathematics. Some of you will need algebra, trigonometry, or pre-calculus before you proceed into the calculus sequence. Others will be required to take a specific liberal arts mathematics course. Some of you will take no further mathematics courses.

But for everyone, mathematics at its best can provide a helpful way of thinking. That is, it offers a framework of values, namely openness, clarity, careful thinking, and strenuous effort to achieve shared understandings that can help you in your comprehension of any situation. It suggests the importance of clearly identifying goals and objectives and expressing them unambiguously. Its standards of openness regarding underlying assumptions and careful examination of purportedly persuasive arguments are ones to which people in any major can aspire. It also points to the use of mathematical tools such as precise definitions, quantification, and mathematical models as a means to gain further understanding.

Some Questions to Think About

My goal here has been to give an overview of mathematics and its place in the college or university curriculum. But along the way I have alluded to some deeper questions that do not admit of easy answers. I'd like to conclude this chapter by mentioning a few of these and leave them with you for further reflection.

- Do social laws analogous to the laws of physics exist? Are they discoverable if they do exist? Are they quantifiable?
- Is there any dimension of human experience that cannot or should not be studied using the methods of mathematics and science? If you believe there is no such dimension, explain why. If you believe there is, what is it and why should it not be pursued in this way?
- Are there forms of knowledge that cannot be acquired by science and mathematics? If your answer is "no," explain why. If "yes," explain how one can "know" such things and why such knowledge ought to be respected.
- Mathematics has obviously affected human societies—especially Western society—deeply. What ethical principles ought to guide its usage in the formation of public policy?
- If, indeed, science and mathematics are unable to provide a basis for choosing among competing norms and values, how are we to make such choices?
- Is the kind of hierarchy of knowledge that characterizes mathematics—starting from axioms and definitions and carefully proceeding to further knowledge—an ideal that is applicable to knowledge in your intended major? Why or why not?

Works Cited

Crombie, Alistair C. *Styles of Scientific Thinking in the European Tradition: The History of Argument and Explanation Especially in the Mathematical and Biomedical Sciences and Arts.* 3 vols. London: Duckworth, 1994.

Davis, Philip J. and Reuben Hersch. *The Mathematical Experience.* Boston: Houghton Mifflin, 1981.

Drake, Stillman. *Discoveries and Opinions of Galileo.* New York: Doubleday Anchor Books, 1957.

14

The Study of Science

Trudy A. Dickneider

My goal is simple. It is complete understanding of the
Universe, why it is as it is and why it exists at all.

Stephen Hawking

THERE IT IS. In just a few words from the man who is definitely
the world's best known, and probably the most respected, scientist of our time, we have a description of what science is, what
scientists do, and why they do it. We haven't quite accomplished
Dr. Hawking's goal; in fact most of us believe we never will,
but the past century was studded with remarkable scientific and
technological accomplishments, moving us closer to the goal of
complete understanding.

In your lifetime alone we have mapped the human genome,
genetically engineered tomatoes, successfully cloned sheep, sent
Sojourner roving across the surface of Mars, and launched Sally
Ride as the first American woman in space. We have placed the
Hubble telescope in space and, after we fixed it, we have mar-
veled at the beauty and majesty of the images of deep space that
it has returned. You have benefited from the rise of the personal
computer and the invention of the CD-ROM. And, of course,
your lives have been affected in innumerable ways by the development of the Internet and the World Wide Web.

But the science in the news that you have seen has not all been
good. You have also seen the space shuttle Challenger explode,
the confusion and fear of the Chernobyl nuclear reactor accident,
and been both saddened and angered by the environmental de-
struction of the Exxon Valdez oil spill. You've also seen earth-
quakes, forest fires, volcanic eruptions, and massive storms, all of

which make it seem as though Mother Nature is bent on destroying herself.

What do all of these events have in common? In order to be understood, in order for the true benefits or risks to be assessed and appreciated, a certain level of scientific literacy is required, and providing that knowledge is one of the main aims of studying science. The opportunity to study science as part of your university career will furnish you with this necessary knowledge. The goal of this chapter is to offer you some insights on the nature of science in general, how it is manifested in the individual scientific disciplines, as well as why and how you should study it.

What Is Science?

Science is both a process and a product. That means you do science to get science. The process of science aims to model reality. A model is an explanation or theory, based on observation and experimentation, that allows us to explain those observations and make predictions about the behavior of the system being studied. The predictions can be the effectiveness of a new pharmaceutical compound, the major product of a chemical reaction, or the needed launch velocity of a space vehicle. They can also involve such things as earthquake predictions and global warming models. These models are often the result of the application of the scientific method. The much-discussed and defined scientific method is a continuing cycle of observation, hypothesis, and testing that you are, no doubt, familiar with from your previous studies of science.

This way of problem solving, which dates from the work of Galileo, is a way of studying not just the world around us, both the macro and the micro, but the entire universe. The process of science, the scientific method, begins with observation and analysis in which a system is studied and the facts are collected. The observations of nature or a controlled experiment must be carefully compiled and reported, describing the observed reality as carefully as possible. The next step is to classify the collected data to deduce the relationships and derive a rule that expresses the dependence of behavior on the variables. It is here that a hypoth-

esis is formed and theories and laws are proposed. These constitute the model. In the final step of this cycle, the model is applied,
resulting in the prediction of new behavior for the original system
or a related one. These predictions become the focus of a new
round of experimental observation as a new analysis phase begins.
This is followed by another synthesis of information that leads to
a revised or expanded model, and the process repeats again and
again.

The goal of this study is an ever-growing understanding of the
universe in all of its parts, learning how it is structured and how
it functions. Indeed, knowledge of structure and function is the
goal of each of the scientific disciplines, whether it is the molecules of chemistry, the organisms of biology, the rock structures
of geology, or the stellar atmospheres of astronomy.

We have already seen that the very process of science is empirical. The work of science rests on observation. These observations
can be of the world around us; birds nesting, air circulation patterns, deep space high-energy physics. Or they can be observations that result from a devised and controlled system when
identified variables are changed—this is an experiment. However,
some experiments can't be done, for example, cosmological studies on topics such as the Big Bang. There is just no way to recreate
that seminal event, even on a small scale. So most of the sciences
now have theoretical branches that make use of sophisticated
computing methods to model such things as stellar evolution and
planetary formation, as well as more terrestrial questions such as
the formation and migration of petroleum in the Gulf of Mexico.

The product of science is knowledge—knowledge about the
workings of the part of the universe being studied, the system.
The information gained leads to another cycle of the scientific
method in search of yet deeper and wider understanding. This is
a never-ending process. Indeed, Sir Isaac Newton, another holder
of the Lucasian chair at Cambridge University now occupied by
Dr. Hawking, once noted that it would be impossible for any one
person or age to explain all nature. We scientists realistically see
our career as time spent as workers in an old vineyard with an
endless future. The fruit of research rests on the structure built by
those who tended the vines before us, and we are building the
basis for the harvest to come long after. We are all working on

another piece in the jigsaw puzzle of nature. Our puzzle piece is the knowledge, the understanding that comes from our observations and calculations, our models.

You will sometimes hear of *scientific truth*. This is mostly a myth of the media. It is a term used by nonscientists writing about science for the layman. Most scientists I know don't know any truth, nor is truth what they are seeking. To the scientist truth is not the goal; it is the outcome of achieving the goal. Truth is not some actual, knowable, attainable thing. It is the product of completely and correctly modeling physical reality. We can't achieve that because there is no way to empirically verify the truth of our models, so even if we got to truth, we wouldn't know it! So the search for truth cannot be the goal of science. Jacob Bronowski has said that we do not look for truth as for a thing, like our notebook or sunglasses. If that were the case, the scientist would be nothing more than a good finder. Rather, scientists constantly correct the picture of reality of the moment with a better one by continuous application of the scientific method. The great scientists we all recognize, Copernicus, Galileo, Harvey, Newton, Einstein, Curie, Bohr, among many others, fit the available data to a much better model. Each iteration of the model moves us one step closer to a truth that is, finally, forever unknowable.

Often, the product of the scientific process will have a practical application in the direct solution of a problem—this is technology. Scientific investigation led to the miniaturization of circuits. The technological application has resulted in laptops and handheld personal data assistants capable of wireless Web surfing. Development of the biomedical telemetry necessary to safely send humans into space has led to advanced medical monitoring devices and sophisticated pacemakers, improving the quality of life for many.

Each of the scientific disciplines examines a different aspect of the physical universe. The individual sciences are related by the progression of the nature of reality that they study. The diagram in figure 13 shows a way to conceptualize the relationships between the sciences (Cassidy, "Sciences and the Humanities"). It shows that the sciences rest on a mathematical foundation. Mathematics (as discussed in chapter 13) provides us with a language for the theoretical and quantitative work of the sciences. The physical sciences model the stuff of the universe, the behavior of matter, whether it is in a distant galaxy or in a chemical synthesis of an important pharmaceutical product. The laws of motion and energy that are the product of physics explain the workings of the universe. The structure and nature of the atomic nucleus is also the province of physics. Chemistry studies matter and the changes that it undergoes, applying the laws of physics. Disciplines such as astronomy and geology apply the understanding of the behavior of matter gained in the two basic disciplines of physics and chemistry to specialized and isolated systems such as stars, planets, rocks, minerals, stratigraphic structures, and meteorites.

We see in this study a progression from the largest system of all, the universe, to smaller and more focused areas of study, such as carbonate geology. We also see a movement from a totally inorganic system consisting of the baryonic matter (protons, neutrons, electrons) of the early universe toward material objects with which we are more familiar, our daily vitamin or a piece of amethyst.

Fig. 13.
The Relationship Between the Scientific Disciplines.

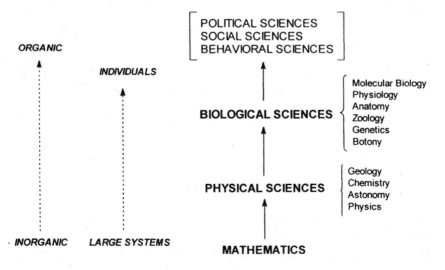

As the progression from large and inorganic systems to smaller and more organic ones continues, the physical sciences develop into the biological sciences. Linking disciplines such as biochemistry and biophysics connect the study of inanimate matter to the sciences that study the structure and behavior of living things— the biological sciences. The biological sciences include disciplines that study plants, animals, microorganisms, and the structure and behavior of the genetic stuff of life itself, as expressed in cellular and molecular biology. These sciences deal with progressively more complicated living systems, their structure, function, and interrelations. However, while these disciplines are concerned with living organisms, they deal only with reflex driven behavior. As the progression of scientific study continues, the large systems develop into organic individuals whose cognitive functions are the objects of study of the behavioral sciences. Psychology deals with the behavior of the individual, while the social sciences are concerned with the actions and interactions of groups of individuals. Finally, the political sciences complete the progression by studying the interactions of large groups.

Figure 13 shows that the physical and biological sciences are related by the progression in the object of their study, and by the fact that the work of each individual discipline uses the understanding gained by the other disciplines. At the same time, each discipline contributes its product to the work of other disciplines. Indeed, as science continues to advance, the lines between the disciplines become less distinct. In fact, the hybrid disciplines, such as geochemistry, planetary geology, bioorganic chemistry, biophysics, and astrobiology are the hottest areas of study and research as scientists come closer and closer to Dr. Hawking's goal of complete understanding. This complete understanding would, of course, obliterate the divisions between disciplines.

Why Study Science?

Hopefully the discussion of the process and product involved in science has convinced you that the pursuit of scientific information is a worthwhile human activity. Many of you will be studying science during your university career because it will become your life's work as a practicing chemist, researcher in biology or geology, an observational astronomer, or theoretical physicist. Some of you are preparing to teach one of the sciences on the elementary or secondary level and recognize the need for a broad foundation in the sciences as a whole.

For others, the required science courses are a part of your preparation for a career in one of the health and medical fields. The study of science is essential for anyone pursuing a career in any of the allied health fields. For example, for a career as a physician or nurse, competency in basic science is necessary in order to understand the structure and function of the human body. But physicians and nurses, as well as physical and occupational therapists, also need to understand the physics of motion and the principles of neurobiology. Medical laboratory scientists, medical technologists, and microbiologists must understand sophisticated laboratory procedures and the operation and use of computers for data analysis and transfer.

For some, your science courses will be taken to fulfill a general education requirement as you pursue a degree in business or the humanities. The business major with a basic level of scientific literacy will be able to understand technological innovations and to maximize interactions and opportunities with scientific aspects. This well-grounded person will be able to benefit from investing opportunities in the sciences on both a corporate and personal level.

Engineering students need to understand not only the physics of energy and motion, but also the principles of material science. Art students, whether they are studio artists or historians, would benefit from an understanding of media developments and the chemical behavior of paints and sculpturing materials. Their understanding of their own discipline would also be enhanced by an understanding of the driving forces of climate change through human history and how it is related to the rise and progression of art as a record of humankind's activities and awareness of the world around us. In a similar manner, students of literature would enrich their understanding through increased appreciation of scientific references and allusions contained in many poetic and fictional works. Along with historians, their interpretation of the cultural grounding of the great writers and political figures would be enhanced by an understanding of the scientific outlook of their times.

If your discipline has been left out of this brief list, you can be sure that it, too, has an aspect that will benefit from a study of the sciences. However, for all of you, these courses offer an opportunity to see how the natural world works, to build on your high school science exposure, and to prepare you to be a well-informed citizen as we move forward into the brave new world of this new century. And not only the professional, but the personal aspect of your life will benefit as well. For certainly the world will not become less scientific or less technologically oriented in the future. You will not be able to function as an informed citizen or maximize the opportunities presented to you in whatever career you pursue without an understanding of and, even more importantly, an appreciation of the sciences. You are going to have much more expected of you than just the ability to program the VCR or properly place the surround sound speakers!

How to Succeed in Science By Really Trying!

The very nature of science as discussed above provides us with hints on how to study it successfully. Science involves a logical thought progression and process of classification that we can use in our techniques to master our science coursework.

Organize Your Study

Science is all about classification and organization and the recognition of patterns in nature. So why not study it that way! As you accumulate lecture notes, worked problems, notes from reading the chapters in your text, and other sources, make notes, charts, and diagrams that show the relationships between the material in a course as it develops. And, of course, it is easiest to do that every day by integrating new material into your notes as it is presented to you, rather than waiting for the famous night before the exam to try to see these patterns.

Look for Connections

No matter which discipline you are studying, each lecture will present ideas that rest on those developed earlier. Examine those connections and use them to increase your understanding. Don't look at science as a bunch of facts to be memorized; see it as a developing story of nature. Make notes from your notes to summarize these connections. These notes will help you not only throughout the semester that the course is studied, but they will also be invaluable as a source of review when you take a course that rests on what you learned in this course.

There are reasons that courses in the sciences have prerequisites. Introductory physics is necessary to do any advanced and applied physics courses, such as optics and acoustics. A firm grounding in the material presented in general biology is needed in order to tackle vertebrate anatomy, genetics, and neurophysiology. General chemistry presents the foundations needed to succeed in organic, and without a grasp of organic chemistry, biochemistry is not understandable. And studies in environmental science and ecology require grounding in basic biology, general, and organic chemistry, and the physics of motion and energy concepts. So your summary notes from each course will not only help you to ace the course final, but also prepare for your next course.

Your class notes should not be just a stenographic record of class lectures and discussions. You should also record your thoughts as topics are developed in class, and note things that connect to other parts of the course. Your notebook should be a very personal record of your developing understanding of the course material. You can make notes to yourself about the importance of different parts of the material, items to look up after class that need more clarification, and even questions that you want to pursue with the course professor during office hours, with the graduate assistant during recitation sections, or with your study partners. The personal nature of your notes is the most important reason to attend every class yourself. You will not get the same benefit from just copying someone else's notes.

Speak the Lingo

The sciences each have their own language. While it may all sound like Greek in the beginning (probably because a good deal of it is Greek!), there are very good reasons for the use of specific language. Often, a term itself tells you what it means; for example a single displacement reaction, or gravitational acceleration. Sometimes the term has its origins deep in the history of the discipline. Others are the original terms coined by the discoverer expressed in their native French, German, Russian, or the Latin or Greek that was used in scholarly pursuits at the time. However they are expressed, these terms all have a precise and specific meaning. They allow for a concise expression and transfer of information. So learn the lingo of the science you are studying, and use it in your notes, questions and answers in class, participation in discussions, recitation sessions, and during the professor's office hours.

It is especially important to use the correct technical term in your answers on exams and in any written work you submit in fulfilling course assignments. Pay attention to the spelling of the terms and the context in which they are used to be sure that you correctly understand their meaning. Pronunciation is also important, so pay attention to how the professor or teaching assistant says the words and write them in your notes in your own version of phonetics so that you will pronounce them correctly when you use them. Your use of the correct scientific term will not only favorably impress your instructors, it will aid in your understanding and mastery of the course material.

Cyberspace Science Tools

Many science texts now come with CD-ROMs that contain expanded course materials, worked problems, and review and study materials. A great deal of work and expense goes into the preparation of these materials, and they are usually of very high quality. So try to integrate them into your study techniques. Often there are Web sites specifically created for your textbook by the author and publisher. These may contain tutorials, links to background material for topics covered in the course, and tips and hints from the authors based on their experience. Visit these sites to see what they offer to aid your study and success. Your professor may have designed a course Web site that contains lecture notes, past exams, expanded problem sets, and even quizzes and assignments to be submitted online. Become familiar with your campus computing system and make full use of these special materials. By using any of the excellent search engines that are readily available on your Internet browser, you can search the topic of your course and find Web sites from similar courses at other universities. These often contain notes and illustrations along with problems and past exams to give you more practice in testing your skills.

Examination Excellence

In order for your professor to evaluate your grasp of the course material, your understanding will be measured by some sort of examination. These may be essay exams, problem sets, multiple-choice questions, or some combination. In essay questions, read the questions carefully and be sure that you understand what the question is actually asking before you begin to answer it. A few seconds spent outlining your answer so that you address all of the parts of a question in a logical manner will always benefit the quality of your final answer. For problems, list the information that is given and write the equations you know which contain the terms using the given information to yield the answer. If you are allowed to use calculators, make sure your batteries are charged and avoid careless mathematical errors that can result in a loss of points. In multiple-choice questions, eliminate obviously wrong choices and then using your understanding of the concepts, select the best answer. It is a good idea to stick with your original answer to a multiple-choice question. Don't second-guess yourself unless you recall some fact or principle that you didn't think of when you arrived at your first answer. Just changing an answer on instinct rarely results in success. Even if you are just guessing, your first guess is usually your best guess!

Learning in the Lab

You will not study science only in the lecture hall. Many of your science courses will have a laboratory component or a related lab course. Since science is an empirical undertaking and rests on observation and experimentation, the lab section of your course is your practical introduction to the process of science. The lab is where you develop techniques and skill in accomplishing lab manipulations, the handling of equipment, and the operation of instrumentation. Lab periods require their own preparation time and techniques. The lab procedure for the day must be read carefully and completely understood. A list of equipment, chemicals, tools, specimens, etc., should be prepared. Any required pre-lab activities must be carefully completed. Usually some sort of lab notebook is used to record the necessary preparation material as well as for the recording and analysis of observations. Again, the lab notebook should allow you to record such things as notes to yourself, questions to ask the lab instructor, and diagrams of the apparatus setup. The notebook also records the data you will need to perform post-lab assignments. As you continue the laboratory apprenticeship, preparation of lab reports for submission will require data analysis. So be concise but complete in recording the details of your experiment. We all learn science by doing science.

And, of course, the library on your campus is meant to serve students in all fields of study. Sometimes we erroneously think that because science is pursued in the lab, scientists will have less reason to visit the library than students in other disciplines. However, the library has much to offer. Besides monographs on every scientific discipline, the scientific literature is stored there in bound copies of scientific journals. Online data searching using subscription services such as Chemical Abstracts Services, Medline, Earthscape, MathSciNet, and SciBase facilitate the use of this record of scientific experimentation.

SCIENCE BEYOND THE THREE LS

Your study of science however, should not be limited to the three Ls: lecture, lab, and library! You can continue your study even outside the lecture hall, labs, and library. The World Wide Web provides you with the opportunity to search for online access to data to exemplify the materials presented in class. Tremendous amounts of raw and interpreted scientific data are catalogued on the Web and are usually freely available. An example of this is the archived data of the Greenland Ice Coring Project, where collected data on the isotope ratio, salinity, ion concentration, even dust particles in the ice cores are easily accessed by an internal search engine. Many science journals offer online access to their tables of contents of article abstracts, and sometimes to full-text articles, although access to the complete article is often restricted to subscribers. You can use these journal sources to read more about the subjects you are studying and to follow literature references made by your professor.

Another important source of information is news and general science journals such as *Science, Nature, American Scientist, Physics Today,* and *Chemical and Engineering News.* These publications provide information on current happenings in the various disciplines of science and in-depth consideration of important concepts and new developments. Your library will subscribe to these and other science journals, and you should make frequent use of these resources as well as the popular science magazines such as *Scientific American* and *Discover.*

Almost every science department sponsors an associated student club. These groups will host lectures, conduct community projects, and sponsor social events. Participation in these clubs is a great way to meet other students who can serve as study partners. You can also get to know the faculty in the department and build resume experience in your discipline. Your club work will help you to quickly integrate into the local university culture. There are often community organizations, such as astronomy or geology clubs, that run observing sessions and field trips. State geological societies are often good sources of information on local collecting areas and often welcome volunteer help from students, as do wildlife organizations and nature preserves. Watch the local newspaper for listings of science related events in your community.

Volunteer as a science tutor in your local high school, junior high, and elementary schools. Often community groups and church groups run after-school centers and include academic work as part of their program. You will discover that you learn really fast when you are trying to explain the basic principles of biology or chemistry to a beginning student.

Take advantage of the area around your university. Students at schools situated in major metropolitan areas will have access to museums, observatories, and zoos, all of which offer the opportunity to study your science outside of the classroom by observation of museum displays or animals in reconstructed habitats. Even small communities often have museums with science collections, and all museums offer an opportunity for volunteer work as a tour guide or helping with curatorial tasks that will expand your scientific horizons. If your university or community has an observatory, watch for public star parties using their facilities, and attend one to see for yourself the fun of observing the stars and planets.

Look for sites near your school that have scientific interest. These include such things as mines and caverns, famous laboratories that are now historic sites open to the public, plants that offer tours, and national and state parks that offer opportunities for ecological study. Take advantage of lectures offered by the various science departments on campus. These talks may range from world famous Nobel Laureates to brown-bag seminars offered by faculty and students in the department. Many science departments have yearly seminar series that are open to students. If your school has a graduate program in the sciences, watch for postings of students presenting their research results as they defend their thesis. This defense is usually the last step before receiving their master's or doctorate degree. They are open to the public and attending will offer a real insight into current topics in science and how research is conducted and reported. It will also make you aware of research topics being pursued by the faculty in your school.

"The Discovery Channel," "Animal Planet," "The Learning Channel," "PBS," and even the "History Channel" offer series and individual program events relevant to many science courses. The visual sophistication of these programs and their use of computer simulations and modeling are often superb, and they can present opportunities to support your classroom study. They frequently afford a chance to see the actual development of the topics you are studying. So, yes, I am telling you to watch TV! And incorporate what you see into your course study and discussions.

However, along with watching TV comes an admonition to read! Read not just your textbook and study guide and the journals mentioned above, but also popular science books. These works, written for the educated layman, are now widely available. Your university bookstore, along with retailers such as Borders and Barnes and Noble, will feature a science and technology section and usually a separate nature section. Also, science books are often found in the new nonfiction section. You will find books covering topics in astronomy, endangered species, the history of science, cosmology, molecular biology and genetics, evolution, space exploration, immunology, dinosaurs, geology, meteorology, and crystallography. These works will augment your study and may make you aware of opportunities for study and research in fields that you had never before considered. A lifelong interest in some area of science or even a career can be sparked in this way. So become a scientific bibliophile; it will enrich your life forever.

But of all the places to study science beyond the three Ls, the most valuable may be participation in research. Werner von Braun, the famous rocket pioneer and father of our space program, once said, "Research is what I am doing when I don't know what I'm doing." And that is when science really is exciting—when you are in the lab working at the edge of science. Yes, this brings you back into the lab, but a research lab is a very different place than an instructional lab where your coursework takes place. The faculty in your science departments will have active research programs underway. These projects often offer opportunities for undergraduate participation. Working in the lab on a research project will immerse you in a discipline. It gives you the opportunity to see how things are really done.

So investigate opportunities available in your department to assist upper-class students with their research, or sign on as a research assistant with a faculty member. Often faculty in biology and geology conduct fieldwork offering many opportunities for student participation at different skill levels, absolute beginners included. Talk to your course professors to determine the areas in which they work, attend seminars, read their publications, and get involved. Many professors include student authors in their publications, so this participation not only builds your resume, but the experience will also develop a mentoring relationship with the director of the research. This can often be a lifelong relationship as you pursue your career. The time spent in the research lab is especially helpful if you decide to pursue graduate work. Besides the preparation, it will also produce good references for you.

This is how working in the lab in this way is very different from the lab component of your course. They both have valuable things to teach you, but research is how science gets done. It is how the field moves forward, discovery by discovery. Each advance leads to the next as the results of the lab or fieldwork are published. This is real science, so why not be part of the process!

SCIENTIFIC CONNECTIONS

All this talk about science could make us think that the sciences are self-contained, although related, disciplines. Nothing could be farther from the truth. The progression of the sciences that we saw earlier continues to relate the objects of scientific study to all areas of human endeavor. In a seminal series of writings, Harold Cassidy *(Sciences and Arts)* tried to answer the apparent problem of the two cultures—the separateness and opposition of the sciences and the humanities—that had been described by C. P. Snow. Cassidy proposed that there was only one culture with two different aspects. He described a circle of knowledge where the progress of human thought continues without beginning or end. An adaptation of this idea is shown in figure 14. The disciplines on the right we have referred to as the sciences, and the subjects on the left we would recognize as the humanities.

An examination of Cassidy's "Circle of Knowledge" shows that logical principles grounded in mathematical reasoning control the rules of language. The languages are used to produce a collected literature of a culture. The art of this literature is one way to express meaning. Drama, painting, the medium of dance, and the other disciplines of the Fine Arts are another way to express the human experience. History is the record of that experience, and history links the humanities to sciences since it is the record of interactions of groups, the study of political science. We can then understand that the differences between the disciplines arise from the object of their study and activities. The sciences do much more analysis, while the main activity in the humanities is synthesis.

It is the goal of the liberal arts institution to provide a grounding education in all of these areas. The product of this education is the "well-rounded person." More importantly, the product of

Fig. 14.
The Relationship of the Sciences to the Humanities.

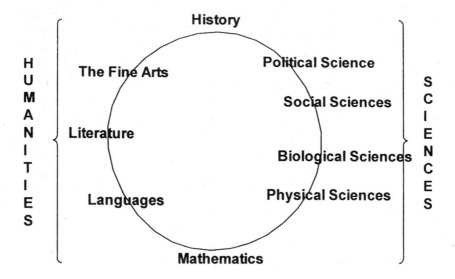

such an education is persons who can relate their discipline to all other areas of study, communicate their field, and understand and appreciate the work of those in other disciplines. They are prepared to cross disciplinary boundaries following research trails that will be beneficial to all. They can meet the mind of others. This is the goal of education, and the study of science is a necessary component.

CONCLUSION

So we've looked at what science is and the various scientific disciplines. We've examined some strategies for success in studying science both in the lecture/lab and outside of it, and we've considered the practical and theoretical values that studying science adds to your education. But what is the real value of education in the sciences? Why study it, even if your chosen career is not as a laboratory scientist? The answer is simple. To study science, even if only for a semester or two, gives you the opportunity to build a foundation to enrich and deepen your understanding of your chosen career. It gives you an opportunity to develop study habits and logical thought processes that will benefit your work in all fields. But more than that, studying the sciences gives you the time to experience the majesty of nature, the astonishing order of physical laws, and the beauties of creation. Even if only for a brief time, you can experience the life of the scientist, described in these words by Rachel Carson in *The Sense of Wonder:*

> Those who dwell as scientists . . . among the beauties and mysteries of the earth are never alone or weary of life. Those who contemplate the beauty of earth find reserves of strength that will endure as long as life lasts (100).

Works Cited

Bronowski, Jacob. *The Origins of Knowledge and Imagination.* New Haven: Yale University Press, 1979.

Carson, Rachel. *The Sense of Wonder.* New York: HarperCollins, 1999.

Cassidy, Harold G. "The Sciences and the Humanities in One World." A presentation at the Connecticut Junior Science and Humanities Symposium, Yale University, 1963.

———. *The Sciences and the Arts: A New Alliance.* New York: Harper, 1962.

Snow, C. P. *The Two Cultures.* New York: Cambridge University Press, 1963.

15

The Goals of a Liberal Education

Wilburn T. Stancil

STUDENTS WHO HAVE READ to this point in this volume have doubtless gained valuable insight about the disciplines of the liberal arts—what they are, how they can be studied, how they can be applied outside the classroom, etc. The contributors to this volume represent not only a wide range of disciplines, but also universities and colleges that are diverse in many ways— geographically (from New York to California, Texas to Michigan), the religious affiliation of the schools, the size of their enrollment, as well as the gender, racial, and economic makeup of their student body. Yet if we focused on differences alone, we might miss the fact that all of these schools share, along with most universities and colleges in the United States, a commitment to the liberal arts. In fact, it would be rare to locate a college or university in the United States that did not express in its mission statement some commitment to the liberal arts.

In making such a commitment, what is it specifically that universities and colleges hope to produce in their graduates? That is, what is it that your college or university wants you to become as a result of your liberal studies? What are the crucial components of a liberal arts education that graduates will benefit from as they complete their formal studies? The following are suggestive of some of the qualities that ideally will emerge from a liberal education.

Respecting Freedom of Inquiry and the Pursuit of Truth

A university is committed to free inquiry. Faculty and students are encouraged to pursue truth in an atmosphere of openness and freedom. The liberal arts seek to "liberate" us from such things as ignorance, provincialism, and limited perspectives. Liberation from these elements requires that we be allowed to follow truth wherever it may lead us. Education dispels ignorance, which breeds fear and mistrust. We fear what we don't understand, and great evils and injustices can occur when people act out of ignorance and fear. Knowledge brings the power to effect change.

Free and open inquiry is a cornerstone of the educational process and makes possible the flourishing of the liberal arts. The respect for freedom of the conscience, a principle supported by both democracy and religion, is fundamental. A liberal education should help us value free inquiry and a respect for the individual's right to make his or her own decisions.

Grounding Education in Values

Colleges and universities with religious missions are not alone in recognizing the importance of grounding education in values. After having been "liberated" through the humanities, the question remains: What now should I do with my life? This question has to do with goals and purpose, and it necessitates moral discernment and reflection on transcendent values. A thorough education in the liberal tradition does not guarantee that we will know how to use the knowledge and skills that result. A liberal education that fails to address the matter of values will also fail to liberate. Like all good things in life, education can be used wisely, it can be wasted, and it can even atrophy through neglect. Without the integration of the intellectual and the moral, education is incomplete.

Developing Critical Thinking and Discernment

Awash in a sea of information, our lives are flooded daily with words, sounds, and images. How should we respond to this bombardment of information that routinely impinges on our lives? There seems to be little hope of even sorting and arranging the ever-increasing data, much less actually assessing and reflecting on it. The liberal arts can help develop our critical skills so that we might exercise that crucial faculty of discernment—discernment of the true from the false, the important from the trivial, the central from the peripheral, the lasting from the ephemeral.

To be educated liberally does not mean we will always discern wisely, but it should mean that we have developed the critical skills to know the difference between the necessary and the unnecessary, the foolish and the wise. Thomas Aquinas once wrote that it is better to know a little of what is important than a lot of what is unimportant. To know goodness, truth, justice, beauty, and to center our lives on them, requires critical thinking and discernment. And while discernment is not guaranteed by a liberal education, it can be greatly enhanced by the liberal arts.

Becoming an Effective Communicator

It is one thing to know, it is something else to be able to articulate that knowledge correctly, with precision, forcefully, and even with eloquence. Every university and college desires to produce graduates who can do so. Becoming an effective communicator takes time and practice. The one who knows but can't express what he or she knows is at a disadvantage in life. The liberal arts is the most sure path in the university to becoming a more forceful and persuasive writer and speaker.

Preparing for Responsible Citizenship

Only a minority of Americans graduate from a college or university. The life-changing experiences afforded by a college education are still, relatively speaking, the privileges of the few. Because university graduates will have such an important influence on matters of civic life, one of the goals of an education is to prepare leaders who will become responsible citizens and agents of change and renewal. Responsible citizenship involves more than simply voting, although it includes that. It means attention to public policy and its implications for the life and well being of all persons, and not simply one's own racial, ethnic, or national group. It means careful attention to the dignity of all persons, again rooted not only in democratic principles embodied in the American ideal, but in a religious vision that all persons are created in God's image. It means social responsibility to the poor, marginalized, and dispossessed. In other words, the liberal arts should set us free from a selfish preoccupation with only our concerns and motivate us to a selfless service to others.

Embracing and Celebrating Diversity

Cultural, religious, and ethnic diversity has been a part of the American landscape for a long time. Only recently, however, have we made the conscious effort to recognize it, celebrate it, and incorporate it into a larger vision of what it is to be an American and a world citizen. For many students, the university provides the first real opportunity to have exposure to the kind of diversity that makes up our world. The experiences of diversity that you obtain at the university, whether through interaction with others or through reading and classroom discussion, can open your mind to a world of differences. This, too, is part of the "liberation" from a narrow perspective that the liberal arts can provide.

Developing the Imagination and Aesthetic Appreciation

The liberal arts introduce us to many different ways of thinking and knowing. While disciplines clearly have methods of inquiry that are often quite different, all require the use of the imagination. Even the disciplines we think of as having the most rigorous methodologies for inquiry, such as the natural sciences, progress by means of imaginative insights into problems and solutions. In fact, to attain the goal of "complete understanding" sought by physicist Stephen Hawking (see chapter 14), one can only guess that such a vision of unity will come about not only as a result of rigorous science, but also by an imaginative vision of the whole.

Since the time of the Greeks, aesthetic value has been attached to the notion of unity and simplicity. This implies that all of the liberal arts are engaged in a kind of search for and appreciation of beauty. At the most fundamental level, the liberal arts help us enjoy life more. Liberating us from the provincialism that limits aesthetic appreciation only to *my* tastes, a liberal education opens up to us the entire world with its variety of cultures and tastes. To develop an aesthetic appreciation for the other is to recognize that beauty, though one in essence, expresses itself in myriad ways.

Becoming an Integrated Person

Ultimately the humanities humanize us. While the focus of the college experience is on the intellectual development, we know that persons are more than simply mind. The term we use for this holistic approach is "integrity," that is, the integration of the whole person. This includes an integrated system of values that speak to the intellectual, spiritual, and moral dimensions of life. Life involves values, and all values are rooted in the head (intellect), the heart (emotion), and the hands (actions). That is, the liberal arts touch us in all three areas—we discover new truth cognitively, we experience it affectively, and we live it with our lives.

In conclusion, the liberal arts can prepare us for a lifetime of learning, not simply for a job. Studying the liberal arts should produce in us a desire to continue growing and learning. Becoming a lifelong learner means that our education only "commences" with graduation. But even our learning is insipid if we fail to use our knowledge wisely. In the end we seek to be wise, and to know what is worth pursuing in life, and to discover to what it is that we should give our lives. We can know much and yet fail to discover the truth; we can have critical skills of analysis and yet fail to live with integrity; we can understand the world and yet fail to understand ourselves.

Poet Rainer Maria Rilke once cautioned a student to be patient with the unresolved questions in his heart. Try to simply love the questions at this stage in your life, he advised. But someday as he matured, Rilke pointed out, the student would be able to move beyond the questions and live out the answers. And that, the poet said, is the point: *to live everything.* The goal of a liberal education is not simply to know, but to live wisely the truths about God, humanity, and the world around us; truths both discovered by us and also given to us as a gift of grace.

ABOUT THE AUTHORS

Roger C. Aikin teaches History of Art at Creighton University in Omaha, Nebraska, where he is an Associate Professor. Dr. Aikin specializes in Renaissance and Baroque art and architecture, and also teaches courses in recent art and art criticism. His publications include articles on American art for the Smithsonian Institution's *American Art* and an exhibition catalogue on the California artists Henrietta Shore and Edward Weston. Dr. Aikin studied with photographer Ansel Adams, and has exhibits of his own photographs of Rome and the West.

C. Randall Bradley is a Professor of Church Music at Baylor University and Director of the Church Music Program where he teaches graduate and undergraduate courses in church music and directs the Baylor Men's Glee Club. He frequently leads conferences on subjects related to conducting, music education, and church music. He has published articles and reviews in professional journals and chapters in books; his revision of the book *Understanding, Preparing For, and Practicing Christian Worship* is a popular resource book for ministers and is used as a textbook at numerous seminaries and colleges. He is particularly interested in the role of music in society and music's effect on human action. He is currently working on a comprehensive resource book for church musicians.

W. James Bradley is a Professor of Mathematics and Computer Science at Calvin College in Grand Rapids, Michigan, where he has taught for sixteen years. He has recently taught courses in statistics, game theory, and differential equations, as well as courses for non-science majors. Dr. Bradley's specialty is applied mathematics in the social sciences. He recently coauthored *The Uses and Misuses of Data and Models* with Kurt Schaefer, an economist, and coedited *Mathematics in a Postmodern Age: A Christian*

Perspective with Russell W. Howell. He also spent eighteen months as a visiting scholar with the U.S. State Department in Washington, D.C. developing mathematical models applicable to arms control issues.

Daniel S. Brown is a Professor of Communication in the Department of English and Communication at Grove City College in Pennsylvania. He holds a doctor of philosophy degree from Louisiana State University and a master's degree from Miami University in Oxford, Ohio. Previously, he was the campus director for Indiana Wesleyan University-Indianapolis and served for many years as an Associate Professor of Communication Arts and Chairman of the Division of Humanities at Bryan College in Dayton, Tennessee. He teaches rhetoric, public relations, public speaking, journalism, and communication theory courses. His reviews and essays have appeared in *Communication Education, Speech Teacher, Christian Library Journal,* and the *Chicago Tribune.* His community activities include marketing and public relations consulting for pregnancy care centers and other non-profit service organizations.

Trudy A. Dickneider is a Professor of Chemistry at the University of Scranton in Pennsylvania, where she has taught for eighteen years. She regularly teaches the introductory and advanced organic chemistry courses and mechanistic organic in the graduate program, as well as courses in environmental geochemistry and industrial chemistry. Recently, she has introduced Peer-Led Team Learning into the organic chemistry program. Dr. Dickneider's research interests are in organic geochemistry where she and her research students characterize paleoenvironments through a study of the organic compounds contained in sediments. She is interested in compounds that indicate past climate changes as well as applications of scanning electron microscopy to analysis of organic sediments and geoarchaeological problems. Her publications in geochemistry include work performed as a guest scientist at the Woods Hole Oceanographic Institution, published in *Organic Geochemistry,* as well as ongoing studies of samples from the K/T boundary layer and the past glacial period in the American southwest. Her most recent publication is contained in *The Great Rift Valleys of Pangea in Eastern North America.*

Philip A. Dynia is Department Chairperson and an Associate Professor of Political Science at Loyola University New Orleans. He teaches courses in American constitutional law, judicial politics, and political theory. His publications include articles in *Cinema Journal* and *Constitutional Commentary* and book reviews in a variety of scholarly journals, including *The American Political Science Review* and *The Journal of Politics.* Most recently, he contributed articles on "Obscenity and Pornography," "Unprotected Speech," and "Dissents" for *The Encyclopedia of the United States Supreme Court.* He is currently writing a book on the perennial questions of American constitutionalism.

Robert D. Hamner is Senior Professor of English and Humanities at Hardin-Simmons University in Abilene, Texas. His Ph.D. is from The University of Texas at Austin. In addition to the papers he has read at many international conferences, he has published numerous articles and reviews in professional journals as well as chapters and introductions to several books. He has edited *Critical Perspectives on V. S. Naipaul, Critical Perspectives on Derek Walcott,* and *Third World Perspectives on Joseph Conrad.* He is the author of *Derek Walcott* and *V. S. Naipaul* in the Twayne World Authors Series and of *Epic of the Dispossessed: Derek Walcott's Omeros.* He teaches undergraduate introductions to writing and literature, two interdisciplinary humanities courses, advanced and graduate courses in Shakespeare and the epic. His primary field of research and publication is Caribbean literature.

Joseph W. Koterski, S.J., is Chair of the Department of Philosophy at Fordham University in Bronx, New York. Ordained a Jesuit priest in 1992, he has also taught at Loyola College (Baltimore) and the University of St. Thomas (Houston). At Fordham, he serves as the Editor-in-Chief of *International Philosophical Quarterly* and works in the area of natural law ethics and the history of medieval philosophy. He recently recorded two series of lectures for The Teaching Company, one on Aristotle's Ethics and one on Natural Law Ethics. Among his recent publications are contributions to the *Cambridge Companion to Karl Jaspers* and to *The Two Wings of Catholic Thought: Essays on* Fides et Ratio.

M. Kathleen Madigan is Department Chairperson of the Classical and Modern Languages Department at Rockhurst University. Her doctorate in Comparative Literature is from the University of North Carolina, Chapel Hill. Her international experience includes teaching at a French university, research in Germany on a DAAD fellowship, and leading study-abroad trips. A regular participant in summer seminars on teaching, most recently in Spain, she teaches courses on language, literature, film, and culture. She is current President of the Greater Kansas City Chapter of the American Association of Teachers of French (AATF). Her publications include articles in *Women in French Studies, Paul Claudel Papers, Religion and Literature,* and the *Dictionary of Literary Biography.*

Robert K. Moore Jr. is Director of Labor Studies and Assistant Professor of Sociology at St. Joseph's University in Philadelphia. He holds a Ph.D. and J.D. from SUNY/Buffalo. Dr. Moore teaches courses in the sociology of work, social inequality, race relations, sociology of law, Appalachian studies, and labor studies. He also teaches a number of service-learning courses involving these subjects. His publications include articles on labor law, industrial relations, and temporary labor. He is currently writing a book on the sociology of work.

Kathleen S. Nash is an Associate Professor of Religious Studies and director of the Core program at Le Moyne College, Syracuse, New York. She is also a faculty member in Le Moyne's Integral Honors and Women's Studies Programs where she teaches courses on the Old Testament/ Hebrew Bible, religion and contemporary film, sexuality and gender, and Biblical Hebrew. Her publications include articles in *The Bible Today,* book reviews in the *Catholic Biblical Quarterly,* and an essay, "The Gospel of Thomas Logion 22: Keeping Momma out of the Kingdom" in Mary Ann Beavis, ed., *The Lost Coin: Parables of Women, Work, and Wisdom.* Currently a member of the editorial board for the revision of the New American Bible Old Testament translation,

Dr. Nash is also completing a research project entitled *Reading the Old Testament Inside and Out.*

James V. Schall, S.J., is a Professor in the Department of Government at Georgetown University. He writes regular columns: "Sense and Nonsense," in *Crisis;* "Schall on Chesterton," in *Gilbert!;* "On Letters and Essays," in the *University Bookman;* and "English Essays," in the *Saint Austin Review.* His most recent book is *On the Unseriousness of Human Affairs.* Other books include *At the Limits of Political Philosophy, Schall on Chesterton,* and *Another Sort of Learning.*

Robert M. Senkewicz is a Professor of History at Santa Clara University, where he also serves as Chair of the University Core Curriculum Committee. He teaches courses on American Colonial and Revolutionary History, California history, Historical Interpretation, and Historical Writing. He is the author of *Vigilantes on Gold Rush San Francisco.* Together with Rose Marie Beebe, he has edited *The History of Alta California,* by Antonio María Osio; *Lands of Promise and Despair: Chronicles of Early California, 1535–1846,* and *A Guide to Manuscripts Concerning Baja California in the Bancroft Library.*

Wilburn T. Stancil is an Associate Professor of Theology and Religious Studies at Rockhurst University and is the director of the Rockhurst University Press. He is coeditor of *Catholicism at the Millennium* (with Gerald L. Miller) and has published more than one hundred chapters in books and articles in journals, most recently contributing dictionary articles to the *New Catholic Encyclopedia,* rev. ed., and a chapter on apocalyptic stained glass windows in *Stained Glass in Catholic Philadelphia.*

Scott VanderStoep is an Associate Professor of Psychology and Director of the Carl Frost Center for Social Science Research at Hope College in Holland, Michigan. He has taught a variety of undergraduate courses in psychology. His research interest is in cognitive psychology, particularly critical thinking and problem solving among college students. He is also interested in how faith beliefs connect with people's understanding of psychological research. Book projects he is currently working on include *Science of the Soul: Christian Perspectives on Psychological Research* and *Learning to Learn: The Skill and Will of College Success.*

INDEX

women's studies resources on, 208, 209
internships
  in communications, 35–36
  in political science, 176
  in sociology, 164–65
interpersonal communication, 25–26, 26f, 35
interpretation
  of art history, 102–3
  of history, 126–28, 131
  of literature, 61, 62–63, 65, 71
  sources of, 128
irony, 69
Islam, 208

James, William, 199
Japanese Noh theater, 69
jazz, 81
Jefferson, Thomas, 105, 123
Jensen, Arthur, 36
Jesus Christ, 3–4
jobs, 160–61
  from art history, 118
  from communication major, 34
  from languages' major, 46–47
  in mathematics, 230
  from political science, 172
  from psychology, 146–47
  from science, 238
  from sociology, 155, 156, 164–65
John Adams (McCullough), 121, 122–23
John Paul II, Pope, 17
Johnson, Elizabeth A., 204
Johnson, Samuel, 16
Joyce, James, 69
Judaism, 208
Jung, Carl, 206

Just What Is It That Makes Today's Homes So Different, So Appealing (Hamilton), 98, *100,* 101, 107

Kagan, Robert, 13–14
Kant, Immanuel, 187, 191, 192, 194, 198
Kivy, Peter, 90–91
knowledge
  axioms and open, 224, 225
  circle of, 247
  as justified true belief, 184–85
  own purpose of, 13
  as product of science, 234–35
  as useful, 13–14
Kurosawa, Akira, 121

laboratory work, 242–43, 246–47
Lamentation on the Death of Christ (Giotto), 108, 109, *110,* 111, 114
Lange, Dale L., 46
language(s)
  adaptability from, 44–45
  children learning, 49
  choosing, 47–48
  classical, 57
  communicative competence with, 43–44, 46
  comparative literature and, 40
  comparison of, 43–44
  context of, 50
  courses in, 41
  culture and, 39–40, 42–44, 45–46, 48, 52–53
  development and living, 42
  expression of meaning in, 39
  fear and, 44
  5 Cs in, 43–44
  fluency goal for, 49